100

GETAWAYS

RUND UM DIE WELT · AROUND THE WORLD · AUTOUR DU MONDE

A–I

TASCHEN

CONTENTS
A–I

100

GETAWAYS

CONTENTS
I–Z

EDITORIAL

HERE'S TO GETTING AWAY FROM IT ALL, TO ESCAPING AND EXPERIENCING NEW THINGS. A place for outdoor adventure, for sport and spa visits, or simply for a book you've been meaning to read for ages: A getaway worthy of this title can be any or all of those things.

So what do we want when we travel for fun today? To experience the natural world aided by local experts? To enjoy a culture of hospitality rather than mere "service"? Or simply to recenter ourselves? Just three of the possibilities offered by the 100 hotels featured within. They were chosen not according to how much they cost or how recently they opened. Which is why a basic Alpine guesthouse rubs shoulders here with a luxury Utah resort and a historic hilltop villa above Florence—and why our selection includes not only genuine newcomers but also TASCHEN favorites with updated details.

Instead, what unites these great destinations and makes them all leaders in their field, be they Vietnamese bungalows or Swedish tree houses, renovated English inns or a Portofino palazzo, is their coherent blend of location, interiors, and cuisine.

Among them, you'll find places for family celebrations alongside hideaways for new lovers, reminders of health tourism's early-1900s heyday alongside unpretentious retreats for today's global citizens. In each case, we've also suggested a parallel destination for your imagination, continuing the tradition begun by Angelika Taschen of recommending a book to go with the hotel. We hope our (hotly debated) choices will be to your liking. Happy traveling!
MARGIT J. MAYER

ALLES HINTER SICH LASSEN, JA FLÜCHTEN, UM NEUE ENTDECKUNGEN ZU MACHEN. Endlich Zeit haben für die Abenteuer der Natur, für Sport oder Spa, für die Lektüre eines schon lange wartenden Romans. Das alles schwingt mit im „Getaway" des Titels dieses Doppelbands.

Wie wollen wir heute reisen? Natur ganz nah erleben und sich dabei von Experten bestens beraten wissen; Kultur der Gastfreundschaft statt nur „Service" genießen; wegfahren, um bei sich anzukommen – in den 100 Hotels auf den Folgeseiten wird genau das möglich.

Sie alle wurden nicht nach Kriterien wie Preis oder Neuheit ausgesucht. Die einfache Bergpension fand ebenso Platz wie das mondäne Resort in Utah oder die Turmvilla in den Hügeln von Florenz. Einige TASCHEN-Hotelklassiker haben wir einem Fakten-Update unterzogen, doch es sind auch absolute Newcomer dabei.

Was diese Orte für gelungene Ferien verbindet und für uns zu Weltstars ihrer Kategorie macht, ist ihre Stimmigkeit in geografischer Lage, Einrichtung und Küche – das gilt für den Urlaubspalazzo in Portofino ebenso wie für die Bungalows in Vietnam, das renovierte Pub in England oder die Baumhäuser in Schweden.

Es sind Plätze für Familienfeste dabei, aber auch solche für ein Wochenende mit der neuen Liebe. Wer sich als Kurgast um 1900 fühlen will, wird fündig werden, aber auch jene, die betont unprätentiös entspannen wollen. Selbst die Reisen im Kopf kommen nicht zu kurz: Wir setzen die von Angelika Taschen begonnene Tradition fort, zu jedem Hotel ein Buch zu empfehlen, und hoffen, dass unsere (viel diskutierte) Auswahl Zustimmung findet. In diesem Sinne: Lassen Sie sich inspirieren! **MARGIT J. MAYER**

TOUT ABANDONNER, FUIR POUR DÉCOUVRIR DE NOUVEAUX HORIZONS. Enfin le temps de vivre des aventures nature, de faire du sport ou d'aller au spa, de lire un roman en attente depuis des lustres. Voilà ce que proment le titre de l'ouvrage.

De nos jours, on veut vivre la nature au plus près, savourer l'hospitalité plutôt que bénéficier d'un simple «service» et partir pour se ressourcer. Dans les 100 hôtels des pages suivantes, cela devient possible. Prix ou nouveauté n'ont pas été des critères de sélection déterminants: une pension familiale à la montagne est ici à sa place au même titre que le complexe hôtelier sélect dans l'Utah ou la villa sur les hauteurs de Florence. Vous retrouverez des classiques des livres TASCHEN sur les hôtels, avec des informations actualisées, mais découvrirez aussi des nouveaux venus.

Ces villégiatures ont un point commun, qui fait d'elles des stars mondiales dans leur catégorie: l'accord parfait entre le site, l'hébergement et la restauration. Cela est vrai aussi bien du palace à Portofino que des bungalows au Vietnam, du pub restauré en Angleterre ou des cabanes dans les arbres en Suède.

Certains hôtels se prêtent à des fêtes de famille, d'autres à un week-end en amoureux. Le voyageur amateur de cures style 1900 trouvera son bonheur, comme celui qui, en citoyen du monde, veut simplement se détendre. Même les voyageurs immobiles seront comblés: perpétuant la tradition initiée par Angelika Taschen, nous suggérons un livre pour chaque hôtel et espérons que nos choix (âprement discutés) vous satisferont. Laissez-vous inspirer.
MARGIT J. MAYER

QASR AL SARAB
DESERT RESORT
ABU DHABI

1 Qasr Al Sarab Road ~ Abu Dhabi ~ United Arab Emirates
Telephone +971 2 886 2088 ~ Fax +971 2 886 2086
infoqas@anantara.com
qasralsarab.anantara.com

A lavishly appointed hideaway on the edge of one of the world's largest sand deserts, the Qasr Al Sarab certainly lives up to its name, which translates as "mirage palace." Crossing the bridge at the entrance, you leave the extreme landscape of endless dunes behind you and step into a world of mosaics, palm trees, and gently bubbling fountains.

Each of the palatial villas boasts beautiful Oriental textiles, artworks with a local connection, and a private pool—a luxury that is particularly welcome in these arid climes. And with everything else taken care of, you can simply relax with a peppermint tea, sit watching the camel trains, and soak up the contrasts of this fairy-tale place. No less unreal is the large library, which contains valuable Arabian artifacts that offer an introduction to the history of the region's desert-dwelling peoples. Proof that there is culture even in the most barren of environments.

Eine opulent ausgestattete Oase in einer der größten Sandwüsten der Welt: Das ist das Qasr Al Sarab, und sein Name – übersetzt „Palast der Fata Morgana" – scheint keinesfalls zu hoch gegriffen. Über die Brücke am Eingang des Resorts kommt der Gast aus einer extremen Landschaft in eine Märchenwelt mit Mosaiken, Palmen und sanft plätschernden Brunnen: ein feudales Fort, eingebettet in die leuchtenden Sanddünen der Rub' al Khali Wüste.

In den Villen warten prächtige orientalische Textilien, Kunst mit Ortsbezug und der (in diesen Dürregefilden doppelt wirkende) Luxus des eigenen Pools. Einen Minztee schlürfen, den Kamelkarawanen zuschauen und die Kontraste des Ortes auf sich wirken lassen, das ist das Einzige, was man hier selbst erledigen muss. Mindestens ebenso unwirklich ist die große Bibliothek, in der wertvolle Artefakte der arabischen Welt den Gast in die Geschichte der Wüstenvölker einführen. Merke: Kultur ist auch dort, wo man erst mal nur Sandberge sieht.

Au cœur de l'un des plus grands déserts de sable du monde, le Qasr Al Sarab est l'oasis par excellence. Ce nom, qui signifie « palais du mirage », donne le ton. En traversant le pont d'accès au complexe hôtelier, le visiteur quitte un paysage aride pour pénétrer dans un univers fabuleux de mosaïques, de palmiers et de fontaines aux doux murmures, celui d'une forteresse féodale nichée dans les dunes lumineuses du désert de Rub' al Khali.

Ornées de somptueuses étoffes orientales et d'œuvres d'art local, les villas bénéficient de piscines privées, un luxe d'autant plus impressionnant dans ce paysage désertique. Il n'y a plus qu'à siroter du thé à la menthe en observant les caravanes de chameaux et en s'imprégnant des contrastes qu'offre le lieu. La grande bibliothèque, tout aussi improbable, abrite de précieux objets d'art qui permettent de s'initier à l'histoire des peuples du désert. La culture ne va-t-elle pas se nicher jusqu'au cœur des dunes les plus reculées ?

LOCATION
150 km/93 miles south of Abu Dhabi in the Rub' al Khali oasis, birthplace of the ruling families of Dubai and Abu Dhabi

RATES
Rooms from $380, suites from $625, villas from $750, breakfast included

ROOMS
154 rooms, 42 private villas, and 10 royal villas

STYLE
Arabian palatial village surrounded by huge dunes

FOOD
Bedouin-style dining at Al Falaj, plus international and Mediterranean cuisine

X FACTOR
Be sure to take one of the sunrise or sunset desert walks in the Empty Quarter and watch the sand dunes turn to golden mountains

BOOK TO PACK
"Finding Nouf" by Zoë Ferraris

LAGE
150 km südlich von Abu Dhabi in der Rub' al Khali Wüste, der Wiege der Herrscherfamilien von Dubai und Abu Dhabi

PREISE
Zimmer ab 290 €, Suiten ab 480 €, Villen ab 750 €, jeweils inklusive Frühstück

ZIMMER
154 Zimmer, 42 Privat-Villen und 10 Royal-Villen

STIL
Arabisches Palastdorf, umgeben von gigantischen Dünen

KÜCHE
Neben dem Beduinen-Restaurant Al Falaj wird international-mediterrane Küche geboten

X-FAKTOR
Keinesfalls entgehen lassen: Sonnenaufgangs- oder Sonnenuntergangs-Wüstenspaziergang ins Gebiet des „Leeren Viertels" – die Dünen werden dann zu Gebirgen aus purem Gold

BUCH ZUM ORT
„Die letzte Sure" von Zoë Ferraris

SITUATION
À 150 km au sud d'Abou Dabi, dans le désert de Rub' al Khali, berceau des dynasties de Dubaï et d'Abou Dabi

PRIX
Chambres à partir de 290 €, suites à partir de 480 €, villas à partir de 750 €; petit déjeuner inclus

CHAMBRES
154 chambres, 42 villas privées et 10 villas royales

STYLE
Palais arabe au milieu de dunes gigantesques

RESTAURATION
Outre le restaurant bédouin Al Falaj, cuisine méditerranéenne internationale

LE « PETIT PLUS »
À ne manquer sous aucun prétexte : la promenade à l'aube ou au crépuscule dans la région du Quart Vide, où les dunes se transforment en montagnes d'or

LIVRE À EMPORTER
« La Disparue du désert » de Zoë Ferraris

"For anyone with a T. E. Lawrence fantasy,
Qasr Al Sarab is the place to stay."

ANNABELLE THORPE, *THE TIMES*

„Das Hotel für alle, die davon träumen, sich einmal wie T. E. Lawrence zu fühlen."

« Au Qasr Al Sarab, les hôtes se sentent l'âme d'un T. E. Lawrence. »

HOTEL DEL CASCO
ARGENTINA

Avenida del Libertador 16.170 ~ B1642CKV San Isidro ~ Buenos Aires ~ Argentina
Telephone & Fax +54 11 4732 3993
info@hoteldelcasco.com.ar
www.hoteldelcasco.com.ar

Situated 15 miles from Buenos Aires, the suburb of San Isidro boasts many historic buildings, one of which is home to the Hotel del Casco. With its external staircase, high windows, and slender columns, this former palazzo in the Beaux Arts style bears more than a passing external resemblance to the mansion housing New York's Frick Collection. The interiors, though, are anything but museum-like, with a central patio whose seating groups are ideal for casual chats and rooms in which local antiques and claw-foot bathtubs create an aristocratic ambience. What you won't find here are the profusions of knick-knacks so beloved of hoteliers in these parts.

Directly opposite the hotel is San Isidro cathedral, alongside which are extensive gardens and parks where guests can experience the melancholy peace of an Argentinean afternoon. And should this suburban idyll occasionally prove too quiet, the hustle and bustle of central Buenos Aires is just under an hour's drive away.

Nur 24 Kilometer von Buenos Aires entfernt liegt der Vorort San Isidro mit seinem historischen Zentrum – und mit dem Hotel del Casco. Die ehemalige Stadtresidenz im Beaux-Arts-Stil wirkt mit ihrer Freitreppe, den hohen Fenstern und schlanken Säulen äußerlich wie eine südamerikanische Frick Collection. Drinnen geht es nicht ganz so museal zu: Im zentralen Patio laden Sitzgruppen zur Plauderei, und die Zimmer mit lokalen Antiquitäten und Badewannen auf Löwenfüßen locken mit aristokratischem Wohnerlebnis. Nippes im Übermaß, wie ihn viele hiesige Hoteliers so lieben, sucht man hier vergebens.

Gleich gegenüber dem Hotel steht die Kathedrale von San Isidro, an deren Mauern man zu großzügigen Gärten und Parks gelangt und so in die melancholische Ruhe des argentinischen Nachmittags eintauchen kann. Und sollte einem das Idyll doch einmal zu ruhig werden, kommt man im Handumdrehen zurück ins urbane Leben: Nach Buenos Aires ist es ja nur eine knappe Stunde Autofahrt.

Situé à 24 kilomètres seulement du centre de Buenos Aires, le quartier historique de San Isidro abrite l'hôtel del Casco. Avec son perron, ses fenêtres hautes et ses colonnes élancées, la façade extérieure de cette ancienne résidence de style Beaux-Arts a des airs de Frick Collection, version sud-américaine. L'intérieur est plus intimiste : dans le patio intérieur, des tables et des fauteuils invitent à la conversation. Les chambres ont beaucoup de classe avec leur baignoire à pattes de lion et les antiquités locales qui les décorent. Ici, point d'accumulation de bibelots comme dans les hôtels voisins.

Juste en face de l'hôtel se dresse la cathédrale de San Isidro. Les jardins luxuriants et les parcs ombragés qui l'entourent vous permettront de profiter du calme mélancolique des après-midi argentins. Si cette tranquillité devait devenir pesante, vous pouvez vous replonger rapidement dans le tourbillon de la vie urbaine : Buenos Aires est à une petite heure de voiture.

LOCATION
Situated 24 km/15 miles northeast of central Buenos Aires, 45 km/28 miles from the airport

RATES
Rooms from $190, suites from $220

ROOMS
20 double rooms and 10 suites

STYLE
Aristocratic summerhouse whose interiors recall the pomp of South America's Gilded Age

FOOD
Traditional Argentinean cuisine given a contemporary international twist

X FACTOR
In keeping with the hotel's thoroughly relaxing atmosphere, the in-house spa's fabulous "jet lag–recovery treatment" purges your body of time zone–related tiredness in just one hour

BOOK TO PACK
"Labyrinths" by Jorge Luis Borges

LAGE
24 km nordöstlich vom Stadtzentrum von Buenos Aires, 45 km vom Flughafen entfernt

PREISE
Zimmer ab 145 €, Suiten ab 170 €

ZIMMER
20 Doppelzimmer und 10 Suiten

STIL
Aristokratisches Sommerhaus, das mit seiner Einrichtung an den Prunk der feudalen Epoche Südamerikas erinnert

KÜCHE
Klassische argentinische Küche, modernisiert durch internationale Akzentuierung

X-FAKTOR
Passt zur absolut entspannenden Atmosphäre des Hauses: Im großartigen *Jetlag Recovery Treatment* des Spa wird der gesamte Körper vom Stress mit den Zeitzonen befreit – und das in nur einer Stunde!

BUCH ZUM ORT
„Labyrinthe" von Jorge Luis Borges

SITUATION
À 24 km au nord-est du centre ville de Buenos Aires, à 45 km de l'aéroport

PRIX
Chambres à partir de 145 €, suites à partir de 170 €

CHAMBRES
20 chambres doubles et 10 suites

STYLE
Résidence d'été aristocratique, dont le mobilier évoque l'âge d'or de l'Amérique Latine

RESTAURATION
Cuisine argentine classique, modernisée par des tendances internationales

LE «PETIT PLUS»
En parfait accord avec l'atmosphère de détente absolue dégagée par le lieu, le fantastique «Jetlag recovery treatment» dispensé dans le spa permet d'évacuer le stress occasionné par le décalage horaire, et ce en une heure seulement!

LIVRE À EMPORTER
«Labyrinthes» de Jorge Luis Borges

TIPILIUKE
ARGENTINA

San Martín de los Andes ~ Patagonia ~ Argentina
Telephone +54 297 242 9466 (lodge) +54 911 4199 2228 (reservations)
info@tipiliuke.com
www.tipiliuke.com

Sometimes you come across hotels that are so beautiful, you barely feel the need to leave them. At Tipiliuke (pronounced "Tip-i-loo-kay") that would be a crying shame—on the doorstep is some of the finest scenery Patagonia has to offer. Two crystal-clear rivers cross the huge estate of which the lodge is part, and guests can fill their days with outdoor pursuits in spectacular surroundings, be it fly-fishing beneath snow-capped peaks, group horse rides to watch the sun set over the Lanín volcano, or vegetable picking in the hotel's own organic garden.

Add in the hospitality of the hosts, the authentic experience of everyday life on a working ranch, and the comforts of the lodge itself, and you have a vacation that combines adventure with a highly congenial atmosphere—at the end of which you may find you really don't want to leave.

Es gibt Hotels, die sind so schön, dass man sie gar nicht verlassen möchte. Im Falle des Tipiliuke (ausgesprochen „Tip-i-lu-kee") liegt die Sache etwas anders: Wer hier nicht rausgeht, verpasst alles, denn vor der Tür liegt eine Art *Best of Patagonia*. Zwei kristallklare Flüsse durchqueren den riesigen Landsitz, zu dem die Lodge gehört. Ob spektakuläres Fliegenfischen im Angesicht schneebedeckter Gipfel, Gruppenausritte zum Sonnenuntergang am Lanín-Vulkan oder auch nur Gemüseernten im hoteleigenen Biogarten – Frischluftakquise in ihrer schönsten Form steht hier jeden Tag auf dem Stundenplan.

Die Herzlichkeit der Gastgeber, die authentische Einbindung in den Alltag der Gauchos auf der Ranch und dazu die luxuriösen Annehmlichkeiten der Lodge, das alles macht den Aufenthalt zum Abenteuer mit Wohlfühlgarantie. Und verlassen möchte man diesen Ort dann natürlich auch nicht mehr.

Certains hôtels sont si beaux qu'on ne ne peut se résoudre à en sortir. Au Tipiliuke (prononcez « Tip-i-lou-ké »), celui qui ne met pas le pied dehors passe à côté de l'essentiel, car il se prive des merveilles de la Patagonie. Deux fleuves à l'eau cristalline traversent l'immense domaine dont fait partie le lodge. Que l'on pratique la pêche à la mouche devant les spectaculaires sommets enneigés, que l'on parte à cheval admirer le soleil couchant sur le volcan Lanín ou que l'on récolte les légumes du jardin bio de l'hôtel, les activités de plein air les plus dépaysantes ne manquent pas.

La grande qualité de l'accueil, le partage de la vie quotidienne des gauchos du ranch, sans oublier les aménagements luxueux du lodge transforment le séjour en une aventure pleine d'agréments. Cet hôtel compte évidemment parmi les lieux que l'on n'a absolument aucune envie de quitter.

LOCATION
From Buenos Aires, it's a 2-hour flight to San Martín de los Andes in the southwest; transfer to the lodge from there takes just 10 minutes

RATES
Singles from $540, doubles from $880, full board and outdoor activities included

ROOMS
9 modern yet rustic rooms in the lodge, plus a 5-room house (can be booked only as a whole)

STYLE
Luxurious country living against the backdrop of spectacular scenery

FOOD
Fine dining with traditional dishes and Argentinean wines

X FACTOR
The working cattle ranch makes this the perfect place for anyone who harbors dreams of being a cowboy—or simply hankers for a great steak

BOOKS TO PACK
"In Patagonia" by Bruce Chatwin and "A Pioneer In Patagonia" by Miguel de Larminat

LAGE
San Martín de los Andes liegt 2 Flugstunden südwestlich von Buenos Aires; der Transfer zur Lodge dauert dann nur mehr 10 Minuten

PREISE
Einzelzimmer ab 400 €, Doppelzimmer ab 650 €, mit Vollpension und Outdoor-Aktivitäten

ZIMMER
9 modern-rustikale Zimmer in der Lodge, 1 Haus mit 5 Zimmern (nur als Einheit zu mieten)

STIL
Gehobenes *country life* vor absolut grandioser Landschaftskulisse

KÜCHE
Hervorragend verfeinerte traditionelle Gerichte und argentinische Weine

X-FAKTOR
Die Rinder-Ranch ist noch in Betrieb; das Haus ist also ideal für jeden, der Neigungen zum Cowboy-Dasein hat – oder auch bloß zu einem exzellenten Steak

BUCH ZUM ORT
„In Patagonien" von Bruce Chatwin

SITUATION
San Martín de los Andes se trouve à 2 heures de vol au sud-ouest de Buenos Aires; le transfert jusqu'au lodge dure 10 minutes

PRIX
Chambres single à partir de 400 €, chambres doubles à partir de 650 €, pension complète et activités en extérieur comprises

CHAMBRES
9 chambres modernes et rustiques dans le lodge, une maison avec 5 chambres (à louer en entier)

STYLE
Country life de luxe dans un paysage absolument grandiose

RESTAURATION
Plats traditionnels très raffinés et vins argentins

LE «PETIT PLUS»
Le ranch de bovins, en service, comblera tous ceux qui sont attirés par la vie de cow-boy ou qui ont envie de déguster un excellent steak

LIVRE À EMPORTER
«En Patagonie» de Bruce Chatwin

LONGITUDE 131°
AUSTRALIA

1 Yulara Dr ~ Yulara NT 0872 ~ Australia
Telephone +61 8 8957 7131 ~ Fax +61 8 8957 7130
reserve@baillielodges.com.au
www.longitude131.com.au

Camping with added glamour, "glamping" is an idea that originated in the U.K. This particularly fine example, though, is in Australia—at Longitude 131° (both the name of the resort and, in the absence of streets, the address).

Situated not far from Uluru, or Ayers Rock as it is better known, these 15 "tents" offer adventure-seeking guests the opportunity to get as close to the outback as possible, without having to sacrifice creature comforts. The canopied cabins are as well equipped as a good hotel room, and the pool outside the Dune House is a rare and welcome sight in the central Australian desert. Such niceties, though, become secondary at dusk, when the setting sun bathes this sacred rock in a spectacular and ever-varying array of colors—leaving an equally special starlit sky in its wake.

Der Begriff „Glamping" bezeichnet eine neue Form des Campings, bei dem das Leben draußen in der Natur mit glamourösem Komfort kombiniert wird. Erfunden haben das zwar die Briten, die Australier jedoch liefern mit dem Longitude 131° ein wahres Musterbeispiel dafür. Der Name ist übrigens gleichzeitig Adresse: Wo es keine Straßen gibt, muss eben der Längengrad als Ortsangabe herhalten.

Unweit des Uluru, besser bekannt als Ayers Rock, stehen hier mitten in der Wüstensteppe 15 Pavillons, in denen abenteuerlustige Gäste das Outback so direkt erfahren wie nirgendwo sonst. Entbehrungen bleiben dennoch außen vor: Die Zeltkabinen müssen sich mit ihrer Ausstattung nicht hinter einem guten Hotelzimmer verstecken, und der Pool vor dem Hauptgebäude ist in der zentralaustralischen Wüste schon etwas Besonderes. Das alles aber ist mit dem Sonnenuntergang vergessen, der den heiligen Berg der Aborigines jeden Abend in neue, wunderbare Farben taucht – gefolgt von einem einzigartigen Sternenhimmel.

Le «glamping» n'est autre qu'une nouvelle forme de camping, combinant la vie en plein air et le confort glamour. Inventée par les Britanniques, cette formule prend véritablement tout son sens avec l'hôtel australien Longitude 131°, dont le nom tient aussi lieu d'adresse : à défaut de rues pour se repérer, seul le degré de longitude permet de localiser l'endroit.

Non loin d'Uluru, plus connu sous le nom d'Ayers Rock, se dressent au beau milieu du désert 15 pavillons en forme de tente, dont les hôtes épris d'aventure font l'expérience de l'outback australien dans des conditions exceptionnelles et sans jamais ressentir la moindre privation. L'aménagement des tentes n'a en effet rien à envier à celui d'une chambre d'hôtel luxueuse, et la piscine située devant le bâtiment principal crée la surprise dans le désert australien. Chaque soir, le soleil couchant éclipse tout et baigne de lumière la montagne sacrée des Aborigènes, donnant à la roche des teintes toujours nouvelles, avant de laisser place à un ciel étoilé étincelant.

LOCATION
In the Australian heartland within view of
UNESCO heritage site Uluru (Ayers Rock)

RATES
Tents from $2,110, minimum stay of 2 nights

ROOMS
15 luxury tents with views of Uluru and the
surrounding desert

STYLE
Glamping (glamorous camping)

FOOD
Modern gourmet cuisine; a dinner under the
starry outback sky is included

X FACTOR
This is no ordinary restaurant terrace: At Table
131°, guests dine in the open desert by the light
of a campfire—and gain a taste of the ancient
indigenous culture at the same time

BOOK TO PACK
"Our Sunshine" by Robert Drewe

LAGE
Im Herzen Australiens in Sichtweite des
UNESCO-Weltkulturerbes Uluru (Ayers Rock)

PREISE
Zelt ab 1550 €, Mindestaufenthalt von 2 Nächten

ZIMMER
15 Luxus-Zelte mit Blick auf den Uluru und die
umliegende Wüste

STIL
Glamping (Glamour + Camping)

KÜCHE
Moderne Gourmet-Cuisine; ein Abendessen
unter dem Sternengefunkel des Outback ist
in der Buchung inbegriffen

X-FAKTOR
Hier gibt es nicht nur irgendein Abendessen
auf der Terrasse: An „Tisch 131°" sitzt man in der
Wüste und wird im Schein des Lagerfeuers mit
der uralten Kultur dieses Ortes vertraut

BUCH ZUM ORT
„Our Sunshine" von Robert Drewe

SITUATION
Au cœur de l'Australie, à proximité d'Ayers Rock,
inscrit au patrimoine mondial de l'UNESCO

PRIX
Tentes à partir de 1550 €, 2 nuits minimum

CHAMBRES
15 tentes de luxe avec vue sur Ayers Rock et
le désert environnant

STYLE
Glamping (glamour + camping)

RESTAURATION
Cuisine moderne raffinée; un dîner à la belle
étoile est compris dans la réservation

LE «PETIT PLUS»
Ici, l'offre ne se limite pas tout simplement
au dîner en terrasse: à la Table 131°, assis au
beau milieu du désert, on se familiarise avec
la culture locale très ancienne à la lueur du
feu de camp

LIVRE À EMPORTER
«Our Sunshine» de Robert Drewe

ON AUGUST 8 19

AURELIO LECH
AUSTRIA

Tannberg 130 ~ 6764 Lech am Arlberg ~ Austria
Telephone +43 5583 2214 ~ Fax +43 5583 3456
reservation@aureliolech.com
www.aureliolech.com

Being a guest at Hotel Aurelio is rather like staying at the chalet of extremely well-heeled friends in the Vorarlberg Alps. Its cozy charm is a result of the virtuoso use of natural materials and of the fact that the rooms and suites—of which there are just 14 and 5, respectively—are spread across several houses. This makes it an ideal venue for either peaceful vacations or private parties. The hotel is particularly proud of its sundeck, which is situated right by the legendary Schlegelkopf piste. In contrast to the dramatic mountain landscape outside, the in-house spa is calm and minimalist, with clean lines, crystal-clear water, and treatments using everything from local herbs to caviar masks. After all, Lech and the Aurelio in particular is not just about Alpine charm; in the skiing season, it's also a popular destination for the haut monde of the pistes.

Wie im Chalet von bestbetuchten Freunden, so fühlt sich der Gast des Hotel Aurelio in den Vorarlberger Alpen von der ersten Minute an. Erzielt wird der gemütliche Charme durch den virtuosen Einsatz von Naturmaterialien und die Aufteilung der lediglich 14 Zimmer und 5 Suiten auf mehrere Häuser – ideal für private Feiern oder auch den wirklich ruhigen Urlaub.

Besonders stolz ist man hier zu Recht auf die Sonnenterrasse, direkt an der legendären Schlegelkopfpiste gelegen. Als Kontrast zur imposanten Bergwelt draußen präsentiert sich der Spa-Bereich beruhigend puristisch. Klare Linien, klares Wasser und dazu Anwendungen mit heimischen Alpenkräutern – oder eben auch Kaviarwickel. Denn bei aller Gemütlichkeit ist das mondäne Örtchen Lech, und hier insbesondere das Aurelio, während der Schneesaison eine Top-Adresse, an der sich die „Ski-ckeria" gerne sehen lässt.

À l'hôtel Aurelio, perché dans les Alpes autrichiennes, on a immédiatement l'impression d'être reçu dans le chalet d'amis très fortunés. Ce charme particulier tient aux matériaux naturels employés avec bonheur et à la répartition sur plusieurs bâtiments des 14 chambres et des 5 suites. Un cadre idéal pour organiser des réceptions privées ou profiter du calme.

La terrasse bien exposée, qui donne directement sur la fameuse piste de Schlegelkopf, fait la fierté des propriétaires, et à juste titre. Contrastant avec l'imposant paysage montagneux, l'architecture du spa est épurée et apaisante, et l'eau y est cristalline. On se relaxe avec des soins aux herbes alpines ainsi que des enveloppements au caviar. Situé dans la station mondaine de Lech, l'hôtel Aurelio est pendant la haute saison une adresse de choix où les skieurs de la haute société aiment se montrer.

LOCATION

Lech is situated in the western Austrian state of Vorarlberg, 94 km/58 miles from Bregenz and 124 km/77 miles from Innsbruck

RATES

Double rooms from $1,140, suites from $2,090

ROOMS

14 rooms and 5 suites

STYLE

Stunning chalet flair in Alpine surroundings; the interiors are by world-renowned London designers Mlinaric, Henry & Zervudachi

FOOD

The spa has its own health bar offering fresh fruit, teas, and snacks

X FACTOR

The Aurelio offers its guests a personal ski butler service; your butler will organize sports equipment and lunches, and even book a helicopter flight if required

BOOK TO PACK

"Women in Love" by D. H. Lawrence

LAGE

Lech liegt im westlichsten österreichischen Bundesland Vorarlberg, 124 km von Innsbruck und 94 km von Bregenz entfernt

PREISE

Doppelzimmer ab 850 €, Suiten ab 1550 €

ZIMMER

14 Zimmer und 5 Suiten

STIL

Fabelhaftes Chalet-Flair in ebensolcher Alpen-Umgebung; die Ausstattung stammt vom welt-bekannten Londoner Interiorbüro Mlinaric, Henry & Zervudachi

KÜCHE

Zum Spa gehört eine Vitalbar, die frische Früchte, Tees und Snacks anbietet

X-FAKTOR

Auf Wunsch bekommt man vom Aurelio einen persönlichen Ski-Butler zugeteilt, der sich um die Bretter kümmert, den Lunch organisiert und bei Bedarf auch einen Heliflug ordert

BUCH ZUM ORT

„Liebende Frauen" von D. H. Lawrence

SITUATION

Lech est situé dans le Land de Voralberg, dans l'ouest de l'Autriche, à 124 km d'Innsbruck et à 94 km de Bregenz

PRIX

Chambres doubles à partir de 850 €, suites à partir de 1550 €

CHAMBRES

14 chambres et 5 suites

STYLE

Dans un cadre alpin féérique, ce chalet de rêve a été aménagé par le célèbre cabinet londonien d'architecture intérieure Mlinaric, Henry & Zervudachi

RESTAURATION

Le « Vitalbar » propose des fruits frais, des thés et infusions, ainsi que des collations

LE « PETIT PLUS »

On peut profiter des services d'un majordome, qui se charge des skis ou du repas de midi ; sur demande, il réserve également les transferts en hélicoptère

LIVRE À EMPORTER

« Femmes amoureuses » de D. H. Lawrence

PRIESTEREGG
AUSTRIA

Sonnberg 22 ~ 5771 Leogang ~ Austria
Telephone +43 6583 825 520 ~ Fax +43 6583 825 54
bergdorf@priesteregg.at
www.priesteregg.at

Even in regions with no shortage of hotels, it's still possible, with a little vision, to create a getaway that stands out—as this resort high up in one of Austria's largest ski areas proves. True to its aim of providing an authentic Alpine experience, guests are greeted on first-name terms from the start and accommodated in individual chalets rather than suites. Breakfast is served in the chalets, which are fitted out in warm Swiss pine and stone and have small en suite wellness areas.

With its 16 houses, pond, and rustic tavern, Priesteregg, which sits 3,600 feet above sea level, feels like a real village, albeit one where there are no cars or power lines, just ample privacy. In spring, fruit trees blossom in front of the houses, while in winter a shuttle service takes guests to the nearest ski lift. The mountain scenery, of course, is a pleasure in any season—just sit on the bench outside your chalet, admire the valley views, and enjoy the life of an Alpine villager.

Visionäre können auch in einer touristisch bestens erschlossenen Region noch ein Ausrufezeichen setzen. So ist mitten in einem der größten Skigebiete Österreichs auf 1100 Höhenmetern mit dem Priesteregg ein Bergdorf entstanden, das sich ganz dem authentischen Bergurlaub verschrieben hat. Der Gast wird hier von der Buchung an geduzt, und die alpine Herzlichkeit ist in jeder der Almhütten, die man hier statt einer Suite bewohnt, zu spüren.

Das Frühstück wird morgens im Chalet angerichtet, jede Hütte verfügt über einen kleinen Wellnessbereich, und die Einrichtung besteht aus Zirbenholz und Naturstein. Mit 16 Häusern, Teich und Gasthaus ist das Priesteregg ein richtiges kleines Dorf geworden, ohne Autos und Strommasten, dafür mit viel Privatsphäre. Im Frühling blühen Obstbäume in den Bauerngärten vor den Chalets, im Winter gibt es einen Shuttle zum nächsten Lift. Zu jeder Jahreszeit kann man auf der Bank vor der eigenen Hütte sitzen und mit Blick ins Tal die Zufriedenheit der Älpler nachempfinden.

Les visionnaires peuvent encore surprendre, même dans une région très touristique. Situé au cœur de l'un des plus grands domaines skiables d'Autriche, Priesteregg est un hameau de montagne créé de toutes pièces à 1100 mètres d'altitude afin de proposer aux amoureux de la nature des vacances à la montagne authentiques. Le tutoiement est de rigueur dès la réservation et la convivialité alpine émane de chaque habitation.

Hébergés dans de petits chalets qui ont tout d'une suite avec leur sauna particulier, les hôtes prennent le petit déjeuner dans le chalet principal. Avec ses 16 maisons construites en pin cembro et en pierre naturelle, son étang et son auberge, Priesteregg est un véritable petit village sans voitures ni pylônes électriques où l'on profite du calme. Au printemps fleurissent les arbres fruitiers. En hiver, une navette conduit les hôtes au téléski le plus proche. En toute saison, on peut s'asseoir sur le banc de son chalet pour profiter de la vue sur la vallée et ressentir la sérénité du lieu.

LOCATION
70 km/43 miles from Salzburg in the Saalbach-Hinterglemm/Leogang piste network, but away from the usual skiing-season hubbub

RATES
Mountain chalets from $270, premium chalets from $325, buffet breakfast included; minimum stay of 3 nights

ROOMS
16 chalets, from a mountain chalet for 2 to a Bogner chalet for 5 with infinity pool

STYLE
Authentic yet luxurious Alpine chalets, each with its own spa

FOOD
First-class cuisine including local specialties such as *Kasnocken* and *Kaiserschmarrn*

X FACTOR
The two woodland bathtubs and massage couches on the edge of the resort offer alfresco relaxation with panoramic Alpine views

BOOK TO PACK
"The Post Office Girl" by Stefan Zweig

LAGE
70 km von Salzburg entfernt im Skigebiet Saalbach-Hinterglemm/Leogang gelegen, doch abseits des typischen Skigebiet-Trubels

PREISE
Berg-Chalets ab 200 €, Premium-Chalets ab 240 €, jeweils inklusive Bergfrühstück; der Mindestaufenthalt beträgt 3 Nächte

ZIMMER
16 Hütten, vom Berg-Chalet für 2 bis zum Bogner-Chalet mit Infinity-Pool für 5 Personen

STIL
Luxuriös-authentische Almhütten, jede mit eigenem Spa

KÜCHE
Exzellente Alpenküche von Kasnocken über geräucherte Forelle bis hin zu Kaiserschmarrn

X-FAKTOR
Am Rand des idyllischen Almdorfes lädt das Waldbad mit zwei Wannen und Massageliegen zum Entspannen vor Alpenpanorama ein

BUCH ZUM ORT
„Rausch der Verwandlung" von Stefan Zweig

SITUATION
À 70 km de Salzbourg, sur le domaine skiable de Saalbach-Hinterglemm/Leogang, loin de l'agitation des stations très fréquentées

PRIX
Chalets à partir de 200 €, chalets supérieurs à partir de 240 €, petit déjeuner inclus; 3 nuits minimum

CHAMBRES
16 chalets, du chalet montagnard pour 2 personnes au Willy-Bogner-Chalet avec piscine à débordement pour 5 personnes

STYLE
Chalets d'alpage authentiques et luxueux, avec spa privé

RESTAURATION
Excellente cuisine alpine dont les *Kasnocken*, la truite fumée et le *Kaiserschmarrn*

LE «PETIT PLUS»
Dans la forêt, une piscine avec deux bassins et des tables de massage invitent à la détente

LIVRE À EMPORTER
«Ivresse de la métamorphose» de Stefan Zweig

LOOSHAUS AM KREUZBERG
AUSTRIA

Kreuzberg 60 ~ 2650 Payerbach ~ Austria
Telephone +43 2666 52911 ~ Fax +43 2666 52911-34
steiner@looshaus.at
www.looshaus.at

Adolf Loos is one of the few architects from the late-19th and early-20th centuries whose aesthetic ethos still stands up today. The country house he built for the industrialist Paul Khuner in 1930 outside Payerbach in Austria was converted into a hotel and restaurant in 1959 and has been in the hands of the same family ever since. It wasn't until the early 1990s, however, that the building was returned to its historic state—fortunately the owners were able to locate much of the original furniture.

With its motto "architecture from the past for the people of today," the hotel is a must for fans of early modernist interiors, though its location in a mountainous region traditionally popular with Viennese tourists means it's also well worth a visit for those with only a passing interest in Loos's cabinetry. The woodland walks are magnificent in summer or winter—as is the fresh fish served up in the evenings by head chef Hanna Sehn.

Adolf Loos ist einer der wenigen Architekten der vorletzten Jahrhundertwende, deren Ästhetikverständnis bis heute Strahlkraft besitzt. Sein 1930 für den Industriellen Paul Khuner fertiggestelltes Landhaus am Kreuzberg ist seit 1959 ein Hotel-Restaurant und wird bis heute als Familienbetrieb geführt. Doch erst Anfang der 1990er-Jahre hat man damit begonnen, das Haus in den historischen Zustand zurückzubauen – zum Glück waren noch viele der originalen Einrichtungsstücke zu finden.

Mit dem Motto „Architektur von damals für Menschen von heute" ist das Looshaus eine Pflichtstation für die Fans von Interiors aus den Anfängen der Moderne. Seine Lage am Fuße des Semmerings, mitten im Wiener Sommerfrische-Gebiet, kann aber auch diejenigen begeistern, die sich für die Loos'schen Einbaumöbel nur am Rande interessieren. Schließlich findet man in dieser alten Kulturlandschaft sommers wie winters herrliche Spazierwege in waldiger Natur. Und abends, dank Küchenchefin Hanna Sehn, eine frische Forelle auf dem Tisch.

Adolf Loos est l'un des rares architectes du début du 20e siècle, dont les conceptions esthétiques ont conservé toute leur prégnance jusqu'à ce jour. C'est en 1930, sur les hauteurs du Kreuzberg, à Payerbach, que Loos construisit cette résidence secondaire pour l'industriel Paul Khuner, laquelle fut transformée en hôtel-restaurant en 1959. Il fallut attendre le début des années 1990 pour que l'on décide de rendre à cette entreprise familiale son aspect d'origine. Heureusement, une grande partie du mobilier avait été conservée.

Prônant l'«architecture d'autrefois pour les hommes d'aujourd'hui», la Looshaus constitue une étape incontournable pour les amoureux des intérieurs du début du mouvement moderne. Situé au pied du Semmering, cet hôtel peut aussi faire le bonheur de ceux qui ne succombent pas au charme du mobilier encastré de Loos. En été comme en hiver, le paysage alentour se prête à de très belles balades en forêt. Le soir, la truite fraîche de Hanna Sehn, aux commandes des fourneaux, ravit les papilles.

LOCATION
Situated approximately 2,950 feet above sea level, close to the Semmering Pass; 100 km/ 62 miles southwest of Vienna

RATES
Rooms from $130, buffet breakfast included

ROOMS
12 rooms with a total of 24 beds

STYLE
Mountain villa by a pioneer of modernism

FOOD
Local classics made with regional ingredients can be enjoyed beneath the high picture window of the hall, the focal point of the house

X FACTOR
The owners' genuine enthusiasm for "their" architect; they are always happy to talk about the restoration and the hunt for original furnishings

BOOK TO PACK
"Why a Man Should Be Well-Dressed: Appearances Can Be Revealing" by Adolf Loos

LAGE
Auf 900 m Höhe mit Blick auf Rax und Schnee-berg inmitten des Semmeringgebiets, 100 km südwestlich von Wien

PREISE
Zimmer ab 97 €, inklusive Frühstücksbuffet

ZIMMER
12 Zimmer mit insgesamt 24 Betten

STIL
Bergvilla von einem Pionier der Moderne

KÜCHE
Heimische Klassiker aus regionalen Zutaten werden vor dem hohen Panoramafenster in der Halle, dem Herzstück des Hauses, serviert

X-FAKTOR
Die handfeste Liebe der Betreiber zu „ihrem" Architekten; sie geben gerne Auskunft über Restauration und stilistische Schatzsuche

BUCH ZUM ORT
„Warum ein Mann gut angezogen sein soll: Enthüllendes über offenbar Verhüllendes" von Adolf Loos

SITUATION
À 900 m d'altitude avec vue sur le Rax et le Schneeberg, au cœur du domaine skiable du Semmering, à 100 km au sud-ouest de Vienne

PRIX
Chambres à partir de 97 €, petit déjeuner-buffet compris

CHAMBRES
12 chambres avec un total de 24 lits

STYLE
Villa montagnarde construite par l'un des pionniers du Mouvement moderne

RESTAURATION
Des plats régionaux classiques avec des produits locaux, servis dans la grande salle avec vue panoramique

LE «PETIT PLUS»
Indéfectiblement attachés à «leur» architecte, les hôteliers sont intarissables sur la restauration de l'hôtel et leur quête d'objets et de mobilier dans le style d'origine

LIVRE À EMPORTER
«Ornement et crime» d'Adolf Loos

"Do not build picturesquely. Leave such
effects to the walls, the mountains, and the sun."

ADOLF LOOS, *RULES FOR ONE WHO BUILDS IN THE MOUNTAINS*, 1913

„Baue nicht malerisch. Überlasse solche Wirkung den Mauern,
den Bergen und der Sonne."

«Ne cherche pas à construire de manière pittoresque. Laisse aux murs,
aux montagnes et au soleil le soin de rendre cet effet. »

MANOIR DE LÉBIOLES
BELGIUM

Domaine de Lébioles 1/5 ~ 4900 Spa (Creppe) ~ Belgium
Telephone +32 87 791 900 ~ Fax +32 87 791 999
manoir@manoirdelebioles.com
www.manoirdelebioles.com

There is more to it than meets the eye—the inscription on the Manoir de Lébioles crest is a fitting motto for the luxury hotel now housed within the manor's walls. The building itself, though, is far from unassuming: Surrounded by the woods of the Ardennes, it was built in the early 20th century by an illegitimate son of King Leopold I, whose aim was to create "le petit Versailles des Ardennes." It was later taken over by a businessman's family and used to host balls and hunts. Since 2006, it has been open to paying guests, who stay in rooms boasting four-poster beds, open fires, and furnishings in aristocratic colors.

As part of the redevelopment, the original flooring was painstakingly restored, along with more than 120 period windows. The service is first-class and agreeably discreet, the chef scored 16 Gault-Millau points, and the grounds are large enough to lose yourself in. An ideal venue for a secret rendezvous, be it for business or pleasure.

„Mehr Sein als Schein" – die Wappeninschrift des Manoir de Lébioles passt auch gut auf seine heutige Verwendung als diskretes Luxushotel in den Wäldern der Ardennen. Wobei das Gebäude an sich nicht gerade unspektakulär ist: Ein unehelicher Sohn König Leopolds I. ließ es zu Beginn des 20. Jahrhunderts als „kleines Versailles der Ardennen" erbauen. Später lud eine Kaufmannsfamilie hier zu Bällen und Jagdveranstaltungen. Erst seit 2006 können zahlende Gäste in den mit Himmelbetten, offenen Kaminen und Textilien in feudalen Farben ausgestatteten Räumen logieren.

Bei der Renovierung wurden mit großem Aufwand die historischen Böden freigelegt und die mehr als 120 Fenster restauriert. Der Service ist ebenso vortrefflich wie unsichtbar, der Koch hat 16 Gault-Millau-Punkte, und der Park ist groß genug, um sich darin zu verlaufen. Genau der richtige Ort für ein geheimes Tête-à-Tête, sei es beruflich oder privat.

«Être plutôt que paraître»: la devise inscrite sur les armoiries du manoir ne saurait mieux résumer la philosophie de cet hôtel de luxe à la splendeur discrète situé est situé dans la forêt des Ardennes. On doit la construction de ce «petit Versailles des Ardennes», qui date du début du 20ᵉ siècle, à un fils naturel de Léopold Iᵉʳ. Plus tard, une famille de commerçants y donna des bals et des parties de chasse. Transformé en hôtel en 2006, le manoir abrite des chambres agrémentées de cheminées, de tentures aux couleurs médiévales et de lits à baldaquin.

Au prix d'un travail minutieux, on a remis en état les sols d'origine et restauré les plus de 120 fenêtres de ce manoir entouré d'un vaste parc. Le service est aussi parfait que discret, et le chef de cuisine s'est vu attribuer 16 points au Gault et Millau. C'est un cadre idéal pour un tête-à-tête professionnel ou privé.

LOCATION
Idyllically situated in the hills surrounding Spa, 130 km/81 miles west of Cologne and 140 km/87 miles east of Brussels

RATES
Rooms from $260, suites from $355, excluding breakfast

ROOMS
16 rooms and suites

STYLE
Stately *maison de plaisance* in the woods

FOOD
The gourmet restaurant serves first-class regional dishes made with fresh ingredients from the market and boasts an exceptionally well-stocked wine cellar

X FACTOR
Once a year, this otherwise-peaceful place gets Grand Prix fever, when the international Formula 1 circus comes to the nearby circuit of Spa-Francorchamps

BOOK TO PACK
"Maigret on Holiday" by Georges Simenon

LAGE
Idyllisch in den Hügeln von Spa gelegen, 130 km westlich von Köln, 140 km östlich von Brüssel

PREISE
Zimmer ab 200 €, Suite ab 270 €, jeweils exklusive Frühstück

ZIMMER
16 Zimmer und Suiten

STIL
Seriöses Lustschloss im Wald

KÜCHE
Das Gourmetrestaurant serviert sehr feine regionale Menüs mit Zutaten frisch vom Markt und kann selbstverständlich auf einen bestens sortierten Weinkeller zurückgreifen

X-FAKTOR
Einmal im Jahr nimmt dieser ruhige Ort Fahrt auf – wenn der internationale Formel-1-Zirkus an der 13 km entfernten Rennstrecke von Spa Station macht

BUCH ZUM ORT
„Maigret macht Ferien" von Georges Simenon

SITUATION
Dans les charmantes collines de Spa, à 130 km à l'ouest de Cologne et à 140 km à l'est de Bruxelles

PRIX
Chambres à partir de 200 €, suites à partir de 270 €, petit déjeuner non compris

CHAMBRES
16 chambres et suites

STYLE
Château de plaisance dans la forêt

RESTAURATION
Le restaurant gastronomique propose des menus régionaux d'une grande finesse, préparés avec des produits du marché, et dispose bien sûr d'une excellente cave à vins

LE «PETIT PLUS»
Une fois par an, cet endroit paisible vit à plus de 300 à l'heure quand le circuit automobile de Spa, situé à 13 km, accueille les bolides du Grand Prix de Formule 1 de Belgique

LIVRE À EMPORTER
«Les Vacances de Maigret» de Georges Simenon

BLANCANEAUX LODGE
BELIZE

Mountain Pine Ridge Forest Reserve
Cayo District ~ Belize
Telephone +501 824 3878
info@coppolaresorts.com
www.coppolaresorts.com

In the early 1980s, Francis Ford Coppola visited Belize (formerly known as British Honduras) and instantly fell in love with this small country on the Caribbean coast. Soon after, the director bought the then-abandoned Blancaneaux Lodge and turned it into a vacation retreat for his extended family. It's not hard to see the attraction—after all, this tropical paradise seems predestined to be a movie location, with lush green rainforest all around, crystal-clear streams and waterfalls, overgrown Maya ruins, and monkeys swinging from the trees.

Since 1993, it has been run as a hotel in which guests stay in straw-roof pavilions that combine a Swiss Family Robinson atmosphere with cosmopolitan interiors featuring Guatemalan fabrics and antiques. Alternatively, guests can book Mr. Coppola's villa itself, which, as you'd expect, has the pick of the views and its own pool.

In den frühen 1980er-Jahren besuchte Francis Ford Coppola Belize und verliebte sich sofort in das kleine Land am karibischen Meer, das früher Britisch-Honduras hieß. Kurzerhand kaufte der Regisseur die verlassene Blancaneaux Lodge im Regenwald und richtete sie als Ferienrefugium für seinen Clan ein. Was uns nicht wundert, die Kulisse ist absolut filmreif: glasklare Bäche und Wasserfälle im Grün des Dschungels, dazu überwachsene Maya-Ruinen und Äffchen in den Bäumen.

Seit 1993 wird die Lodge als Hotel geführt, die Gäste wohnen in einer Handvoll strohgedeckter Pavillons, die ein Lebensgefühl à la Schweizer Familie Robinson vermitteln und kosmopolitisch mit guatemaltekischen Stoffen und Antiquitäten ausgestattet wurden. Sogar die Villa von Mr. Coppola *himself* kann man buchen, standesgemäß natürlich mit eigenem Pool und der besten Aussicht über dieses kleine Tropenparadies.

Au début des années 1980, Francis Ford Coppola se rendit au Belize et tomba amoureux de ce petit pays, anciennement Honduras britannique, situé sur la mer des Antilles. Sans plus attendre, le cinéaste acheta dans la forêt tropicale un lodge abandonné, qu'il transforma en refuge privé. Rien de moins surprenant, car le site a tout d'un décor de cinéma avec ses cascades et ses ruisseaux aux eaux cristallines sur fond de jungle et de ruines mayas, sans oublier la compagnie des petits singes dans les arbres.

Devenu hôtel en 1993, le lodge accueille ses hôtes dans des *cabañas* au toit de chaume ornées d'étoffes et d'antiquités guatémaltèques, leur donnant ainsi l'impression de vivre les aventures de la famille du *Robinson suisse*. On peut même louer la villa avec piscine du célèbre propriétaire, qui bénéficie bien sûr de la plus belle vue sur ce petit paradis tropical.

LOCATION
Situated by Privassion Creek in the Maya Mountains; the nearest town is San Ignacio (115 km/71 miles southwest of Belize City)

RATES
Cabanas from $268, villas from $525, breakfast included

ROOMS
20 cabanas and villas

STYLE
For globe-trotters who want adventure now (without the air of apocalypse)

FOOD
Montagna Restaurant serves Italian dishes cooked according to Coppola family recipes, and there is also a Guatemalan tavern

X FACTOR
Definitely the waterfall spa—you'll be hard put to find a more perfect and refreshing setting for a massage

BOOK TO PACK
"Maya: Divine Kings of the Rainforest" by Nikolai Grube

LAGE
Am Privassion Creek in den Maya Mountains; die nächste Stadt ist San Ignacio, das 115 km südwestlich von Belize City liegt

PREISE
Cabaña ab 200 €, Villa ab 390 €, inklusive Frühstück

ZIMMER
20 Cabañas und Villen

STIL
Für Zivilisationsmüde, die *Abenteuer Now* ohne Komfort-Apokalypse suchen

KÜCHE
Im Montagna Restaurant wird nach italienischen Rezepten der Coppolas gekocht, aber es gibt auch ein guatemaltekisches Lokal

X-FAKTOR
Eindeutig das Wasserfall-Spa – nie zuvor wurde man in so einem perfekten und vor allem zutiefst erfrischenden Ambiente massiert

BUCH ZUM ORT
„Maya. Gottkönige im Regenwald" von Nikolai Grube

SITUATION
Privassion Creek dans les monts Maya; la ville la plus proche est San Ignacio (à 115 km au sud-ouest de Belize City)

PRIX
Cabañas à partir de 200 €, villas à partir de 390 €, petit déjeuner inclus

CHAMBRES
20 cabañas et villas

STYLE
Pour ceux qui veulent se couper du monde sans avoir à composer avec un confort apocalyptique

RESTAURATION
Le Montagna Restaurant, qui prépare les plats d'après les recettes italiennes des Coppola, et un restaurant guatémaltèque

LE « PETIT PLUS »
Le spa à cascade : jamais on ne s'était fait masser dans une ambiance aussi rafraîchissante

LIVRE À EMPORTER
« Mayas – Les dieux sacrés de la forêt tropicale » de Nicolai Grube

"It's like being on location
for a movie—you just bring everything
with you or build it yourself."

FRANCIS FORD COPPOLA

„Es ist wie am entlegenen Drehort eines Films: Alles wird herangeschleppt
oder einfach selbst gebaut."

« C'est comme sur un lieu de tournage au bout du monde :
on emporte tout avec soi ou on construit tout sur place. »

UMA BY COMO
BHUTAN

P.O. Box 222 ~ Paro ~ Bhutan
Telephone +975 827 1597 ~ Fax +975 827 1513
uma.paro@comohotels.com
www.comohotels.com/umaparo

If there were such a thing as a hideaway for the soul, then this would surely be the place. White magnolia blossoms twinkle against the backdrop of the garden's Himalayan pines and cypresses, small colored flags flap in the mountain breeze, and the sun blazes in a cobalt-blue sky.

In Paro Valley, meditation is part of everyday life and the sound of distant prayer bells is ever present. In the 8th century, Guru Rinpoche is said to have come here in order to release the people from the curse of angry spirits and to convert them to Buddhism; now the spot where he landed after flying over the Himalayas on the back of a tigress is marked by the Taktsang monastery, which perches precariously on the side of a mountain. Unwind by the fire, green tea martini or chai-spiced hot chocolate in hand, after visiting one of the many such holy sites, then enjoy a hot stone treatment with local herbs—sheer bliss for both body and soul.

Wenn es so etwas wie ein *hideout* für die Seele gibt, dann muss es genau hier sein. Wie weiße Sterne leuchten die Blüten der Magnolien im Garten zwischen Tränenkiefern und Himalaja-Zypressen, knallbunt flattern kleine Fahnen im Bergwind, kobaltblau strahlt der Himmel über dem Paro-Tal. Allgegenwärtig ist das ferne Klingeln der Gebetsmühlen. Meditation ist hier Alltag.

Im 8. Jahrhundert soll Religionsstifter Guru Rinpoche nach seinem Flug über den Himalaja auf dem Rücken einer Tigerin hier gelandet sein, um die Menschen vom Fluch der aufgebrachten Naturgeister zu befreien und sie zum Buddhismus zu bekehren. Nun kleben an dieser Stelle die Mauern des Taktsang-Klosters in der steilen Felswand. Nach einem Ausflug zu einem der vielen Klöster am Kaminfeuer des Salons einen Green Tea Martini oder eine mit Chai gewürzte heiße Schokolade trinken, sich im Spa auf heißen Steinen mit einheimischen Kräutern behandeln lassen – das genügt an diesem Ort völlig. Der Rest ist Weite und Atem.

S'il existe un refuge pour l'âme, c'est bien ici qu'il se trouve. Sur le fond bleu cobalt du ciel de la vallée de Paro, les étoiles blanches des fleurs de magnolia scintillent entre les pins et les cyprès de l'Himalaya et les petits drapeaux colorés flottent au gré du vent. Le tintement lointain des moulins à prière est omniprésent dans ce pays où la méditation est une pratique quotidienne.

Au VIIIe siècle, le maître bouddhiste Padmasambhava serait arrivé ici après avoir franchi l'Himalaya à dos de tigresse. Il aurait alors libéré les habitants du sortilège lancé par les esprits courroucés de la nature et les aurait convertis au bouddhisme. C'est à cette falaise qu'est accroché le monastère de Taktshang. Après avoir visité l'un des nombreux monastères de la région, un martini au thé vert ou un chocolat chaud au *chai* devant un bon feu de bois, puis un soin aux herbes locales prodigué sur des pierres chaudes dans l'espace de remise en forme, suffiront à combler vos désirs.

LOCATION
On the southeastern edge of the Himalayas in the kingdom of Bhutan, just a 10-minute drive from Paro Airport

RATES
Rooms from $395, villas from $590

ROOMS
29 guest rooms and suites, including 9 villas

STYLE
A modern take on Bhutanese arts and crafts, with stone, wood, and tile interiors, furniture painted by local artists, and Nepalese rugs

FOOD
Bhutanese, Indian, and international cuisine made with locally sourced ingredients

X FACTOR
Yoga pioneers such as Judy Krupp and Eileen Hall are regular visitors to Uma by Como. After one of their intensive courses in the open yoga pavilion, you are lost for pretentiously esoteric yoga classes at home

BOOK TO PACK
"Beyond the Sky and Earth" by Jamie Zeppa

LAGE
An den südöstlichen Ausläufern des Himalajas im Königreich Bhutan gelegen, 10 Minuten Autofahrt von Paro Airport

PREISE
Zimmer ab 300 €, Villen ab 450 €

ZIMMER
29 Gästezimmer und Suiten, davon 9 Villen

STIL
Heutige Interpretation von Bhutans Tradition: Stein, Holz und Fliesen, von einheimischen Künstlern bemalte Möbel, Teppiche aus Nepal

KÜCHE
Mit regionalen Zutaten wird bhutanisch, indisch und international gekocht

X-FAKTOR
Yoga-Vordenker wie Judy Krupp oder Eileen Hall machen regelmäßig Station im Uma by Como und bieten Intensivkurse im offenen Yoga-Pavillon an. Danach ist man für esoterische La-di-da-Gymnastik verloren

BUCH ZUM ORT
„Mein Leben in Bhutan" von Jamie Zeppa

SITUATION
Sur les contreforts sud-est de l'Himalaya, dans le royaume du Bhoutan, à 10 minutes de l'aéroport de Paro

PRIX
Chambres à partir de 300 €, villas dès 450 €

CHAMBRES
29 chambres et suites, dont 9 villas

STYLE
Tradition bhoutanaise revisitée : pierre, bois et carrelage, meubles peints par des artistes locaux, tapis du Népal

RESTAURATION
Cuisine bhoutanaise, indienne et internationale préparée avec des produits locaux

LE « PETIT PLUS »
Des maîtres à penser du yoga, comme Judy Krupp et Eileen Hall, animent régulièrement des stages dans le pavillon de yoga. De quoi devenir accro à ces cours teintés d'ésotérisme !

LIVRE À EMPORTER
« Bhoutan – Voyage au pays de Bouddha » de Michaël Pitiot

"Christina Ong [Uma by Como's founder]
brings the East to the West, and the West to the East.
That's pretty global."
DONNA KARAN

„Christina Ong (die Gründerin des Hotels) bringt den Osten in den Westen
und den Westen in den Osten. Das nenne ich globales Denken."

« Christina Ong (fondatrice de l'hôtel) apporte l'Orient en Occident et l'Occident en Orient.
C'est ce que j'appelle la mentalité globale. »

SAN CAMP
BOTSWANA

Makgadikgadi Salt Pans ~ Botswana
Telephone +27 11 447 1605
reservations@unchartedafrica.com
www.unchartedafrica.com

Sometimes it's so quiet here, you can hear the sound of your own blood pumping, say the operators of San Camp. Aside from enjoying a tranquillity that is broken only by the occasional animal call, guests at this Kalahari Desert retreat can take walks with local bushmen, explore the vast Makgadikgadi Salt Pans via quad bike, and even interact with a family of human-habituated meerkats.

The camp itself was founded by the scions of a famous family of big-game hunters and conjures up images of glorious historical expeditions. The six white tents, standing majestically amid desert palms, boast feather bedding, hot-water bottles, paraffin lamps lamps, and Persian carpets—plus, of course, en suite bathrooms. And on the subject of quiet: The vistas of endless grasslands or starry night skies afforded by the veranda are wonders best enjoyed in reverential silence.

Hier sei es oft so still, dass man das eigene Blut rauschen höre, sagen die Betreiber des San Camp über ihren Standort in der Kalahari. Neben dem Genuss dieser Ruhe, die nur von den gelegentlichen Lauten der Tiere durchbrochen wird, bieten sich dem Gast von Einheimischen geführte Touren durch die Wüste oder Quad-Trips zu den weitläufigen Makgadikgadi-Salzpfannen an. Im Camp selbst sorgt eine zahme Erdmännchen-Familie für vergnügliche Begegnungen.

San Camp wurde von Sprösslingen einer ruhmreichen Großwildjäger-Familie eingerichtet und beschwört die wunderbare Welt historischer Expeditionen herauf. Zwischen Oasenpalmen stehen majestätisch sechs weiße Zelte, darin finden sich Federbetten mit Wärmflaschen, Paraffinlampen und Perserteppiche; und natürlich auch En-suite-Bäder. Apropos Stille: Die grandiose Weite, die man von der Veranda aus überblickt, und der Sternenhimmel funktionieren ohne Worte am besten.

Ici, le calme est tel qu'on peut entendre son propre sang couler dans ses veines. C'est du moins ce qu'affirment les propriétaires du San Camp. En plus de jouir d'une quiétude rompue seulement par les cris occasionnels des animaux, les hôtes de ce refuge planté dans le désert du Kalahari peuvent faire des balades à pied avec les Bochimans du cru, explorer au guidon d'un quad l'immensité du pan de Makgadikgadi, et même jouer avec une famille de suricates habitués à la présence des humains.

Aménagé par les descendants d'une célèbre famille de chasseurs de gros gibier, le lodge évoque les aventures merveilleuses d'expéditions historiques. Entre les palmiers se dressent majestueusement six tentes blanches pourvues de couettes et de bouillottes, de lampe à huile de paraffine, de tapis persans et, bien sûr, d'une salle d'eau individuelle. Pour en revenir au silence : le paysage grandiose sur lequel on a vue depuis la véranda et la voûte étoilée se passent parfaitement de mots.

LOCATION
In the Kalahari desert, on the edge of the Makgadikgadi Salt Pans

RATES
From $1,170 per person per night, all meals, beverages, and expeditions included

ROOMS
2 double and 4 twin tents, each with its own bathroom and veranda

STYLE
Inside, a contemporary take on colonial style that Ralph Lauren would surely adore; outside, "God's own minimalism" (A. A. Gill)

FOOD
The meals served up in the camp's mess tent are worthy of a luxury-hotel restaurant

X FACTOR
The morning walk with Zu/'hoasi bushmen is an experience you'll remember (and reminisce about) for a very long time

BOOK TO PACK
"The No. 1 Ladies' Detective Agency" by Alexander McCall Smith

LAGE
In der Wüste Kalahari, am Rande der riesigen Makgadikgadi-Salzpfanne

PREISE
Ab 860 € pro Person und Nacht; alle Getränke, Speisen und Ausflüge sind inbegriffen

ZIMMER
4 Doppel- und 2 Zweibettzimmer, jeweils mit eigenem Bad und Veranda

STIL
Drinnen ein Update des Kolonialstils, wie ihn Ralph Lauren lieben würde; draußen „God's own minimalism" (A. A. Gill)

KÜCHE
Was im *mess tent* des Camps serviert wird, hält dem Vergleich mit Luxushotels stand

X-FAKTOR
Ein Erlebnis, von dem man noch lange zehrt (und erzählt): Morgenwanderung gemeinsam mit den Zu'hoasi-Buschmännern

BUCH ZUM ORT
„Ein Krokodil für Mma Ramotswe" von Alexander McCall Smith

SITUATION
Dans le désert du Kalahari, en bordure de l'immense pan de Makgadikgadi

PRIX
À partir de 860 € par personne et par nuit, boissons, repas et excursions inclus

CHAMBRES
4 chambres doubles et 2 chambres à lits jumeaux, avec salle d'eau et véranda

STYLE
À l'intérieur, un style colonial revisité qui plairait à Ralph Lauren; à l'extérieur, « le minimalisme de Dieu » (A. A. Gill)

RESTAURATION
Servis dans la tente commune, les repas sont dignes des grands hôtels

LE « PETIT PLUS »
La promenade le matin avec les Bushmen Zu'hoasi nourrira longtemps l'imaginaire et les conversations

LIVRE À EMPORTER
« Mma Ramotswe détective » d'Alexander McCall Smith

ZARAFA CAMP
BOTSWANA

Selinda Reserve ~ Kasane ~ Botswana
Telephone +27 21 434 5208 ~ Fax +27 86 671 7610
reservations@greatplainsconservation.com
www.greatplainsconservation.com

It sounds almost surreal, but at this small camp in the Botswanan savanna you can watch elephants stroll by as you relax in a copper bathtub. Situated by a lagoon and next to a forest of ebony trees, the camp offers an old-style British safari experience: accommodation is spread across four separate tents, each outfitted with sturdy campaign furniture.

The camp's impeccable environmental credentials, on the other hand, are rather more contemporary, with all electricity generated by solar power, while the maximum human occupancy of eight ensures the fauna always gets the attention it deserves. What's more, the only shooting around here is of the photographic variety—an SLR camera and zoom lens, perfect for capturing the buffalo, zebra, and hippos in and around the lagoon, is provided for each tent. The resulting photos are then burned on a DVD as a souvenir from the wilderness.

Klingt schon leicht exzentrisch: in einer Kupferbadewanne sitzen und dabei beobachten, wie Elefanten durch das Camp ziehen. Genau diesen Zeitvertreib ermöglicht das kleine Zarafa Camp, gelegen zwischen Savanne, Wasserstelle und einem Wald von Ebenholzbäumen. Ganz dem britischen Safari-Erbe verpflichtet, beherbergen hier vier Zelte, eingerichtet mit robuster *campaign furniture*, die Gäste. Durchaus heutig aber ist der Öko-Gedanke, der mustergültig exerziert wird; so wird das Camp zum Beispiel komplett mit Solarstrom betrieben.

Da die Maximalbelegung acht menschliche Gäste beträgt, hat die Tierwelt hier immer die Aufmerksamkeit, die sie verdient. Geschossen wird nur mit der Linse – in jedem der Zelte wartet eine Spiegelreflexkamera mit Zoom, mit der man das Treiben von Büffel, Zebra und Hippo an oder in der Lagune dokumentieren kann. Die Bilder gibt's dann als Gruß aus der Wildnis auf DVD gebrannt.

Qu'y a-t-il de plus surréaliste que de prendre son bain dans une baignoire en cuivre tout en regardant les éléphants passer devant le lodge? C'est précisément l'une des distractions que propose le Zarafa Camp, situé entre la savane, un lagon et une forêt d'ébéniers. Dans l'esprit des premiers safaris britanniques, quatre tentes pourvues d'un mobilier de voyage robuste sont mises à la disposition des hôtes. Particulièrement soucieux de l'environnement, les fondateurs du lodge l'ont équipé de panneaux solaires.

Le lieu ne pouvant accueillir plus de huit personnes, les animaux sont au centre de toutes les attentions. Le téléobjectif de l'appareil photo reflex mis à disposition sous chaque tente est le seul viseur autorisé pour prendre sur le vif les buffles, les zèbres ou les hippopotames vivant dans le lagon ou venant s'y abreuver. Un DVD des photos est ensuite offert à leurs auteurs en souvenir de la savane.

LOCATION
Overlooking Zibadianja Lagoon in the Selinda
Reserve (northeast of the Okavango Delta);
50 minutes by plane, to the southwest of Kasane

RATES
Tents from $1,945 (single) or $2,880 (double)
per day, full board and morning and late-after-
noon game drives included

ROOMS
Four 1,000 sq. ft. tents, each with bedroom,
bathroom, lounge, and veranda with plunge pool

STYLE
Safari club on decks of old railroad ties

FOOD
Breakfast, brunch, afternoon tea, and dinner
are served in the main tent

X FACTOR
With their eerie noises and never-ending skies,
the nighttime safaris by Land Cruiser offer the
kind of African experience you'd otherwise get
only in nature documentaries

BOOK TO PACK
"Botswana Time" by Will Randall

LAGE
An der Zibadianja-Lagune im Selinda-Reservat
gelegen (nordöstlich des Okavango-Deltas),
50 Flugminuten südwestlich von Kasane

PREISE
Zelt pro Tag ab 1440 € bei Einzel- und 2130 €
bei Doppelbelegung, inklusive Vollpension und
Game-Drives am Morgen und Spätnachmittag

ZIMMER
Vier 93-m²-Zelte mit Bad, Wohn- und Schlaf-
raum plus Veranda mit Tauchpool

STIL
Safari-Club auf Plateaus aus Ex-Bahntrassen

KÜCHE
Im Hauptzelt werden frühes Frühstück, Brunch,
Nachmittagstee und Abendessen serviert

X-FAKTOR
Unheimliche Geräusche und unfassbar hoher
Sternenhimmel: Besonders die Nachtsafaris
im Land Cruiser bieten ein Afrika-Erlebnis, wie
man es sonst nur mehr in Büchern findet

BUCH ZUM ORT
„Ein Engländer in Botswana" von Will Randall

SITUATION
Au bord du lagon de Zibadianja dans la réserve
de Selinda (au nord-est du delta de l'Okavango),
à 50 minutes de vol au sud-est de Kasane

PRIX
À partir de 1440 € par personne, à partir de
2130 € la tente pour deux, pension complète
et safaris inclus

CHAMBRES
4 tentes de 93 m² (salon, chambre et véranda
avec piscine privative)

STYLE
Inspiration Safari Club sur des plateaux réalisés
à partir d'anciennes traverses de chemin de fer

RESTAURATION
Le petit déjeuner, le brunch, le thé et le dîner
sont servis dans la tente principale

LE « PETIT PLUS »
Des bruits insolites et une voûte étoilée infinie :
les safaris nocturnes sont inoubliables

LIVRE À EMPORTER
« Vague à l'âme au Botswana » d'Alexander
McCall Smith

HOTEL SANTA TERESA
BRAZIL

Rua Almirante Alexandrino 660 ~ Santa Teresa
20241-260 Rio de Janeiro ~ RJ ~ Brazil
Telephone +55 213 380 0200
reservas@santateresahotel.com
www.santa-teresa-hotel.com

Guests at this Relais & Châteaux hotel needn't worry: Rio de Janeiro's Santa Teresa district is peaceful and safe. Situated on a hill up above downtown Rio, this historic neighborhood holds the cultural soul of the city and is home to one of the best hotels in South America.

A former plantation owner's mansion from the glorious age of cocoa and coffee trade, it combines a historic ambience with an urban ethnic vibe. The tropical garden, meanwhile, is the perfect place to don that white linen suit, sip redberry caipirinhas, and watch marmosets gamboling in the trees. Cocoa still plays a role today, albeit chiefly in the spa, which offers divine Brazil-nut-and-cocoa-butter treatments—after which you'll feel reinvigorated and ready for a trip into the pulsating city below.

Keine Sorge, das Viertel Santa Teresa oberhalb der City ist sicher und ruhig. Hier schlägt das kulturelle und historische Herz von Rio de Janeiro, und mittendrin wartet eines der besten Hotels Südamerikas, in dem man noch die gloriose Zeit des Kakao- und Kaffeehandels atmen kann.

Aus dem einstigen Herrenhaus einer Kaffeeplantage wurde ein Relais-&-Châteaux-Hotel, das sich einem urbanen Ethno-Stil verpflichtet hat. Genau das richtige Umfeld, um den weißen Leinenanzug im tropischen Garten auszuführen und bei einem Red-Berry-Caipirinha die Seidenäffchen in den Bäumen zu beobachten. Kakao gibt es heute natürlich auch noch, allerdings vor allem im Spa, wo Anwendungen mit Kakao- und Paranussbutter angeboten werden – ein Erlebnis zum Dahinschmelzen, das Kraft spendet für Ausflüge in die pulsierende Metropole unterhalb.

Aucune crainte à avoir : le quartier Santa Teresa, sur les hauteurs de Rio de Janeiro, est sûr et calme. Ce cœur historique et culturel de la ville abrite l'un des meilleurs hôtels d'Amérique du Sud où l'on peut encore s'imprégner de la grande époque du commerce du café et du cacao.

L'ancienne maison de maître d'une plantation de café est devenue cet hôtel Relais & Châteaux au style ethno-urbain. C'est le lieu idéal pour se promener vêtu de lin blanc dans le jardin tropical ou pour siroter une caïpirinha aux fruits rouges en observant les ouistitis dans les arbres. Le cacao est toujours d'actualité, mais il est surtout employé dans le spa, où l'on prodigue des soins à base de cacao et de noix du Brésil. C'est une expérience très relaxante qui permet de reprendre des forces avant d'aller arpenter les rues des quartiers trépidants de la métropole.

LOCATION
On a hill in the upscale Santa Teresa district, 12 miles from Galeão International Airport

RATES
Rooms from $460, suites from $825

ROOMS
28 rooms and 12 suites

STYLE
International interior design meets local influences, with wood, linen, and animal statues

FOOD
The excellent hotel restaurant Térèze combines fine French cuisine with Brazilian flavors

X FACTOR
Those fortunate enough to have a room with its own private veranda won't be able to get enough of the view—the panoramic vistas of the bay, the bustling city, and the mountains beyond are simply sensational

BOOK TO PACK
"Brazil" by John Updike

LAGE
Auf einem Hügel im noblen Viertel Santa Teresa gelegen, 20 km vom Galeão International Airport entfernt

PREISE
Zimmer ab 340 €, Suiten ab 610 €

ZIMMER
28 Zimmer und 12 Suiten

STIL
Globales Interiordesign mit lokalem Akzent: Massivholz, Leinen, Tierfiguren aus Holz

KÜCHE
Das ausgezeichnete Restaurant Térèze verbindet feine französische Küche und brasilianische Aromen

X-FAKTOR
Wer hier ein Zimmer mit eigener Veranda ergattert, will sich nicht mehr fortbewegen: Der Blick über die erstaunliche Metropole und das Meer ist immer wieder aufs Neue von majestätischer Schönheit

BUCH ZUM ORT
„Brasilien" von John Updike

SITUATION
Sur une colline, dans le quartier résidentiel de Santa Teresa, à 20 km de l'aéroport international de Rio de Janeiro-Galeão

PRIX
Chambres à partir de 340 €, suites à partir de 610 €

CHAMBRES
28 chambres et 12 suites

STYLE
International, avec une tonalité locale : bois massif, lin, sculptures animalières en bois

RESTAURATION
L'excellent restaurant Térèze marie le raffinement de la cuisine française et les saveurs du Brésil

LE « PETIT PLUS »
Ceux qui ont le privilège de loger dans une chambre avec véranda n'auront plus envie d'en sortir : la vue sur l'étonnante métropole et sur la mer est d'une beauté majestueuse

LIVRE À EMPORTER
« Brésil » de John Updike

VILA NAIÁ
BRAZIL

Corumbau ~ Bahia ~ Brazil
Telephone & Fax +55 73 573 1006
info@vilanaia.com.br
www.vilanaia.com.br

How to find it is one of the many things Vila Naiá's guests needn't worry about: The only way to get there is with the aid of a local. Situated near Corumbau on the edge of Brazil's Monte Pascoal national park, this small resort designed by architect Renato Marques and owner Renata Mellão seems far removed from the noise of Bahia, thanks to a soundtrack of rustling palm fronds and lapping waves.

Its suites, meanwhile, are as simple and unpretentious as the surroundings, without being too "back to nature" or sacrificing too much in the way of luxury. The four apartments and four houses are clearly structured and sparingly furnished, with colorful Eames chairs. Hammocks and orchid-hued ceilings provide a touch of Rio flair. The food, too, keeps things simple. Maria Alice Solimene creates delicious Brazilian dishes using whatever the fishermen deliver each morning plus fresh produce from the resort's own garden. The final ingredient in this extra-special sensory experience? The salty tang of the ever-present sea breeze.

Schon bei der Anfahrt hat man eine Sorge weniger: Wer ins Vila Naiá möchte, muss dem Orientierungssinn eines Einheimischen vertrauen. Das kleine Resort liegt an der Atlantikküste bei Corumbau am Rand des Nationalparks Monte Pascoal. Das laute Bahia ist hier ganz fern; dafür sind der Wind in den Palmen und das Wellenrauschen nah. Sie unterstreichen akustisch das kleine Wunder, das Architekt Renato Marques und Besitzerin Renata Mellão hier vollbracht haben: wohnliche Suiten und Bäder, ursprünglich und luxuriös.

Die vier Apartments und vier Häuser sind klar organisiert und sparsam möbliert. Für den Rio-Touch reichen farbige Eames-Stühle, Hängematten und Decken in Orchideentönen. Ohne Schnörkel kommt auch die Küche aus – Maria Alice Solimene verarbeitet das, was die Fischer jeden Morgen anliefern und der Garten hergibt, zu großartiger brasilianischer Küche. Die sensorische Abrundung ihrer Menüs besorgt die Natur: mit der hauchzarten Brise salziger Meeresluft, die man hier immer spürt.

Pour se rendre à la Vila Naiá, petit hôtel situé sur la côte atlantique près de Corumbau, en bordure du parc national de Monte Pascoal, il faut s'en remettre au sens de l'orientation d'un autochtone. La trépidante ville de Bahia semble être à des années-lumière. Ici, on n'entend que le bruissement du vent dans les palmiers et le roulement des vagues. Pour ce magnifique hôtel, l'architecte Renato Marques et la propriétaire Renata Mellão ont voulu créer des suites aussi simples et authentiques que la nature environnante, sans pour autant tomber dans l'écologie à outrance, mais dotées d'un certain luxe.

Les quatre appartements et les quatre maisons sont bien distribués et meublés sans exubérance. Les chaises Eames, les hamacs et les plafonds dans les tons orchidée sont les seules touches de couleur évoquant Rio. Également sans chichis, les délicieux plats brésiliens de Maria Alice Solimene sont préparés avec les légumes du jardin et la pêche du jour. La douce brise chargée d'embruns achève de combler vos sens.

LOCATION
Situated 60 km/37 miles south of Porto Seguro airport. Transfer to the resort by light aircraft (20 minutes), SUV (approx. 4 hours), or SUV and boat (just under 3 hours)

RATES
Apartment for 2 from $595, full board included

ROOMS
4 apartments for 1 to 2 persons, 4 houses for up to 3 persons

STYLE
Modern ethnic look with thoughtful details

FOOD
Gourmet-standard Brazilian dishes made with the freshest ingredients; delicious homemade flatbread

X FACTOR
Ultra-friendly staff; the fact that meals are served wherever guests want them, be it by the pool or in the apartment

BOOK TO PACK
"Captains of the Sand" by Jorge Amado

LAGE
60 km südlich des Flughafens Porto Seguro gelegen; Transfer zum Resort per Kleinflugzeug (20 Minuten), Landrover (4 Stunden) oder SUV und Boot (knapp 3 Stunden)

PREISE
Apartment für 2 ab 440 €, inklusive Vollpension

ZIMMER
4 Apartments für max. 2 Personen, 4 Häuser für max. 3 Personen

STIL
Moderner Ethno-Charme mit liebevollen Details

KÜCHE
Brasilianische Gerichte aus knackfrischen Zutaten, auf Gourmet-Niveau zubereitet; herrliches, selbst gebackenes Fladenbrot

X-FAKTOR
Überaus freundliches Personal, das Mahlzeiten dort serviert, wo man gerade Lust hat, sei es am Pool oder im Apartment

BUCH ZUM ORT
„Herren des Strandes" von Jorge Amado

SITUATION
À 60 km au sud de l'aéroport de Porto Seguro ; transfert en petit avion (20 minutes), en 4x4 (4 heures) ou en 4x4 et en bateau (3 heures)

PRIX
Appartement pour 2 personnes à partir de 440 € en pension complète

CHAMBRES
4 appartements pour 2 personnes, 4 maisons pour 3 personnes

STYLE
Charme ethno-moderne avec de séduisants détails

RESTAURATION
Plats brésiliens avec des produits de toute première fraîcheur, cuisine gastronomique ; délicieuses galettes de pain maison

LE « PETIT PLUS »
Un personnel particulièrement chaleureux, qui sert les plats où on le souhaite, que ce soit au bord de la piscine ou dans l'appartement

LIVRE À EMPORTER
« Capitaines des sables » de Jorge Amado

GOLDEN ROCK
CARIBBEAN

P.O. Box 493 ~ Charlestown ~ Nevis, West Indies
Telephone +1 869 469 3346 ~ Fax +1 869 469 2113
info@goldenrocknevis.com
www.goldenrocknevis.com

On the island of Nevis, the Caribbean still feels almost entirely unspoiled. There's not a building taller than a palm tree, and the slow pace of life follows the rhythm of the sun and the waves. Once, though, this was the bustling heart of a thriving sugarcane industry, and it's to this era that the buildings of the Golden Rock Inn date back. The old sugar mill and the surrounding cottages now house guest accommodations that have been beautifully decorated by the present-day owners, the New York artist Brice Marden and his wife, Helen, while the tropical greenery is dotted with the remains of old walls that make for a highly picturesque backdrop.

The furniture is mostly by local craftsmen, complemented by some of the owners' favorite design pieces. Above all, though, the ambience is influenced by the lavish tropical flowers that seem to accompany one's every step. A fragrant paradise for monkeys, hummingbirds—and a few lucky guests.

Auf der Insel Nevis ist die Karibik noch ganz bei sich. Kein Gebäude ist höher als eine Palme, und die Tage vergehen gemächlich im Rhythmus von Sonne und Wellen. Dabei ging es hier schon mal richtig heiß her: Nevis war einst das Herz der florierenden Zuckerrohrindustrie. Auch das Gelände des heutigen Golden Rock Inn stammt aus dieser großen Zeit. Seine Besitzer – der New Yorker Künstler Brice Marden und seine Frau Helen – schufen im Turm der alten Zuckermühle und in den umliegenden Cottages wirklich herausragende Gästezimmer, denen die Reste alter Mauern im tropischen Grün eine äußerst malerische Kulisse geben.

Das Mobiliar stammt größtenteils von einheimischen Handwerkern, dazu gesellen sich Design-Favoriten der Hausherren. Am wichtigsten für die Atmosphäre sind jedoch die tropischen Blumen, die in verschwenderischer Pracht jeden Schritt begleiten. Ein duftendes Paradies für Meerkatzen, Kolibris – und ein paar glückliche Besucher.

Nevis est une île des Petites Antilles plutôt typique : les maisons ne sont pas plus hautes que les palmiers et les journées se déroulent au rythme du soleil et des vagues. Pourtant, Nevis fut autrefois le centre de l'industrie florissante de la canne à sucre. Le complexe du Golden Rock date d'ailleurs de cette grande époque. Ses propriétaires, l'artiste new-yorkais Brice Marden et sa femme Helen, ont aménagé des chambres d'hôtes superbes dans la tour de l'ancien moulin à canne à sucre et dans les bâtiments annexes. Les vestiges d'anciennes bâtisses sur fond de paysage tropical sont particulièrement pittoresques.

Réalisé en grande partie par des artisans locaux, le mobilier compte aussi quelques pièces des designers favoris des propriétaires. Les fleurs tropicales à profusion créent ici une atmosphère envoûtante, un véritable paradis de couleurs et de senteurs peuplé par les cercopithèques, les colibris et... les quelques heureux visiteurs.

LOCATION
Situated in the hills of Nevis, 28 km/17 miles from the island's airport

RATES
Cottages from $210, breakfast included

ROOMS
7 garden cottages for 1 to 5 persons plus 1 mill tower room

STYLE
Idyllic Caribbean refuge

FOOD
The restaurant uses fresh ingredients to create Caribbean dishes that reference and refine traditional West Indian cuisine

X FACTOR
A word of warning: The rum punch served at the Golden Rock's bar is renowned throughout the island for its potency. Still, it tastes great, and, as a guest, you at least don't have to worry about getting home afterward

BOOK TO PACK
"The Star-Apple Kingdom" by Derek Walcott

LAGE
In den Hügeln von Nevis gelegen, 28 km südlich des Flughafens der Antilleninsel

PREISE
Cottage ab 160 €, inklusive Frühstück

ZIMMER
7 Gartencottages für jeweils 1 bis 5 Gäste, 1 Zimmer im Mühlturm

STIL
Verträumtes Karibikrefugium

KÜCHE
Im Restaurant wird mit frischen Zutaten die karibische Küche der Westindischen Inseln nachempfunden und weiterentwickelt

X-FAKTOR
Aufpassen! Der Rum-Punsch, der an der Bar des Golden Rock serviert wird, ist auf der ganzen Insel für seine durchschlagende Wirkung bekannt. Köstlich ist er trotzdem, und als Gast muss man danach ja nicht mehr heimfinden

BUCH ZUM ORT
„Das Königreich des Sternapfels" von Derek Walcott

SITUATION
Collines de Nevis, à 28 km au sud de l'aéroport de cette île des Petites Antilles

PRIX
Cottage à partir de 160 €, petit déjeuner inclus

CHAMBRES
7 cottages (1–5 personnes) et 1 chambre dans la tour du moulin

STYLE
Refuge idyllique aux Antilles

RESTAURATION
Le restaurant propose des plats inspirés de la cuisine des Antilles britanniques préparés avec des produits frais

LE « PETIT PLUS »
Attention ! S'il est succulent, le punch servi au bar du Golden Rock a la réputation sur toute l'île de faire tourner la tête. Heureusement, les hôtes n'ont que quelques pas à faire pour rentrer chez eux …

LIVRE À EMPORTER
« Le Royaume du fruit-étoile » de Derek Walcott

LE SERENO
CARIBBEAN

Grand Cul-de-Sac BP 19 ~ Saint-Barthélemy ~ 97133 French West Indies
Telephone +59 05 90 29 83 00 ~ Fax +59 05 90 27 75 47
info@lesereno.com
www.lesereno.com

When discussing the most beautiful beaches in the world, it's never long before the name St. Barth crops up. This small Caribbean island remains largely free from mass tourism and hotel chains, instead boasting hotel gems such as Le Sereno, previously the legendary Sereno Beach Hotel. Its rebirth was overseen by star Parisian designer Christian Liaigre, a fact that is reflected in the flawless natural modernist aesthetic of the suites as well as in grounds that never attempt to upstage the beautiful surroundings.

For kiteboarders, the glorious bay is an added attraction, though the spa (stocked, of course, with products from the St. Barth range) and the commitment to first-class cuisine mean Le Sereno is also a perfect refuge for those simply wanting to read, relax, and ride the crests of their imagination.

Wenn es um die schönsten Strände der Welt geht, fällt bald auch der Name St. Barth. Die kleine Karibikinsel ist von Massentouristik und Hotelketten bisher weitgehend verschont geblieben, dafür finden sich hier echte Hotelsensationen wie das Le Sereno. Diese Auferstehung des legendären Sereno Beach Hotel wurde vom Pariser Interior-Weltstar Christian Liaigre begleitet, was sich in der fehlerlosen Natur-Moderne der Suiten sowie in einer Außenanlage ausdrückt, die sich jederzeit vor der grandiosen Umgebung verneigt.

Für Kite-Surfer ist die Lage in einer malerischen Bucht besonders interessant. Doch das Spa (mit Produkten der Kosmetiklinie St. Barth, was sonst) und das besondere Augenmerk auf erstklassige Küche machen das Sereno auch zur idealen Fluchtadresse für jene, denen es völlig reicht, mit ein paar Büchern auf den Wellen ihrer Fantasie dahinzugleiten.

Les plages de Saint-Barthélemy comptent sans aucun doute parmi les plus belles du monde. Épargnée par le tourisme de masse et les chaînes d'hôtels, cette petite île des Antilles abrite quelques établissements d'exception comme Le Sereno. On doit le nouvel aménagement de ce lieu légendaire au très renommé designer parisien Christian Liaigre, dont le style mariant le moderne et les éléments naturels est immédiatement reconnaissable dans les superbes suites et les espaces extérieurs. La nature grandiose se charge du reste.

Pour les adeptes du kitesurf, la petite baie pittoresque qui borde l'hôtel est un vrai bonheur. Mais le spa (qui utilise bien sûr des produits cosmétiques de la ligne St Barth), ainsi que l'excellente cuisine, font du Sereno une adresse idéale pour tous – y compris pour ceux qui préfèrent s'adonner à la lecture en laissant leur imagination surfer sur les vagues.

LOCATION
On a bay at the eastern end of the island, protected by a coral reef

RATES
Suites from $715, breakfast included

ROOMS
37 one- to three-room suites and villas

STYLE
Caribbean *savoir-vivre*

FOOD
A look out the window tells you all you need to know about the cuisine—fans of freshly caught seafood will never go hungry here

X FACTOR
Another locally sourced treat for Le Sereno's guests to enjoy is the famous Ligne St. Barth cosmetics range. Ingredients include the seeds of the native roucou tree, a time-tested natural sun screen

BOOK TO PACK
"A Caribbean Mystery" by Agatha Christie

LAGE
An einer von einem Korallenriff geschützten Bucht am östlichen Ende der Insel

PREISE
Suiten ab 550 €, inklusive Frühstück

ZIMMER
37 Ein- bis Drei-Zimmer-Suiten und Villen

STIL
Karibisches Savoir-vivre

KÜCHE
Ein Blick aus dem Fenster sagt alles: Wer frisch gefangenes Meeresgetier mag, wird hier auf jeden Fall satt

X-FAKTOR
Es gibt hier ein ganz besonderes, regionales Produkt: die renommierte Kosmetik von Ligne St. Barth. Sie verwendet zum Beispiel Samen des einheimischen Ruku-Strauches als altbewährtes Sonnenschutzmittel

BUCH ZUM ORT
„Karibische Affäre" von Agatha Christie

SITUATION
Dans une baie protégée par un récif corallien, à la pointe est de l'île

PRIX
Suites à partir de 550 €, petit déjeuner inclus

CHAMBRES
37 suites (1 à 3 pièces) et villas

STYLE
Le savoir-vivre antillais

RESTAURATION
Il suffit de jeter un coup d'œil par la fenêtre pour comprendre que les amateurs de poissons et de fruits de mer sont comblés

LE «PETIT PLUS»
Produit star de la région, la ligne cosmétique St Barth proposée par l'hôtel utilise notamment les graines du roucou, un arbuste endémique, reconnues depuis les temps anciens pour leurs vertus protectrices contre le soleil

LIVRE À EMPORTER
«Le major parlait trop» d'Agatha Christie

PARROT CAY BY COMO
CARIBBEAN

P.O. Box 164 ~ Providenciales, Turks & Caicos Islands ~ British West Indies
Telephone +1 649 946 7788 ~ Fax +1 649 946 7789
parrotcay@comohotels.com
www.comohotels.com/parrotcay

Outside it is well more than 86 degrees Fahrenheit; inside the fan whirrs, and the sweating guests hold their Downward Facing Dog poses. Was that not more than five breaths? So unfair. Why not quit the yoga class and amble over to the bar for a drink? But then the almost unnatural blue of the Caribbean or a visit to the world's most elegant spa quickly calms the chakras.

Besides, why rebel? There is no escape route off this small private island, to which one can easily imagine James Bond retiring. And why would you want to leave anyway? The resort's personal butlers fulfill your every wish, and the scent of hibiscus flowers hangs heavy in the air above its floodlit tennis courts and infinity pool. It's a place popular with both supermodels and world-famous yogis (plus devotees), who come to enjoy peace and harmony against a backdrop of rhythmically rolling waves.

Draußen sind es über 30 Grad, drinnen surrt der Ventilator, schwitzend harrt die Yoga-Klasse im „Herabschauenden Hund" aus. Waren das nicht schon mehr als fünf Atemzüge? Frechheit. Warum nicht zusammenpacken und hinüber an die Bar schlendern auf einen Drink? Doch das fast schon verstörend blaue Blau der Karibik oder ein Besuch im elegantesten Spa der Welt besänftigen schnell die aufgebrachten Chakras. Was sollte Rebellion hier auch nützen? Es gibt kein Entkommen von dieser kleinen Privatinsel, die in der Karibik liegt, als warte sie nur darauf, dass James Bond sich auf ihr als Rentner niederlässt.

Wirklich weg will ohnehin keiner, warum auch? Suitenbutler erfüllen jeden Wunsch, schwer hängt der Duft von Hibiskusblüten über den Tennisplätzen und dem Infinity-Pool. Models und weltberühmte Yogis sowie die Anhänger beider Personengruppen flüchten hierher, um beim naturgegebenen Soundtrack der rhythmisch zischenden Gischt zu genießen, was am kostbarsten ist: Frieden und Harmonie.

À l'extérieur, le mercure affiche plus de 30 °C; à l'intérieur, le ventilateur bourdonne. Les hôtes en nage gardent stoïquement la posture yoga du «chien tête en bas». Mais cela fait plus de cinq respirations, non? Comme c'est injuste! Qui n'aurait pas envie de plier bagage pour aller prendre un verre au bar? Cependant, le bleu presque irréel des Antilles ou une séance dans le spa le plus élégant du monde suffisent à calmer les esprits. D'ailleurs, à quoi bon se rebeller? On ne s'évade pas si facilement de cette petite île privée, posée là sur la mer des Antilles, comme si elle attendait que James Bond vienne y prendre sa retraite.

Et puis, pourquoi s'enfuir? Un maître d'hôtel satisfait vos moindres désirs, le parfum lourd des fleurs d'hibiscus plane au-dessus des courts de tennis et de la piscine à débordement. Topmodèles, grands maîtres de yoga et leurs disciples viennent se réfugier ici et, avec le frémissement de l'écume comme fond sonore, ils profitent de l'essentiel: la paix et l'harmonie.

LOCATION
One of the 40 small Turks & Caicos Islands southeast of Miami. About 70 minutes by plane from there, then boat transfer from the main island of Providenciales

RATES
Rooms from $475, beach houses from $2,050

ROOMS
74 rooms including beach houses and villas

STYLE
Caribbean meets East Asia: louvred doors, teak, rattan, and white cotton quilts

FOOD
Caribbean, Southeast Asian, Continental, Italian —you name it, you can have it

X FACTOR
The hotel's own records reveal that the sun shines on 350 days a year at Parrot Cay, making it the perfect vacation destination for those who don't like to take chances with the weather

BOOK TO PACK
"Dr. No" by Ian Fleming

LAGE
Eine der 40 kleinen Turks- und Caicosinseln, etwa 70-minütige Flugzeit südöstlich von Miami gelegen. Flughafentransfer von der Hauptinsel Providenciales per Boot

PREISE
Zimmer ab 360 €, Strandhäuser ab 1515 €

ZIMMER
74 Zimmer inklusive Strandhäuser und Villen

STIL
Karibik meets Asien: Lamellentüren, Teak und Rattan, Quiltdecken aus weißer Baumwolle

KÜCHE
Karibisch, südostasiatisch, kontinental, italienisch – *you name it, you can have it*

X-FAKTOR
Die Wetteraufzeichnungen des Hotels verraten es: Hier scheint an 350 Tagen im Jahr die Sonne. Ein ziemlich überzeugendes Argument für alle, die beim nächsten Urlaub auf Nummer sicher gehen möchten

BUCHTIPP
„James Bond jagt Dr. No" von Ian Fleming

SITUATION
Une des 40 petites îles Turques-et-Caïques, à environ 70 minutes de vol au sud-est de Miami ; transfert par bateau de Providenciales

PRIX
Chambres à partir de 360 €, maisons en bord de mer à partir de 1515 €

CHAMBRES
74 chambres, maisons en bord de mer et villas comprises

STYLE
Caraïbes et Asie : portes à claire-voie, teck et rotin, courtepointes en coton blanc

RESTAURATION
Cuisine antillaise, du Sud-Est asiatique, française ou italienne – *you name it, you can have it*

LE «PETIT PLUS»
Les relevés météorologiques de l'hôtel le prouvent : ici, le soleil brille 350 jours par an. Un argument de taille pour ceux qui veulent être sûrs de passer des vacances au soleil

LIVRE À EMPORTER
«Docteur No» de Ian Fleming

VICEROY ANGUILLA
CARIBBEAN

Barnes Bay ~ P.O. Box 8028, West End ~ AI-2640 Anguilla
Telephone +1 264 497 7000 ~ Fax +1 264 497 7100
viceroyanguillaltc@viceroyanguilla.com
www.viceroyhotelsandresorts.com/en/anguilla

Despite being just 32 km/20 miles from celebrity hangout St. Barth, Anguilla is a far calmer place, one free from cruise ships and camera-phone-toting VIP hunters. This long coral island cuts an eel-like path (hence the name) through the turquoise Caribbean waters and boasts 33 flawless beaches.

The Viceroy is ideally located between Meads and Barnes bays and, with its low-slung pavilion-like architecture and earth-tone interiors, blends surprisingly well with the landscape. For Californian decorator Kelly Wearstler, renowned for her unashamedly decadent and theatrical compositions, this was the perfect stage: Sculptures by local artists thus stand alongside Indian metalwork, while driftwood lamps contrast with jet-set-style furniture from the 1970s. All the same, interior design is unlikely to be the main topic of conversation among the guests, who will probably be too busy swapping snorkeling stories and discussing whether the kitchen has enough locally caught lobster for dinner.

Obwohl nur 32 Kilometer von der Promi-Insel St. Barth entfernt, ist Anguilla ein Ort der Ruhe: keine Kreuzfahrtschiffe, keine schnatternden Horden auf der Handy-Jagd nach VIPs. Die Koralleninsel mit ihren 33 makellosen Stränden schlängelt sich auf 25 Kilometern Länge wie ein Aal (daher auch der Name) durchs türkise Wasser. Das Resort liegt dabei höchst vorteilhaft zwischen der Meads- und der Barnes-Bucht; flach wie ein Pavillon und innen in Erdtönen gehalten, fügt es sich in die Landschaft ein.

Die Ausstattung stammt von der Kalifornierin Kelly Wearstler, deren ungeniert neureiche Material-Theatralik hier eine ideale Bühne vorfand: Skulpturen einheimischer Künstler stehen neben Metallarbeiten aus Indien, „natürliche" Treibholzlampen kontrastieren mit Mobiliar im Jetset-Look der 1970er. Wobei, ehrlich gesagt: Interiordesign ist in diesem Viceroy kaum Gesprächsthema Nummer eins. Eher die Erlebnisse beim Schnorcheln und die Frage, ob der Koch von den Inselfischern auch genug Hummer bekommen hat.

Bien que 32 km seulement la séparent de l'île de Saint-Barthélemy si courue, Anguilla est un lieu calme, sans bateau de croisière ni hordes jacassantes traquant les célébrités avec leurs téléphones portables. Avec ses 33 plages immaculées, cette île corallienne s'étend sur 25 km telle une anguille (d'où son nom) sur l'eau turquoise. L'hôtel est situé entre les baies idylliques de Meads et de Barnes. Avec son toit plat et son intérieur dans les tons ocre, il s'intègre parfaitement au paysage.

On doit la décoration intérieure à la Californienne Kelly Wearstler, qui met en scène les matériaux avec une superbe désinvolture : les sculptures d'artistes locaux côtoient des œuvres en métal indiennes, des lampes en bois flottant « naturelles » contrastent avec le mobilier jet-set des années 1970. Mais pour être honnête, ce n'est pas ce qui délie le plus les langues ici. On s'intéresse davantage aux expériences de plongée et au fait de savoir si le cuisinier s'est fait livrer suffisamment de homards par les pêcheurs de l'île.

LOCATION
At the western end of the island, 10 km/6 miles from the airport

RATES
Studios from $625, suites from $1,025

ROOMS
166 studios, suites, and villas

STYLE
Luxury hideaway for fans of the good life; star designer Kelly Wearstler proves that natural hues and decadent chic can go hand in hand

FOOD
A top-class mix—everything from gourmet dinners to beachfront steak barbecues and spa cuisine

X FACTOR
Surprisingly for such a high-end resort, the Viceroy offers an impressive range of activities for children. Whether they're hunting for treasure or building a hut, younger guests are guaranteed a fabulous time too

BOOK TO PACK
"Islands in the Stream" by Ernest Hemingway

LAGE
Am westlichen Ende der Insel gelegen, 10 km vom Flughafen entfernt

PREISE
Studios ab 480 €, Suiten ab 785 €

ZIMMER
166 Studios, Suiten und Villen

STIL
Super-Hideaway für Verwöhnte; Stardesignerin Kelly Wearstler beweist, dass sich Bio-Töne und dekadenter Chic bestens vertragen können

KÜCHE
High-End-Mischung – vom Steakgrillen am Strand über Gourmet-Dinner bis Spa Cuisine

X-FAKTOR
Die Überraschung in so einem Top-Resort ist das wirklich ambitionierte Programm, das es im Viceroy für Kinder gibt. Ob Schatzsuchen oder Hüttenbauen, hier bekommt auch der Nachwuchs seine Traumferien

BUCH ZUM ORT
„Inseln im Strom" von Ernest Hemingway

SITUATION
À la pointe ouest de l'île, à 10 km de l'aéroport

PRIX
Studios à partir de 480 €, suites à partir de 785 €

CHAMBRES
166 studios, suites et villas

STYLE
Refuge idéal pour hôtes exigeants. Kelly Wearstler, décoratrice réputée, prouve que les tons naturels et le chic bohème font bon ménage

RESTAURATION
Cuisine de grande qualité : steaks au gril sur la plage, dîners gastronomiques, cuisine vitalité

LE «PETIT PLUS»
La richesse des activités proposées aux enfants crée la surprise dans un hôtel de ce niveau. Entre chasses au trésor et construction de cabanes, les plus jeunes passent des vacances de rêve

LIVRE À EMPORTER
«Îles à la dérive» d'Ernest Hemingway

HOTEL ANTUMALAL
CHILE

Km 2 Camino Pucón-Villarrica ~ Pucón ~ Chile
Telephone +56 45 244 1011
info@antumalal.com
www.antumalal.com

In 1938, fleeing the turmoil and warmongering of Europe, young newlyweds Guillermo and Catalina Pollak swapped Prague for Pucón to begin a new life in Chile. Misfortune struck when volcanic eruption and fire destroyed their first establishment, but 10 years later they went on to create one of the most spectacular guesthouses in all of South America. Built by the Chilean architect Jorge Elton on a rocky plateau above Lake Villarrica, this midcentury hotel offers views across the 12-acre grounds and the lake to the mountains beyond—who needs movies when the world beyond the full-height windows is as captivating as this?

Wooden paneling, rope-back chairs, and bench seating recall the Bohemian style of the 1950s, while each room has its own fireplace. Antumalal's current owners (the hotel is still in private hands) continue to do nothing by halves: When the pool area was converted into a spa in 2010, they had a new hydromassage pool hewn into the natural rock.

Aus den europäischen Kriegswirren flüchtend, kam 1938 ein junges Paar aus Prag nach Pucón, um sich ein neues Leben in Chile aufzubauen. Guillermo und Catalina Pollak hatten aber erstmal Pech: Ein Vulkanausbruch und ein Feuer zerstörten ihr ursprüngliches Hotel. Zehn Jahre später aber schufen sie mit dem chilenischen Architekten Jorge Elton auf einem Felsplateau über dem Lake Villarrica eine der spektakulärsten Gästeresidenzen in ganz Südamerika.

Der Midcentury-Bau bietet Ausblicke über fünf Hektar Privatgarten und den See, bis hin zu Bergen am anderen Ufer – die Panoramafenster sind besser als Kino. Holztäfelungen, Stühle mit Kordellehne und Polsterbänke erinnern an den Boheme-Salonlook der Fifties, jedes Zimmer hat eine eigene Feuerstelle. Und auch im 21. Jahrhundert werden in dem nach wie vor privat geführten Haus keine halben Sachen gemacht: Als man 2010 den Poolbereich zum Spa erweiterte, wurde eigens ein Hydromassage-Pool in den Felsen gehauen.

Fuyant l'Europe agitée par les menaces de guerre, un couple de jeunes Pragois gagna le Chili en 1938 pour repartir de zéro dans la ville de Pucón. Malheureusement, une éruption volcanique et un incendie détruisirent le premier hôtel de Guillermo et Catalina Pollak. Dix ans plus tard, avec l'aide de l'architecte chilien Jorge Elton, ils construisirent sur un promontoire rocheux l'un des hôtels les plus spectaculaires d'Amérique du Sud.

Avec ses immenses baies vitrées, cet hôtel datant du milieu du 20e siècle offre une vue panoramique sur les cinq hectares de jardin, le lac et les montagnes qui se dressent au-delà. Les boiseries, les chaises à dossier en cordage et les banquettes évoquent le style bohème des années 1950. Chaque chambre dispose d'une cheminée. Les récentes modernisations n'ont rien à envier aux précédentes : en 2010, on créa un spa en adjoignant à la piscine un bassin à hydromassage creusé dans la roche.

LOCATION
125 km/78 miles southeast of Temuco airport, domestic flights to there from Santiago. 90-minute transfer to hotel on request

RATES
Rooms from $250, suites from $340, and chalets from $530

ROOMS
11 double rooms, 2 suites, and 2 chalets

STYLE
Chilean take on the home of James Mason's character in Hitchcock's "The Third Man"

FOOD
Restaurant Parque Antumalal serves Czech-Chilean fusion cuisine, while Bar Don Guillermo is a often-frequented watering hole

X FACTOR
The counter at the bar—it measures exactly 13 feet and was sawn from a single block of wood

BOOK TO PACK
"Ways of Going Home" by Alejandro Zambra

LAGE
125 km südöstlich des Flughafens Temuco; Inlandsflüge dorthin ab Santiago, 90-minütiger Transfer zum Hotel auf Wunsch

PREISE
Zimmer ab 190 €, Suiten ab 260 € und Chalets ab 410 €

ZIMMER
11 Doppelzimmer, 2 Suiten und 2 Chalets

STIL
Chilenische Version des Hauses von James Mason in Hitchcocks „Der unsichtbare Dritte"

KÜCHE
Restaurant Parque Antumalal mit tschechisch-chilenischer Küche. Außerdem (und besonders gut besucht): Bar Don Guillermo

X-FAKTOR
Die Bar, denn sie ist genau 3,99 m lang und wurde aus einem einzigen Stück Holz gesägt

BUCH ZUM ORT
„Die Erfindung der Kindheit" von Alejandro Zambra

SITUATION
À 125 km au sud-est de l'aéroport de Temuco (vols intérieurs à partir de Santiago); transfert de 90 minutes sur demande

PRIX
Chambres à partir de 190 €, suites à partir de 260 € et chalets à partir de 410 €

CHAMBRES
11 chambres doubles, 2 suites et 2 chalets

STYLE
Version chilienne de la maison de James Mason dans «La Mort aux trousses» d'Alfred Hitchcock

RESTAURATION
Cuisine tchéco-chilienne au Restaurant Parque Antumalal; à noter également: le Bar Don Guillermo très couru

LE «PETIT PLUS»
Le bar de 3,99 mètres de long taillé dans un tronc d'arbre

LIVRE À EMPORTER
«Personnages secondaires» d'Alejandro Zambra

"The Antumalal is in such pristine condition
that it looks as if the windows
must have been papered up just as the hotel opened."

OLIVER SCHWANER-ALBRIGHT, *CONDÉ NAST TRAVELER*

„Das Antumalal ist derart gut erhalten, dass man meinen könnte, es wäre sofort nach
seiner Eröffnung verpackt und erst kürzlich wieder ausgepackt worden."

« L'hôtel Antumalal est dans un état de conservation tel qu'il donne
l'impression d'avoir ouvert ses portes tout récemment. »

HOTEL CASA REAL
CHILE

Camino Padre Hurtado 0695 ~ Alto Jahuel ~ Santiago ~ Chile
Telephone +56 2 821 9966
hotelcasareal@santarita.cl
www.santarita.com/international/casa-real-hotel

An air of mystery surrounds this hotel at the foot of the Andes, its website giving few details. That doesn't seem to harm bookings—it is particularly popular for wedding parties and exclusive groups. Situated in the Santa Rita vineyard about an hour to the south of Santiago, this neoclassical villa was converted into a hotel in the 1990s. Its 16 comfortable rooms, furnished with antiques and agreeably subtle designer items, aim first and foremost to offer guests absolute peace and a blissfully deep sleep.

The neo-Gothic chapel, meanwhile, is rather more opulent, as are the hotel's reception areas, which bear testimony to the lavish lifestyles of large landowners in the 19th century. The almost-100-acre park in which the building stands dates back to the same era, and, with its olive, almond, lemon, and cedar trees, is an ideal place for picnics and romantic walks—and not just for newlyweds.

Ein wenig geheimnisvoll geht es in dieser Residenz am Fuße der Anden zu, gelegen etwa eine Stunde südlich von Santiago. Die Auskünfte auf der Homepage sind spärlich, die Buchungsliste ist trotzdem erstaunlich voll – besonders Hochzeitsgesellschaften und elitäre Cliquen treffen sich gerne in der Casa Real, die zum Gelände des Santa-Rita-Weingutes gehört. Dessen Besitzer ließ die neoklassizistische Villa in den 1990ern zum Hotel umbauen, wobei die 16 komfortablen Zimmer mit Antiquitäten und angenehm dezenten Designerstücken vor allem eines garantieren sollen: absolute Ungestörtheit und selig tiefen Schlummer.

Prunkvoll sind dagegen die neugotische Kapelle und die Empfangsräume des Hotels, die noch vom üppigen Leben der Großgrundbesitzer im vorletzten Jahrhundert erzählen. Aus deren Epoche stammt auch der 40 Hektar große Park, der die Gebäude umgibt und mit seinen Zedern, Oliven-, Mandel- und Zitronenbäumen einen erstklassigen Rahmen für Picknicks und romantische Spaziergänge bietet.

Située au pied des Andes, à environ une heure au sud de Santiago, cette résidence est enveloppée de mystère : son site Internet n'en dit guère long à son sujet, mais son carnet de réservations est étonnamment plein. Appartenant au domaine viticole de Santa Rita, Casa Real accueille surtout des mariages et des groupes d'amis privilégiés. Dans les années 1990, son propriétaire a transformé en hôtel cette villa néoclassique. Les 16 chambres confortables ornées d'antiquités et d'œuvres discrètes de designers offrent à leurs hôtes un calme absolu, qui leur permet de dormir en toute quiétude.

Témoignant de la vie fastueuse menée au 19e siècle par le propriétaire des lieux, la chapelle néogothique et les salles de réception de l'hôtel sont particulièrement luxueuses. Créé à la même époque, le parc de 40 hectares abrite des cèdres, des oliviers, des amandiers et des citronniers. Il se prête idéalement aux pique-niques et aux promenades romantiques.

LOCATION
Situated 42 km/26 miles south of Santiago

RATES
Double rooms from $430, suites from $480, breakfast and winery tour included

ROOMS
10 doubles, 6 suites

STYLE
A little too much gold and heavy drapery for Europeans, but the architecture is fabulous

FOOD
Doña Paula, the estate's own restaurant, serves regional and international cuisine, and there's also an in-house wine store

X FACTOR
The Casa Real cabernet sauvignon is one of South America's finest reds. It is produced only in exceptional years, so a little luck is required to be on hand for a new vintage. For earlier examples, all you need is the necessary small change

BOOK TO PACK
"The House of the Spirits" by Isabel Allende

LAGE
42 km südlich von Santiago gelegen

PREISE
Doppelzimmer ab 315 €, Suiten ab 350 €, inklusive Frühstück und Weingut-Führung

ZIMMER
10 Doppelzimmer, 6 Suiten

STIL
Für Europäer etwas zu viel Gold und schwere Draperien, aber zauberhafte Architektur

KÜCHE
Doña Paula, das Restaurant des Weingutes, bietet regionale und internationale Küche; hauseigene Vinothek

X-FAKTOR
Der Cabernet Sauvignon Casa Real zählt zu den besten Weinen Südamerikas. Er wird nur mit außerordentlichen Jahrgängen produziert – man braucht also etwas Glück, um als Gast bei seiner Entstehung dabei zu sein. Um ihn zu genießen, reicht dagegen das nötige Kleingeld

BUCH ZUM ORT
„Das Geisterhaus" von Isabel Allende

SITUATION
À 42 km au sud de Santiago

PRIX
Chambres doubles à partir de 315 €, suites à partir de 350 €, petit déjeuner et visite du vignoble inclus

CHAMBRES
10 chambres doubles et 6 suites

STYLE
Ornementation un peu trop chargée au goût des Européens, mais architecture envoûtante

RESTAURATION
Le restaurant du vignoble, le Doña Paula, propose une cuisine locale et internationale ; la maison a sa propre cave

LE « PETIT PLUS »
Le cabernet sauvignon Casa Real compte parmi les meilleurs vins d'Amérique du Sud. Il n'est produit qu'avec les plus grands millésimes. Les hôtes chanceux pourront assister à son élaboration

LIVRE À EMPORTER
« La Maison aux esprits » d'Isabel Allende

CASA GANGOTENA
ECUADOR

Bolivar Oe6-41 y Cuenca ~ Quito ~ Ecuador
Telephone +59 32 400 8000
info@casagangotena.com
www.casagangotena.com

Travelers visiting Quito have more reason to send postcards than most: At 2,850m/9,350 feet above sea level, it is the highest capital city in the world (or the second highest if you count Tibet as a country) and the only one almost exactly on the equator. The old quarter has long been a world heritage site, and Casa Gangotena lies at its heart.

Today, this historic mansion, built on top of the foundations of an ancient Incan temple, contains 31 cozy rooms boasting views of the picturesque Plaza San Francisco and its restored colonial architecture. The building was once the seat of the influential Gangotena family, a past to which beaux arts and Art Deco features bear testimony, and remains an important fixture in the social life of the city today. Guests can begin their exploration of Quito's nightlife right in the lobby, though they may find it hard to tear themselves away from the bar's delicious *aguas frescas*, made with verbena, mint, and rose essence.

Hier lohnt sich das Postkartenschreiben wirklich: Immerhin ist Quito mit 2850 Metern über dem Meer die höchste (für jene, die Tibet als eigenes Land zählen, die zweithöchste) Hauptstadt der Welt und die einzige, die fast direkt am Äquator liegt. Die Altstadt wurde schon früh zum Weltkulturerbe erklärt. Dort steht auch die historische Villa Gangotena, auf den Fundamenten eines alten Inka-Tempels.

Wo einst die Inka ihren Kakao tranken, warten heute 31 Zimmer, *cosy* eingerichtet und mit Aussicht auf die malerische Plaza San Francisco und ihre restaurierten Kolonialhäuser. Beaux-Arts- und Art-déco-Elemente erzählen von der glanzvollen Vergangenheit des Hauses, das Stammsitz der einflussreichen Familie Gangotena war. Wie damals ist das Gebäude fest im gesellschaftlichen Alltag der Stadt verankert. Abends kann man als Gast bereits in der Lobby ins Nachtleben Quitos eintauchen – sofern man sich überhaupt losreißen will vom *aguas frescas* des Hotels, einem Getränke aus Verveine, Minze, Rosenessenz und anderen Spezereien.

N'hésitez pas à envoyer des cartes postales de Quito: située à 2 850 m d'altitude, c'est la plus haute capitale du monde (ou la deuxième plus haute si l'on considère le Tibet comme un pays), et la seule à être sur la ligne de l'équateur. Inscrite depuis 1978 sur la Liste du patrimoine mondial, la vieille ville abrite la Casa Gangotena, qui repose sur les fondations d'un temple inca.

À l'endroit où les Incas dégustaient leur cacao, on a aménagé 31 chambres cosy. Elles donnent sur la pittoresque place San Francisco bordée de maisons coloniales restaurées. Les éléments de style Beaux-Arts et Art déco témoignent du brillant passé de la maison, qui fut la résidence de l'influente famille Gangotena. Comme autrefois, le bâtiment est aux premières loges pour profiter de la ville. Le soir, du hall de l'hôtel aux hauts lieux de la vie nocturne de Quito, il n'y a qu'un pas, à condition d'avoir le courage de renoncer à l' *aguas frescas*, une boisson à base de verveine, de menthe, d'essence de rose et d'épices servie à l'hôtel.

LOCATION
Right on Plaza San Francisco in the heart of Quito's old quarter, which has been listed as an UNESCO world heritage site since 1978

RATES
Rooms from $450, breakfast and afternoon coffee included

ROOMS
31 rooms and suites

STYLE
Handsome mansion offering five-star luxury

FOOD
First-class updates of national specialties such as lamb, turnovers, and thick soups; the chocolate is a must

X FACTOR
Quiteños love a good cup of coffee, and the hotel offers "high tea" Ecuadorian style—served with coffee of such quality, you'd be hard put to find better in Europe

BOOK TO PACK
"The Villagers (Huasipungo)" by Jorge Icaza

LAGE
Direkt an der Plaza San Francisco mitten in der Altstadt Quitos, die bereits im Jahr 1978 zum UNESCO-Weltkulturerbe ernannt wurde

PREISE
Zimmer ab 345 €, inklusive Frühstück und Nachmittagskaffee

ZIMMER
31 Zimmer und Suiten

STIL
Reizender Stadtpalast mit 5-Sterne-Komfort

KÜCHE
Hervorragende Updates nationaler Spezialitäten wie Lamm, Teigtaschen oder sämige Suppen; ein *Must-try* ist die Schokolade

X-FAKTOR
Die Quiteños lieben eine gute Tasse Kaffee, also wird „High Tea im ecuadorianischen Stil" angeboten – mit Kaffee in einer Qualität, nach der man in Europa lange suchen muss

BUCH ZUM ORT
„Huasipungo: Unser kleines Stückchen Erde" von Jorge Icaza

SITUATION
Sur la place San Francisco au cœur de la vieille ville de Quito, inscrite depuis 1978 au patrimoine mondial de l'UNESCO

PRIX
Chambres à partir de 345 €, petit déjeuner et café de l'après-midi inclus

CHAMBRES
31 chambres et suites

STYLE
Ravissant palais urbain offrant un confort cinq étoiles

RESTAURATION
Des spécialités équatoriennes comme l'agneau, les *empañadas* et les veloutés sont revisitées avec brio; il faut absolument goûter le chocolat

LE «PETIT PLUS»
Les habitants de Quito boivent volontiers une bonne tasse de café. L'hôtel propose un «goûter à l'équatorienne» avec une qualité de café quasiment introuvable en Europe

LIVRE À EMPORTER
«Huasipungo» de Jorge Icaza

PÄDASTE MANOR
ESTONIA

Muhu Island 94716 ~ Estonia
Telephone +372 45 48 800 ~ Fax +372 45 48 811
info@padaste.ee
www.padaste.ee

Northern intensity, simple colors, and pure air are what it's all about at Pädaste Manor on the charming Estonian island of Muhu. Here, guests can enjoy an altogether slower pace of life, thanks to the uncluttered architecture of the manor house, once the seat of a German-Baltic family of aristocrats; a cuisine that is mercifully free of frippery; and a superb spa whose highlights include a wood-fired sauna and a treatment involving dried birch twigs.

There are no unwanted distractions, the mainland is far in the distance, and the only nightlife hot spot on those long summer evenings is the outdoor tub, in which guests can lie back and count stars instead of sheep.

Die Intensität des Nordens, die Sauberkeit der Farben und die Reinheit der Luft – das sind die Werte, denen man sich im Pädaste Manor verpflichtet hat. Für den Gast bedeutet ein Aufenthalt auf der charmanten Ostseeinsel Muhu deswegen eine Lektion in Entschleunigung. Dafür sorgen die klare Architektur des Herrenhauses, das einst Sitz einer deutsch-baltischen Adelsfamilie war, ebenso wie seine Küche, die sich nicht mit Spielereien aufhält, sowie das ausgezeichnete Spa mit holzbefeuerter Sauna und einer Birkenreisig-Kur im Angebot.

Nichts lenkt hier vom Wesentlichen ab, das Festland ist weit, und das Nachtleben beschränkt sich in den hellen Sommernächten auf ein heißes Bad unter freiem Himmel. Dort kann man Sterne zählen statt Schäfchen – und wird dabei garantiert nicht müde.

Le Nord dans toute sa splendeur, l'éclat des couleurs et la pureté de l'air, telle est la philosophie du Pädaste Manor. Les hôtes qui posent leurs valises à Muhu, charmante île de la mer Baltique, y apprennent à lever le pied. L'architecture épurée de ce manoir, qui fut autrefois la résidence d'un baron allemand de la Baltique, sa cuisine qui va droit au but, ainsi que son spa extraordinaire doté d'un sauna chauffé au bois, avec en prime une friction aux brindilles de bouleau, contribueront à vous détendre.

Ici, rien ne détourne de l'essentiel, le continent est loin et, pendant les belles nuits d'été, les activités nocturnes se limitent à un bain chaud à ciel ouvert. On peut ensuite compter les étoiles au lieu des moutons, sans sombrer dans le sommeil.

LOCATION
Situated on Pädaste Bay, Muhu Island, off the west coast of Estonia. The journey from Tallinn by car and ferry takes 2 hours

RATES
Rooms from $280, suites from $560

ROOMS
11 rooms, 12 suites, and a farmhouse that sleeps 2 to 5

STYLE
Historic manor with a distinctly Scandinavian influence

FOOD
The hotel restaurant Alexander offers Nordic Islands cuisine made with vegetables and herbs from its own garden. In summer, lunches are served on the Sea House Terrace

X FACTOR
Suite number 15, from which a ladder leads up to a "poetry loft" featuring a first-class collection of literature

BOOK TO PACK
"Purge" by Sofi Oksanen

LAGE
An der Pädaste-Bucht der Insel Muhu vor der Westküste Estlands gelegen. Der Transfer per Auto und Fähre ab Tallinn dauert 2 Stunden

PREISE
Zimmer ab 210 €, Suiten ab 420 €

ZIMMER
11 Zimmer und 12 Suiten; dazu ein Bauernhaus für 2 bis 5 Gäste

STIL
Historischer Gutshof mit deutlichen skandinavischen Einflüssen

KÜCHE
Gemüse und Kräuter für die nordischen Menüs im Restaurant Alexander stammen aus dem eigenen Garten. Im Sommer genießt man den Lunch auf der Sea House Terrace

X-FAKTOR
Suite Nummer 15. Dazu gehört ein „poetry loft", das über eine Leiter zu erreichen ist; am Ziel wartet dann eine feine Sammlung Literatur

BUCH ZUM ORT
„Fegefeuer" von Sofi Oksanen

SITUATION
Baie de Pädaste sur l'île de Muhu, au large de la côte ouest de L'Estonie; le transfert en voiture et en bac depuis Tallinn dure 2 heures

PRIX
Chambres à partir de 210 €, suites à partir de 420 €

CHAMBRES
11 chambres et 12 suites; une ferme (2–5 personnes)

STYLE
Ancien manoir aux influences scandinaves

RESTAURATION
Les légumes et les herbes aromatiques qui composent les menus nordiques du restaurant Alexander proviennent du jardin. En été, le déjeuner est servi au Sea House Terrace

LE «PETIT PLUS»
La suite n° 15, qui abrite une «mansarde poétique» accessible par une échelle. De la littérature choisie vous y attend

LIVRE À EMPORTER
«Purge» de Sofi Oksanen

CAP ESTEL
FRANCE

1312, Avenue Raymond-Poincaré ~ 06360 Èze-Bord-de-Mer ~ France
Telephone +33 493 76 2929 ~ Fax +33 493 015 520
contact@capestel.com
www.capestel.com

This French Riviera hotel is blessed (there's no other word for it) with a spectacular location. Situated on a peninsula between Nice and Monte Carlo, its four villas boast stunning views of the Mediterranean, while also offering high levels of privacy. That, no doubt, is why the Cap Estel has long been a popular hideaway among more discerning members of the international jet set. The hotel was built in 1900 by Frank Harris, an Irish journalist and friend of Oscar Wilde. He was succeeded as owner by Baron Stroganoff, who, in turn, was followed by shipping dynasty scion and surrealist poet Andréas Embiricos.

The ocean views are not the only natural attraction, however—the grounds to the rear are full of rare trees. The suites' interiors, meanwhile, offer the kind of grand Mediterranean style that never fails to lift the spirits after a day in the sun. Alternatively, guests can cool off in the seafront saltwater infinity pool—the perfect place to lie back and think of love, life, and money.

Man kann es nicht anders nennen: Das Cap Estel liegt in gebenedeiter Lage. Auf einer Halbinsel zwischen Nizza und Monte Carlo eröffnen seine vier Villen den Suitenbewohnern sagenhafte Aussichten aufs Mittelmeer und bieten zugleich viel Privatsphäre. Wohl deshalb ist das Kap schon lange Anlaufstelle für Teilnehmer des kultivierten Jetsets. Bauherr im Jahre 1900 war Frank Harris, ein irischer Journalist und Freund Oscar Wildes, ihm folgten ein Baron Stroganoff sowie der griechische Reederei-Erbe und surrealistische Dichter Andréas Embiricos.

Hier ist nicht nur der Meerblick hinreißend, sondern auch die Rückseite mit einem Park voll ausgesucht seltener Bäume. Die Zimmer sind in jener mediterranen Noblesse eingerichtet, die am Ende eines Tags an der Sonne so aufmunternd wirkt. Natürlich kann man auch in den Infinity-Salzwasserpool steigen, der mit seiner grandios exponierten Lage dazu einlädt, sich schwerelos treiben zu lassen und über das Leben, die Liebe und das Geld nachzudenken, irgendwo zwischen Nizza und Monte Carlo.

Le Cap Estel jouit indéniablement d'une situation géographique privilégiée. Trônant sur une presqu'île entre Nice et Monte-Carlo, ses quatre villas offrent une vue sublime sur la mer Méditerranée et beaucoup d'intimité. C'est pourquoi le Cap Estel accueille depuis longtemps les représentants de la jet-set distinguée. Construit en 1900 par Frank Harris, journaliste irlandais et ami d'Oscar Wilde, le domaine a plus tard appartenu au baron Stroganoff puis à Andréas Embiríkos, poète surréaliste et héritier d'une dynastie d'armateurs grecs.

Si côté mer, la vue est magique, elle est tout aussi somptueuse côté jardin, avec le parc planté d'essences rares. Les chambres sont aménagées avec raffinement dans cet esprit méditerranéen chaleureux qui requinque après une journée au soleil. On peut aussi profiter bien sûr de la piscine d'eau de mer à débordement qui invite à se laisser bercer par l'apesanteur pour méditer sur la vie, l'amour et l'argent – quelque part entre Nice et Monte-Carlo.

LOCATION
Hidden away below the medieval village of Èze and barely marked; the hotel is just 20 km/ 12 miles from Nice airport and yet worlds away from the tourist hordes along the coast

RATES
Rooms from $1,250, suites from $1,330

ROOMS
4 rooms, 14 suites

STYLE
International luxury, but underpinned with traces of the old Riviera flair of the '30s, '40s, and '50s—especially in the gardens

FOOD
The aromatic Mediterranean cuisine is served in the pool house or in your room

X FACTOR
Perhaps not relevant for every guest, but a key factor for the hotel's movie and music industry regulars: Sunbathers on the Cap Estel's private beach are safe from paparazzi lenses

BOOK TO PACK
"My Life and Loves" by Frank Harris

LAGE
Kaum ausgeschildert unterhalb des mittelalterlichen Ortes Èze gelegen, liegt das Hotel nur 20 km vom Flughafen Nizza, jedoch Welten entfernt vom Touristentrubel der Küste

PREISE
Zimmer ab 930 €, Suiten ab 990 €

ZIMMER
4 Zimmer, 14 Suiten

STIL
Globalisierungs-Luxus, unter dem – vor allem im Garten – noch das Flair der alten, großen Riviera der 1930er bis 1950er spürbar ist

KÜCHE
Die aromatischen mediterranen Menüs werden im Poolhaus oder im Zimmer serviert

X-FAKTOR
Vielleicht nicht für jeden relevant, aber für Stammgäste aus der Film- oder Musikbranche ein wichtiges Argument: Der private kleine Sandstrand des Cap Estel ist Paparazzi-sicher

BUCH ZUM ORT
„Mein Leben und Lieben" von Frank Harris

SITUATION
En contrebas du village perché d'Èze, à 20 km de l'aéroport de Nice et à l'écart de l'agitation touristique de la côte

PRIX
Chambres à partir de 930 €, suites à partir de 990 €

CHAMBRES
4 chambres et 14 suites

STYLE
Luxe teinté de mondialisation et encore pénétré du charme de la Côte d'Azur des années 1930 et 1950, surtout dans le jardin

RESTAURATION
Des menus méditerranéens savoureux sont servis au poolhouse ou dans les chambres

LE «PETIT PLUS»
Un petit détail qui peut avoir son importance, surtout pour les hôtes qui travaillent dans le cinéma ou la musique: la petite plage de sable privée du Cap Estel est à l'abri des paparazzi

LIVRE À EMPORTER
«Ma vie et mes amours» de Frank Harris

CHÂTEAU DES ALPILLES
FRANCE

Départementale 31 ~ 13210 Saint-Rémy-de-Provence ~ France
Telephone +33 490 920 333 ~ Fax +33 490 924 517
chateau.alpilles@wanadoo.fr
www.chateaudesalpilles.com

This country residence was once owned by the family of French novelist Amédée Pichot, whose guests included politicians and artists. Now a hotel run by a mother-and-daughter team, the château nonetheless remains a destination for *le tout* Paris. For most, a walk in the enchanting park is the first priority on arrival. Covering 17 acres, this estate on the edge of the Alpine foothills is full of old plane trees and secret places that will leave you yearning for a bit of Proust—a feeling that only intensifies when sitting in front of the fire (there's one in every room), surrounded by antiques.

Thankfully, there are more contemporary diversions on offer too—the modern Provençal cuisine, for instance, or the pool by which guests can enjoy something probably unknown to Proust and his peers: chilling out.

Einst gehörte dieser Landsitz der Familie des Romanciers Amédée Pichot, der hier französische Politiker und Künstler zu Gast hatte. Heute empfängt ein Mutter-Tochter-Gespann die Gäste, zu denen immer noch *le tout Paris* gehört. Noch vor dem Kofferauspacken steht für die meisten ein Spaziergang durch den zauberhaften Park an. Am Fuß der Voralpen erstreckt sich auf sieben Hektar diese bemerkenswerte Anlage; alte Platanen und viele klandestine Plätzchen zum Verweilen sorgen für das dringende Verlangen, anschließend Proust zu lesen. Ein Gefühl, das im Herrenhaus, mit seinen Antiquitäten und einem Kamin in jedem Zimmer, nicht gerade schwächer wird.

Nur gut, dass es dann doch ein bisschen zeitgenössische Ablenkung gibt – die moderne provenzalische Küche des Hauses etwa, oder einen Pool, wo man etwas tut, das es zu Prousts Zeiten noch gar nicht gab: relaxen.

Cette propriété appartenait autrefois à la famille du romancier Amédée Pichot, qui accueillait ici des personnalités du monde politique et artistique. Aujourd'hui, un duo mère-fille y reçoit encore le Tout-Paris. Avant même de défaire ses bagages, on se doit de faire une promenade dans le magnifique parc de sept hectares qui s'étend au pied des Alpilles. Ses platanes et ses nombreux refuges ombragés invitent à la rêverie et suscitent le besoin urgent de relire Proust ; et ce besoin n'en est que plus vif quand on pénètre à l'intérieur de l'hôtel meublé d'antiquités, dont chaque chambre dispose d'une cheminée.

Par bonheur, les plaisirs contemporains ne sont pas tout à fait exclus, l'établissement proposant notamment de la cuisine provençale moderne et une piscine où s'adonner à une activité encore inconnue au temps de Proust : la relaxation.

LOCATION

The 17-acre estate lies on the edge of
Saint-Rémy-de-Provence, 90 km/56 miles
northwest of Marseille airport

RATES

Rooms from $270, suites from $405,
excluding breakfast

ROOMS

21 rooms and suites in the château itself and in
the more modern Mas du Cyprès farmhouse,
plus 2 cottages in the grounds

STYLE

Like the home of well-to-do friends of the family

FOOD

Quality Provençal specialties made from ultra-
fresh ingredients and fine herbs. There are also
occasional cooking courses

X FACTOR

The air of grand-bourgeois nonchalance so
admirably cultivated by the château's owners

BOOK TO PACK

"Quicksands: A Memoir" by Sybille Bedford

LAGE

Das 7 ha große Grundstück liegt am Rand von
Saint-Rémy-de-Provence, 90 km nordwestlich
des Flughafens Marseille

PREISE

Zimmer ab 200 €, Suiten ab 300 €,
ohne Frühstück

ZIMMER

21 Zimmer und Suiten im Château und dem
moderner gehaltenen Nebengebäude Mas du
Cyprès, außerdem 2 Häuschen im Park

STIL

Als wäre man zu Gast bei Freunden der Eltern

KÜCHE

Provenzalisch raffiniert, aus frischesten Zutaten
und wunderbar mit Kräutern abgeschmeckt;
gelegentlich gibt es sogar Kochkurse

X-FAKTOR

Die großbürgerliche französische Lässigkeit,
die die Betreiberfamilie hier so beneidenswert
vorlebt

BUCH ZUM ORT

„Treibsand" von Sybille Bedford

SITUATION

En bordure de Saint-Rémy-de-Provence, à 90 km
au nord-ouest de l'aéroport de Marseille

PRIX

Chambres à partir de 200 €, suites à partir
de 300 €, petit déjeuner non compris

CHAMBRES

21 chambres et suites au château et dans
l'annexe plus moderne, le Mas du Cyprès,
2 petites maisons dans le parc

STYLE

Comme si l'on était invité chez des amis
de ses parents

RESTAURATION

Cuisine provençale raffinée avec des produits
frais agrémentés d'herbes aromatiques. Des
cours de cuisine sont régulièrement proposés

LE «PETIT PLUS»

Cette décontraction typique de la grande
bourgeoisie française que le maître de lieux
cultive ici admirablement

LIVRE À EMPORTER

«Sables mouvants» de Sybille Bedford

HÔTEL DU CAP-EDEN-ROC
FRANCE

Boulevard John F Kennedy, BP 29 ~ 06601 Antibes ~ France
Telephone +33 493 613 901 ~ Fax +33 493 677 604
reservation@hdcer.com
www.hotel-du-cap-eden-roc.com

There are hotels that seem more than the sum of their parts, and then there's the Cap-Eden-Roc, where everything seems straight out of a dream. Cream-colored residence by the sea. Perfectly manicured grounds with a path (a catwalk?) to the coast. Seafront pool carved into the rock, by which guests sunbathe in almost obligatory Eres bikinis. Suites with Louis XVI–style interiors. Not forgetting the restaurant with yacht-deck-like terrace and the stunning piano bar. No wonder Leonardo DiCaprio, Cate Blanchett, and Sean Connery all hole up at this Cap d'Antibes hideaway during the Cannes Film Festival.

Behind the scenes, everything here runs like clockwork: the Cap-Eden-Roc is a celebration of the hotelier's art and of old-school Riviera luxury. Until a few years ago, it had no in-room TVs, provided hair dryers only on request, and didn't take credit cards. This is a place where other things matter more: absolute discretion, for example, or the private-club atmosphere.

Es gibt Hotels, die mehr sind als die Summe ihrer Annehmlichkeiten ... und noch darüber schwebt das Cap-Eden-Roc. Ein cremefarbener Palast am Meer, ein makellos manikürter Park, durch den ein Weg, nein: Laufsteg zur Küste mit einem Felsenpool führt, an dessen Rand man gefälligst im Eres-Bikini sonnenbadet. Nicht zu vergessen Suiten im Louis-XVI-Stil, ein Restaurant mit einem veritablen Jachtdeck von Terrasse und eine hinreißende Pianobar.

Kein Wunder, dass während des Filmfestivals in Cannes hier Leonardo DiCaprio, Cate Blanchett und Sean Connery verweilen. Wie in den Filmstudios läuft hinter den Kulissen eine wahre Präzisionsmaschine: Das Haus am Cap d'Antibes zelebriert die Hotellerie alter Schule, als Sehnsuchtsort klassischer Riviera-Sommerfrische. Bis vor wenigen Jahren kamen die Zimmer ohne Fernseher aus, Haartrockner wurden nur auf Wunsch gebracht und Kreditkarten nicht akzeptiert. In diesen Hallen setzt man eben auf andere Werte: zum Beispiel auf formvollendete Diskretion und Club-Gefühl.

Certains hôtels offrent plus encore que ce qu'ils annoncent. Le Cap-Eden-Roc va même au-delà. Un palais couleur crème, un parc tiré à quatre épingles traversé par un chemin, ou plutôt un « tapis rouge » bis menant à une piscine creusée dans la roche au-dessus de la mer et sur les bords de laquelle il est de bon ton de prendre un bain de soleil en bikini Eres. Sans oublier les suites de style Louis XVI, un restaurant avec un pont de yacht en guise de terrasse et un merveilleux piano-bar.

Pas étonnant que Leonardo DiCaprio, Cate Blanchett et Sean Connery s'y attardent pendant le Festival de Cannes. Comme dans les studios de cinéma, c'est une machine de précision qui fonctionne dans les coulisses : ce lieu mythique de la villégiature classique sur la Côte d'Azur perpétue la tradition hôtelière à l'ancienne. Il y a quelques années encore, les chambres n'avaient pas de téléviseur, le sèche-cheveux était apporté sur demande et les cartes bancaires n'étaient pas acceptées. Ici, c'est la discrétion absolue et l'ambiance club qui priment.

LOCATION
25 km/16 miles south of Nice airport

RATES
Rooms from $1,080, suites from $2,200

ROOMS
118 rooms, suites and villas offer state-of-the-art amenities, private bars and marble bathrooms

STYLE
Garden of Eden beneath pine trees

FOOD
Mediterranean at the Eden-Roc; tapas and sushi at the Grill & Lounge Bar; everything from Negroni to Pimm's Royal at the two bars

X FACTOR
The genius loci: From 1887, the then Villa Soleil, built by the publisher of *Le Figaro*, served as a retreat for the likes of Orson Welles, Marlene Dietrich, and the Duke and Duchess of Windsor

BOOK TO PACK
"Tender is the Night" by F. Scott Fitzgerald (the Cap-Eden-Roc of the 1920s was the inspiration for the "Hôtel des Etrangers")

LAGE
25 km südlich vom Flughafen Nizza gelegen

PREISE
Zimmer ab 800 €, Suiten ab 1630 €

ZIMMER
118 Zimmer, Suiten und Villen mit luxuriöser Ausstattung, eigener Bar und Marmorbädern

STIL
Garten Eden hinter Pinienbäumen

KÜCHE
Das Eden Roc serviert Haute Cuisine, die Grill & Lounge Bar Tapas und Sushi, die zwei Bars flüssige Leckereien von Negroni bis Pimm's Royal

X-FAKTOR
Der Genius Loci: 1870 vom Verleger des *Figaro* als Villa Soleil erbaut, seit 1887 eine Zuflucht für Leute wie Orson Welles, Marlene Dietrich oder die Windsors (samt Cairn Terrier)

BUCH ZUM ORT
„Zärtlich ist die Nacht" von F. Scott Fitzgerald (das Cap-Eden-Roc der 1920er war Vorbild für dessen „Hôtel des Étrangers")

SITUATION
À 25 km au sud-ouest de l'aéroport de Nice

PRIX
Chambres à partir de 800 €, suite à partir de 1630 €

CHAMBRES
118 chambres, suites et villas dotées d'équipements de pointe, de bars privés et de salles de bains en marbre

STYLE
Jardin d'Éden caché dans une pinède

RESTAURATION
L' Eden-Roc sert de la grande cuisine, le Grill & Lounge Bar des tapas et des sushis, les deux bars des boissons divines tels le Negroni et le Pimm's royal

LE « PETIT PLUS »
Construite en 1870 par le propriétaire du *Figaro*, la Villa Soleil sert depuis 1887 de refuge à des personnalités (Orson Welles, Marlene Dietrich, les Windsor ...)

LIVRE À EMPORTER
« Tendre est la nuit » de F. Scott Fitzgerald

MONTE-CARLO BEACH HOTEL
FRANCE

Avenue Princesse Grace ~ 06190 Roquebrune-Cap-Martin ~ France
Telephone +377 98 062 525 ~ Fax +377 98 062 626
resort@sbm.mc
www.monte-carlo-beach.com

In 1929, modernism arrived with a bang on the Côte d'Azur, courtesy of a luxury beach hotel that suddenly made the stuccoed grand hotels of old look overdressed. Built by celebrated architect Roger Séassal for the Société des Bains de Mer, it had the curves of a Bugatti, the sleek lines of a Garçonne haircut, and an Olympic pool with diving tower—a facility that, just as at the new resorts then being built in the United States, was as much about flirting over cocktails as about sporting endeavor.

Eight decades later, Parisian interior designer India Mahdavi completed a redesign of this Art Deco gem that draws on the Côte's avant-garde past—on Matisse, Cocteau, Eileen Gray, and even gossip queen Elsa Maxwell, who once organized the hotel's opening ball. On the subject of parties, the waterfront Sea Lounge ensures the hotel still features prominently on Monaco's social circuit. Some things never change—thankfully!

1929 zog die Moderne an der Côte d'Azur ein, und zwar mit einem echten Knaller. Im Auftrag der Société des Bains de Mer hatte der renommierte Architekt Roger Séassal ein Luxushotel an die Küste gestellt, das die Grandhotels mit ihren Stuckgirlanden auf einmal tantig wirken ließ: kurvig wie ein Bugatti, schnittig wie eine Garçonne-Frisur und mit Wettkampfpool samt Sprungturm ganz dem Sport und dem Flirten bei Cocktails gewidmet, genau wie die gleichzeitig entstehenden Resorts in den USA.

Zeitsprung in die 2000er. Die Pariser Interiordesignerin India Mahdavi wird mit der Neugestaltung des Art-déco-Juwels betraut und ruft als Inspiration prompt die Geister der Côte-Avantgarde auf – von Matisse, Cocteau und Eileen Gray bis zur Klatschdiva Elsa Maxwell, die einst den Eröffnungsball organisierte. Apropos: Dank der Sea Lounge direkt am Meer gehört das Hotel immer noch zu Monacos besten Partyplätzen. Manche Dinge ändern sich eben nie. Zum Glück!

En 1929, l'apparition de l'architecture moderne sur la Côte d'Azur fit l'effet d'une bombe. Le célèbre architecte Roger Séassal avait été chargé par la Société des Bains de Mer de réaliser un hôtel de luxe, à côté duquel les grands hôtels croulant sous le stuc feraient soudain mauvais genre. Arborant les courbes d'une Bugatti, ce palace doté d'une piscine de compétition et d'un plongeoir devait être voué au sport et au flirt autour de cocktails, exactement comme les grands hôtels américains de la même époque.

Plus tard, dans les années 2000, l'architecte d'intérieur parisienne India Mahdavi, qui se voit confier le réaménagement de ce bijou Art déco, s'inspire de l'avant-garde de la Côte d'Azur – de Matisse à Elsa Maxwell, qui organisa autrefois le bal d'ouverture, en passant par Cocteau et Eileen Gray. Grâce au Sea Lounge donnant sur la mer, cet hôtel compte toujours parmi les hauts lieux des fêtes monégasques. Heureusement, il est des choses qui ne changent pas.

LOCATION
30 km/19 miles east of Nice airport

RATES
Rooms from $320, suites from $780

ROOMS
26 rooms and 14 suites

STYLE
The ultimate in Riviera chic

FOOD
In addition to the Sea Lounge and the restaurant Elsa, there is the more informal poolside atmosphere of Le Deck and La Vigie for buffet lunches and dinners in summer

X FACTOR
As part of the 2009 overhaul, the grounds of the Monte-Carlo Beach Hotel were also given a new look—by French landscape design maestro Jean Mus. His highly aesthetic ensemble of palms, pines, and grasses is now well and truly established and ranks as an attraction in its own right

BOOK TO PACK
"Loser Takes All" by Graham Greene

LAGE
30 km östlich des Flughafens Nizza gelegen

PREISE
Zimmer ab 240 €, Suiten ab 580 €

ZIMMER
26 Zimmer und 14 Suiten

STIL
Best of Riviera-Chic

KÜCHE
Neben dem Restaurant Elsa und der Sea Lounge gibt es das legere Le Deck am Pool sowie das im Sommer geöffnete La Vigie mit Lunch- und Dinnerbuffets

X-FAKTOR
Bei der großen Renovierung im Jahr 2009 wurden auch die Außenanlagen des Beach Hotel neu gestaltet – diese Veredelung übernahm damals Altmeister Jean Mus persönlich. Jetzt ist sein Werk aus Palmen, Pinien und Gräsern endlich perfekt eingewachsen und mittlerweile eine Sehenswürdigkeit für sich

BUCH ZUM ORT
„Heirate nie in Monte Carlo" von Graham Greene

SITUATION
À 30 km à l'est de l'aéroport de Nice

PRIX
Chambres à partir de 240 €, suites à partir de 580 €

CHAMBRES
26 chambres et 14 suites

STYLE
Le chic du chic de la Côte d'Azur

RESTAURATION
Outre le restaurant Elsa et le Sea Lounge, il y a aussi Le Deck au bord de la piscine et La Vigie en été, qui propose des buffets midi et soir

LE « PETIT PLUS »
Lors de la grande rénovation de 2009, les espaces extérieurs du Beach Hotel ont été également réaménagés par l'architecte paysagiste Jean Mus. Les palmiers, les pins parasols et les plantes ont si vite pris possession des lieux que le jardin constitue une véritable curiosité en soi

LIVRE À EMPORTER
« Qui perd gagne » de Graham Greene

"The sea—its colors, its shapes—was supposed to have the lead in the story we wanted to tell."

INDIA MAHDAVI, ARTISTIC DIRECTOR

„Die Hauptrolle in der Story, die wir bei diesem Projekt erzählen wollten, hatte immer das Meer – seine Farben, seine Formen."

« Le rôle principal de l'histoire que nous voulions raconter ici était tenu par la mer, ses couleurs et ses ondulations. »

DAS KRANZBACH
GERMANY

Kranzbach 1 ~ 82493 Kranzbach bei Garmisch-Partenkirchen ~ Germany
Telephone +49 8823 928 000 ~ Fax +49 8823 928 00900
info@daskranzbach.de
www.daskranzbach.de

Its name, literally translated, means "garland brook," and the Kranzbach is every bit as picturesque as that sounds. Located in the most southeasterly corner of Germany, the hotel sits amid 32 acres of Alpine meadow between the Zugspitze and Karwendel peaks. It was built in the Arts and Crafts style by Mary Portman, a wealthy British aristocrat, and is surely the only English country house in the whole of Bavaria. The interiors, meanwhile, were recently given a suitably high-class update by London interior designer Ilse Crawford.

For the current owners, authentic quality is key, be it in the contemporary coziness for which the Kranzbach is renowned, the fine cuisine, or the unfussy wellness center that even boasts a roof terrace for naturists. Whether you choose to spend it naked on the roof, wrapped snugly in feather duvets, or out on the Alpine meadows, you'll find a weekend at the Kranzbach is always supremely relaxing.

Genauso gemütlich, wie sein Name klingt, ist das Kranzbach auch. Hinterfangen von Karwendelgebirge und Zugspitze liegt es in der äußersten Südecke Deutschlands, umgeben von nichts als 13 Hektar Bergwiese. Von der reichen Britin Mary Portman erbaut, ist es wohl das einzige Country House in Bayern, das diesen Titel wirklich verdient. Bevorzugter Stil der Hausherrin war damals *Arts and Crafts,* und dank der Londoner Interiordesignerin Ilse Crawford erfuhr dessen Charme bei der Generalrenovierung ein vorbildliches Update.

Die jetzigen Gastgeber legen großen Wert auf authentische Qualität – es ist jene zeitgemäße Geborgenheit, die den guten Ruf des Kranzbach ausmacht. Dazu gehört erstklassige Versorgung aus der Küche ebenso wie ein schnörkelloser Wellnesstrakt, der sogar mit einer Dachterrasse für Naturisten aufwarten kann. Egal ob nackt, in der Daunendecke oder auf der Bergwiese: Bei einem Wochenende im Kranzbach entspannt man jedenfalls kolossal.

Le Kranzbach est un lieu très agréable. Avec pour toile de fond le massif du Karwendel et la Zugspitze, cet hôtel situé dans l'extrême sud de l'Allemagne est entouré de pas moins de 13 hectares d'alpages. Construit par la Britannique Mary Portman, c'est la seule «country house» de Bavière digne de ce nom. Le style Arts & Crafts est celui pour lequel avait opté l'ancienne propriétaire. Complètement rénové et modernisé par l'architecte d'intérieur londonienne Ilse Crawford, l'endroit n'a rien perdu de son charme.

Les propriétaires actuels accordent beaucoup d'importance à la qualité de leurs prestations. C'est d'ailleurs ce qui fait la réputation du Kranzbach. L'excellente cuisine y contribue ainsi que l'aile réservée à l'espace de remise en forme, pourvue d'un toit-terrasse pour les naturistes. Que vous soyez nu ou pas sous la couette ou dans les prés, un week-end passé ici vous permettra de retrouver une forme olympique.

LOCATION
15 km/9 miles from Garmisch-Partenkirchen
at the foot of the German Alps

RATES
Rooms from $200, suites from $250, tree
house from $425

ROOMS
129 rooms, one tree house, and one gatehouse

STYLE
Elegant British interiors by Ilse Crawford in the
main house; modern chalet chic in garden wing

FOOD
Light cuisine or hearty fare, organic steaks
or vegetarian creations—there's something here
for everyone. Half-board includes buffet breakfast, soup-and-salad lunches with farmhouse
bread, and 5-course à la carte evening meals

X FACTOR
The hotel invites first-timers to sleep with
the windows open—just to prove how peaceful
the surroundings are

BOOK TO PACK
"A Room of One's Own" by Virginia Woolf

LAGE
15 km von Garmisch-Partenkirchen am Fuß der
Alpen in Süddeutschland gelegen

PREISE
Zimmer ab 145 €, Suiten ab 185 €, Baumhaus
ab 245 €

ZIMMER
129 Zimmer, 1 Baumhaus und 1 Torhaus

STIL
Im Haupthaus *British Chic* (Interiors von Ilse
Crawford), im Gartenflügel Chalet-Moderne

KÜCHE
Ob vegetarisch oder Bio-Steak, leicht oder herz-
haft, hier wird jeder glücklich. Ein Hoch auf die
Genießer-Halbpension: morgens Frühstücksbuffet, mittags Suppe & Salate mit Bauernbrot,
abends 5 Gänge nach Wahl von der Karte

X-FAKTOR
Das traut sich nicht jeder Gastgeber: Das Hotel
fordert Neulinge auf, bei geöffnetem Fenster zu
schlafen – als Test der Ruhe draußen

BUCH ZUM ORT
„Ein Zimmer für sich allein" von Virginia Woolf

SITUATION
Au pied des Alpes, dans le sud de l'Allemagne,
à 15 km de Garmisch-Partenkirchen

PRIX
Chambres à partir de 145 €, suites à partir de
185 €, cabane dans les arbres à partir de 245 €

CHAMBRES
129 chambres, 1 cabane dans les arbres
et 1 porterie

STYLE
Chic britannique dans le bâtiment principal
(intérieurs d'Ilse Crawford), chalet moderne
dans l'aile donnant sur le jardin

RESTAURATION
La demi-pension est soignée : buffet au petit
déjeuner, soupe et salade avec du pain de campagne au déjeuner et 5 plats à choisir sur la
carte au dîner

LE «PETIT PLUS»
Le calme absolu : l'hôtel encourage même
à dormir avec la fenêtre ouverte !

LIVRE À EMPORTER
«Une chambre à soi» de Virginia Woolf

GRÄFLICHER PARK
GERMANY

Brunnenallee 1 ~ 33014 Bad Driburg ~ Germany
Telephone +49 525 395 230 ~ Fax +49 525 395 232 05
info@graeflicher-park.de
www.graeflicher-park.de

At this aristocratic estate, which has been in the same family's hands for seven generations, the lady of the manor herself takes responsibility for maintaining the unique ambience. Established by Caspar Heinrich von Sierstorpff, Gräflicher Park has served as a place for those in search of rest and relaxation since the 18th century.

Bad Driburg has long been known for its naturally carbonated spring waters—their therapeutic effect was described by poet Friedrich Hölderlin—and this 158-acre park, laid out in the style of an English landscape garden, is home to three such springs. Guests can take the waters in the hotel's garden spa, whose charming bathhouse offers an impressive range of treatments. The restaurant's combination of baroque welcome and contemporary cuisine, meanwhile, can only further enhance your sense of well-being. Bathing, feasting, and strolling in the grounds— Gräflicher Park is a treat for all the senses.

Hier sorgt die Gräfin noch selbst fürs richtige Ambiente – und das in der siebten Generation. Seit dem 18. Jahrhundert dient der Gräfliche Park, den einst Caspar Heinrich von Sierstorpff anlegte, als Ziel für Sommerfrischler und Erholungssuchende. Selbst Friedrich Hölderlin kam nicht umhin, die wohltuende Wirkung des kohlensäurehaltigen Heilwassers von Bad Driburg in Briefen lobend zu erwähnen.

Gleich drei Quellen davon sprudeln in dem 64 Hektar großen englischen Landschaftspark. In ihren Genuss kommt man als Gast des gräflichen Hotels im Garten-Spa mit reizendem Badehaus, wo man aus einer beeindruckenden Vielfalt an Heilanwendungen wählen kann. Ganzheitlich wohl wird einem spätestens beim Abendessen, wo sich barocke Gastlichkeit und zeitgemäße Kulinarik aufs Trefflichste verbinden. Baden, Schmausen und Flanieren – wahrlich ein Platz für alle Sinne.

C'est toujours la comtesse qui donne le ton dans cette propriété, et cela dure depuis sept générations. Aménagé autrefois par Caspar Heinrich Sierstorpff, le Gräflicher Park est un lieu de villégiature et de détente depuis le 18e siècle. Le poète et philosophe Friedrich Hölderlin lui-même fit l'éloge dans ses lettres des effets bienfaisants de l'eau thermale gazeuse de Bad Driburg.

Dans le grand parc à l'anglaise qui s'étend sur 64 hectares jaillissent pas moins de trois sources dont les hôtes peuvent agréablement profiter en fréquentant le spa pourvu de bains ravissants. Là, ils peuvent choisir parmi une palette impressionnante de soins. Leur bien-être sera assurément à son comble au moment du dîner, où la convivialité baroque et la cuisine moderne s'associent pour le meilleur. Se baigner, se délecter et flâner. Ici, tous les sens sont en éveil.

LOCATION
30 km/19 miles east of Paderborn; 200 km/
124 miles southwest of Düsseldorf airport

RATES
Rooms from $160, junior suites from $320

ROOMS
135 rooms and junior suites

STYLE
Outside: half-timbered splendor, graceful
stuccoed spa architecture, and contemporary
glass; inside: comfort for the soul

FOOD
Caspar's Restaurant serves seasonal cuisine;
Pferdestall, in a stable block from 1860, is a grill
with a show kitchen

X FACTOR
Moor-mud baths may not sound very dignified,
but they are a real miracle cure. Thoroughly
renewed, you can then admire the park's huge
exotic trees with pooch in tow—four-legged
friends are welcome in one of the guesthouses

BOOK TO PACK
"Selected Poems" by Friedrich Hölderlin

LAGE
30 km östlich von Paderborn; der Flughafen
Düsseldorf ist 200 km entfernt

PREISE
Zimmer ab 120 €, Junior-Suiten ab 240 €

ZIMMER
135 Zimmer und Junior-Suiten

STIL
Außen Fachwerk-Noblesse, anmutiger Bäder-
stuck und gläserne Gegenwart; drinnen ein
Komfort, der auch der Seele guttut

KÜCHE
Caspar's Restaurant serviert saisonale Menüs.
Der 1860 erbaute Pferdestall ist ein uriges
Grillrestaurant mit Schauküche

X-FAKTOR
Klingt unelegant, ist aber ein echtes Wundermit-
tel: Moorbäder. Und danach wie frisch geboren
mit dem Dackel an der Leine die riesigen Baum-
exoten bewundern. In einem der Gästehäuser
sind nämlich auch Vierbeiner wohlgelitten!

BUCH ZUM ORT
„Sämtliche Gedichte" von Friedrich Hölderlin

SITUATION
À 30 km à l'est de Paderborn et à 200 km
de l'aéroport de Düsseldorf

PRIX
Chambres à partir de 120 €, suites juniors
à partir de 240 €

CHAMBRES
135 chambres et suites juniors

STYLE
À l'extérieur, élégants colombages, charmants
bains en stuc et architecture contemporaine
en verre; à l'intérieur, un confort apaisant

RESTAURATION
Le Caspar's Restaurant propose des menus
avec des produits de saison. La rôtisserie du
Pferdestall, construite en 1860, se visite

LE « PETIT PLUS »
Les miraculeux bains de boue font des miracles!
Promenez-vous sous les arbres avec votre teckel
en laisse. Dans l'une des résidences, les animaux
sont en effet les bienvenus!

LIVRE À EMPORTER
« Poèmes : 1806–1843 » de Friedrich Hölderlin

HOFGUT HAFNERLEITEN
GERMANY

Brunndobl 16 ~ 84364 Bad Birnbach ~ Germany
Telephone +49 8563 91511 ~ Fax +49 8563 91512
post@hofgut.info
www.hofgut.info

The melancholy hills around the Rott valley are not exactly the place you'd expect to come across a highly successful hospitality experiment. It's here, though, that we find Hofgut Hafnerleiten, a retreat that soothes all the senses. Its owners first established a cookery school here, then, in 2005, built their first cabins, creating individual refuges that are wonderfully peaceful and close to nature—yet also offer the option of getting together with other guests.

The couple themselves are incredibly welcoming and have chosen to focus on their guests' basic needs: to eat well, sleep well, and be well looked after. The sustainable architecture offers plenty of space and yet has cozier areas too, and there's even a tree house for those who really want to get away from it all (the ground included). Today, there are also larger, long-stay cabins—perfect for freelancers seeking creative inspiration in Lower Bavaria's Tuscany.

In der melancholischen Rottaler Hügelland-schaft hätte man derlei nicht unbedingt vermu-tet: ein äußerst geglücktes Hotelexperiment, das sich mit Sinn und Sinnlichkeit um seine Gäste bemüht. Das Hofgut Hafnerleiten war zunächst nur eine Kochschule. 2005 folgten die ersten Themenhäuschen und begründeten einen Ort, der wunderbar ruhige und naturnahe Rückzugsräume bietet – aber auch die Möglich-keit, sich mit anderen zu treffen.

Das rührend bemühte Betreiberpaar hat sich darauf konzentriert, seinen Hof rund um die elementaren Ansprüche eines Gastes zu bauen: gut essen, gut schlafen und gut umsorgt werden. Die nachhaltige Architektur bietet viel Freiraum, dabei trotzdem gemütliche Ecken; und sogar ein Baumhaus für diejenigen, die mal alles unter sich lassen wollen. Inzwischen gibt es auch drei „Langhäuser" für Gäste, die ein bisschen länger bleiben wollen. Zum Beispiel, weil sie als Freibe-rufler festgestellt haben, dass es sich hier in der niederbayerischen Toskana auch sehr gut krea-tiv arbeiten lässt.

Dans ce paysage mélancolique de la vallée de la Rott, on ne soupçonnerait pas forcément la présence d'un tel concept Hôtelier totalement dédié au bien-être. Le succès est pourtant bel et bien au rendez-vous. À l'origine, le Hofgut Hafnerleiten donnait des cours de cuisine. En 2005 apparurent les premières maisons à thème, dotant ainsi ce lieu aussi bien de lieux propices au calme et proches de la nature que d'espaces conviviaux, permettant de se retrou-ver à plusieurs.

Le couple de propriétaires a à cœur de répondre au mieux aux besoins élémentaires de ses hôtes : bien manger, bien dormir et être dorlotés. L'architecture durable offre une grande liberté et des coins douillets, ainsi qu'une cabane dans un arbre pour ceux qui veulent prendre de la hauteur. Trois « longères » sont mises à la disposition de ceux qui, tels les artistes indé-pendants, veulent prolonger leur séjour au Hofgut Hafnerleiten parce qu'ils ont compris combien la « Toscane bavaroise » est propice à la création.

LOCATION
In the district of Rottal-Inn, 1.5 hours from Munich, Salzburg, and Linz airports

RATES
From $210 per person per night, breakfast included

ROOMS
3 long-stay cabins, seven themed cabins, and two poolside suites

STYLE
Innovative rural architecture

FOOD
The motto is fresh ingredients, honest recipes. The results, inevitably, are Mediterranean

X FACTOR
The *pasta alla famiglia* served to all the guests every Thursday at the main building's long family dining table. Guests can also hone their own cookery and barista skills with Hofgut Hafnerleiten's in-house courses

BOOK TO PACK
"The Life of My Mother" by Oskar Maria Graf

LAGE
Im Rottal-Inn, jeweils 1,5 Stunden von den Flughäfen München, Salzburg und Linz entfernt

PREISE
Übernachtung inklusive Frühstück ab 160 € pro Person und Tag

ZIMMER
3 Rottaler Langhäuser, 7 Themenhäuser und 2 Teichsuiten

STIL
Innovative Landarchitektur

KÜCHE
Motto: Frische Lebensmittel, ehrlich zubereitet. Da landet man zwangsläufig bei Mediterranem

X-FAKTOR
Die *pasta alla famiglia*, die jeden Donnerstagabend im Haupthaus mit allen Hausgästen an der großen Familientafel stattfindet; derselbe Genussgeist weht auch durch die Barista- und Kochkurse, die hier angeboten werden

BUCH ZUM ORT
„Das Leben meiner Mutter" von Oskar Maria Graf

SITUATION
Vallée de la Rott, à 1 heure 30 des aéroports de Munich, de Salzbourg et de Linz

PRIX
160 € par personne et par jour, petit déjeuner inclus

CHAMBRES
3 longères dans le style local, 7 maisons à thème et 2 suites

STYLE
Architecture rurale innovante

RESTAURATION
Des produits frais merveilleusement préparés. Les plats ont des saveurs méditerranéennes

LE «PETIT PLUS»
La *pasta alla famiglia* qui est servie le jeudi soir dans la maison principale à tous les hôtes réunis autour de la table; la même convivialité règne pendant les cours de barista et de cuisine donnés sur place

LIVRE À EMPORTER
«Dans la forêt de Bavière» d'Adalbert Stifter

BELVEDERE
GREECE

Belvedere Hotel ~ School of Fine Arts District ~ 84600 Mykonos ~ Greece
Telephone +30 228 902 5122 ~ Fax +30 228 902 5126
contact@belvederehotel.com
www.belvederehotel.com

From afar, the white buildings of this Mykonos hotel complex resemble a traditional Cycladic village. Inside, though, they are unexpectedly urbane. The architects of the Rockwell Group drew inspiration from contemporary yacht design in their painstaking 2009 renovation, decorating the rooms with furnishings you definitely wouldn't find in the local *kafenion*. The upscale nature of the Belvedere is evident elsewhere too—in the staff uniforms by British designer Neil Barrett, for example, or the fact that the signature cocktails are exclusive to the hotel bar, a popular meeting place for the island's trendy young things.

Despite the hip vibe, there's plenty of traditional Aegean magic to enjoy too. The interiors are bathed in soft sunlight, the courtyard bougainvillea exudes a seductive scent, and the suites' terraces afford fantastic views of the sunset—surely the real experience at this very special hotel.

Aus der Ferne betrachtet wirken die weißen Häuser dieser bemerkenswerten Hotelanlage wie ein traditionelles Kykladen-Dorf. Doch das Innenleben ist überraschend urban: Bei ihrer sorgfältigen Renovierung im Jahr 2009 haben sich die Architekten der Rockwell Group von zeitgenössischem Bootsdesign inspirieren lassen und das Belvedere mit Möbeln ausgestattet, wie man sie definitiv nicht im nächsten Kafenion antrifft. Auch sonst folgt hier alles einem eher elitären Konzept – die Uniformen der Angestellten kommen vom britischen Designer Neil Barrett, und die Haus-Cocktails gibt es nur hier an der Bar, an der sich abends das junge Mykonos ein Stelldichein gibt.

Trotz dieser hippen Atmosphäre kommt im Belvedere der Zauber der Ägäis nie zu kurz. Alles ist vom weichen Sonnenlicht durchflutet, die Bougainvilleen im Innenhof duften verführerisch, und der Sonnenuntergang, betrachtet von einer der Suite-Terrassen, ist wahrlich das schönste Ereignis des Hotels.

Vues de loin, les maisons blanches de ce très bel hôtel évoquent un village traditionnel des Cyclades, mais leur aménagement intérieur est étonnamment urbain. Lors de la rénovation soignée de 2009, les architectes du Rockwell Group se sont inspirés du design nautique contemporain pour doter le Belvedere d'un mobilier aux lignes épurées qui n'a absolument rien à voir avec celui du *kafenion* du coin. Tout ici relève d'une conception plutôt élitiste. Les tenues des employés ont été créés par le styliste britannique Neil Barret, et les cocktails maison sont la spécialité du bar où la jeunesse de Mykonos se donne rendez-vous le soir.

En dépit de cette atmosphère branchée, le charme de la mer Égée est profondément perceptible au Belvedere, baigné de soleil. La cour intérieure embaume du parfum des bougainvilliers, et le soleil couchant sur la terrasse des suites est sans doute l'un des moments les plus forts dont on peut faire l'expérience lors d'un séjour dans ces lieux.

LOCATION
Situated above Mykonos Chora, 2 km/1.2 miles to the northwest of the island's airport

RATES
Rooms from $175, suites from $610, breakfast included

ROOMS
35 rooms and 8 suites, some with private terraces

STYLE
Hip location in Mykonos white

FOOD
Japanese/South American dishes at the world-famous Matsuhisa Mykonos; The Belvedere Club has innovative Greek cuisine

X FACTOR
The hotel's special sunset service: Invite friends over to your suite and celebrate sundown with divine drinks and great music—the perfect way to warm up for an evening on the town

BOOK TO PACK
"The Magus" by John Fowles

LAGE
Über Mykonos Chora gelegen, 2 km nordwestlich vom Flughafen der Insel

PREISE
Zimmer ab 130 €, Suite ab 450 €, inklusive Frühstück

ZIMMER
35 Zimmer und 8 Suiten, einige davon mit privaten Terrassen

STIL
It-Place ganz in Mykonos-Weiß

KÜCHE
Das japanisch-südamerikanische Matsuhisa Mykonos ist weltberühmt; innovative griechische Kost serviert The Belvedere Club

X-FAKTOR
Der besondere *Sunset*-Service: Freunde in die Suite einladen und mit besonderen Drinks und Musik den Sonnenuntergang zelebrieren. Perfekt als atmosphärischer Kick-Start vor dem Ausgehen in die Altstadt

BUCH ZUM ORT
„Der Magus" von John Fowles

SITUATION
Au-dessus de la ville de Mykonos Chora, à 2 km à l'ouest de l'aéroport de l'île

PRIX
Chambres à partir de 130 €, suites à partir de 450 €, petit déjeuner inclus

CHAMBRES
35 chambres et 8 suites, dont certaines avec terrasse privée

STYLE
LE lieu où il faut être, dans la blanche Mykonos

RESTAURATION
Le restaurant japonais-sud-américain Matsuhisa Mykonos est de réputation mondiale; plats grecs inventifs au Belvedere Club

LE «PETIT PLUS»
Le service «Sunset»: inviter des amis dans sa suite et célébrer le soleil couchant avec des boissons originales et de la musique. Un début de soirée parfait avant de sortir dans la vieille ville

LIVRE À EMPORTER
«Le Mage» de John Fowles

PERIVOLAS
GREECE

Oía 84702 ~ Santorini ~ Greece
Telephone +30 228 607 1308 ~ Fax +30 228 607 1309
info@perivolas.gr
www.perivolas.gr

On Santorini, the setting sun is the star of the show, transforming the summer evening sky with a stunning display of colors before disappearing into the Aegean Sea. Sadly, this highly romantic sight is one most visitors have to share with the countless other onlookers setting up their cameras on the crater's rim or jostling for places in the local bars.

Those fortunate enough to be staying at Perivolas, however, can watch the sun set from the comfort of their own verandas. These private terraces belong to cave-like dwellings that were once carved into the hillside and have since been transformed by Costis Psychas and his parents into unique hideaways with white-washed ceilings, colorful fabrics, and furniture made on the island itself.

To swap privacy for company, stroll over to the spectacular pool, where the water seems to flow straight into the sea, or take a seat at the guests-only poolside restaurant, at which Mediterranean cuisine is served by candle-light—once the celestial spectacle is over.

Der Star von Santorin ist die Sonne. Sie liefert jeden Abend eine Show der Superlative, an deren Ende sie in die Ägäis abtaucht. Ein hochromantisches Schauspiel – das man nur leider mit ungezählten anderen Bewunderern teilt, die am Kraterrand ihre Fotoapparate aufbauen oder mit denen man um Plätze in den Bars kämpfen muss.

Es sei denn, man genießt das Privileg, im Perivolas zu wohnen, denn dann erlebt man den Sonnenuntergang exklusiv von der privaten Veranda aus. Diese Veranden gehören zu höhlenartigen Häusern, die einst in den Berg gegraben wurden. Costis Psychas und seine Eltern haben sie in einzigartige *Hideaways* verwandelt, mit weiß getünchten Decken, farbigen Stoffen und auf der Insel gefertigten Möbeln. Wer trotz aller Romantik Gesellschaft sucht, wandert zum spektakulären Pool, der direkt ins Meer zu fließen scheint. Gleich daneben ist das Restaurant, das abends nur für Hotelgäste mediterrane Menüs serviert. Gegessen wird bei Kerzenlicht – nach dem Abgang des Inselstars.

À Santorin, le coucher du soleil est un rendez-vous à ne pas manquer. Cette véritable féerie s'achève avec le soleil plongeant dans la mer. Un spectacle romantique que l'on doit partager avec d'innombrables admirateurs ayant installé le trépied de leurs appareils photo au bord du cratère ou luttant pour avoir les meilleures places dans les bars.

À moins que vous n'ayez le privilège de séjourner au Perivolas, où vous pourrez assister au coucher de soleil depuis votre véranda. Ces demeures troglodytiques ont été autrefois aménagées dans la montagne. Costis Psychas et ses parents les ont transformées en refuges aux plafonds blanchis à la chaux, aux meubles de fabrication locale et aux étoffes colorées. Si vous recherchez la compagnie de vos pairs, vous pourrez faire un tour à la piscine spectaculaire qui semble se déverser dans la mer. À côté, le restaurant propose le soir des menus méditerranéens, réservés aux résidents. On y dîne à la lueur des bougies, une fois que la star de l'île a tiré sa révérence.

LOCATION
Located near Oía, 30 minutes from the airport, 40 minutes from Santorini harbor. There's privacy galore, although no private beach

RATES
Studios from $570, suites from $760

ROOMS
20 dwellings of between 270 and 1,500 sq. ft. (depending on category). All have terraces

STYLE
Ancient meets elegant

FOOD
Dionysos be praised: The restaurant is housed in a former wine cellar

X FACTOR
Even the most seasoned travelers will get a kick out of turning back time and sleeping in caves as our early ancestors once did. The strange rock dwellings at Perivolas may not quite be Stone Age (they are around 300 years old) but still...

BOOK TO PACK
"The Colossus of Maroussi" by Henry Miller

LAGE
Bei Oía, 30 Minuten vom Flughafen und 40 Minuten vom Hafen Santorin entfernt; das Hotel bietet vieles, nur keinen eigenen Strand

PREISE
Studios ab 420 €, Suiten ab 560 €

ZIMMER
20 private Häuser, je nach Kategorie 25 bis 140 m² groß, alle mit privater Terrasse

STIL
Archaische Eleganz

KÜCHE
Danke, Dionysos: Als Restaurant wird eine ehemalige Weinkellerei genutzt

X-FAKTOR
Der evolutionäre Kitzel, der selbst den abgebrühtesten Gast erfasst, wenn er oder sie wie zu Urzeiten in einer Höhle wohnen darf. Die bizarren Felsnischen des Perivolas sind allerdings nicht steinzeitlich, sondern vor etwa 300 Jahren entstanden. Aber immerhin!

BUCH ZUM ORT
„Der Koloss von Maroussi" von Henry Miller

SITUATION
À Oía, à 30 minutes de l'aéroport et à 40 minutes du port de Santorin; l'hôtel propose de multiples activités, mais il n'a pas de plage privée

PRIX
Studios à partir de 420 €, suites à partir de 560 €, petit déjeuner inclus

CHAMBRES
20 habitations privées entre 25 et 140 m² selon les prix, toutes avec une terrasse privée

STYLE
Élégance archaïque

RESTAURATION
Dionysos soit loué! Le restaurant est situé dans une ancienne cave à vin

LE «PETIT PLUS»
L'excitation qui gagne même l'hôte le plus endurci à l'idée de vivre dans une grotte. Certes les habitations troglodytiques du Perivolas ne datent pas de l'âge de pierre – elles ont 300 ans –, mais quand même!

LIVRE À EMPORTER
«Le Colosse de Maroussi» de Henry Miller

THE OLD PHOENIX
GREECE

Finikas-Sfakion ~ 73013 Crete ~ Greece
Telephone +30 282 509 1257 ~ Fax +30 282 509 1126
info@old-phoenix.com
www.old-phoenix.com

The most spectacular stretches of Crete's 600-plus miles of coastline are to be found along the island's south coast. Here, the cliffs are steep, rough, and furrowed, and the White Mountains are cut through with canyons such as the legendary Samaria Gorge, a must-see for many tourists.

The Old Phoenix in the nearby bay of Finix, on the other hand, is a well-kept secret. Only accessible by boat, it is a simply and authentically styled hotel with plain blue shutters at the windows. But then who needs opulent interiors when you've got a balcony with breathtaking views of the Libyan Sea? On the hotel terrace below, guests can enjoy exactly the kind of fuss-free cuisine you'd hope for in such a place. The fish is home-caught, and the cheese is from the hotel's own herds of goat and sheep. Siestas, meanwhile, are best enjoyed à deux beneath a parasol on the pebble beach, far away from the hustle and bustle along the other 599 miles of coast.

Kretas Küstenlinie ist mehr als 1000 Kilometer lang, die spektakulärsten finden sich am Süd-rand der Insel. Dort sind die Felsen steil, rau und zerfurcht, und durch die Weißen Berge schneiden Canyons wie die Samaria-Schlucht, deren Erkundung für viele Touristen zum Pflicht-programm gehört.

Ein echter Geheimtipp ist hingegen in der nahen Bucht von Finix zu finden. Nur per Boot erreichbar steht hier The Old Phoenix, ein schlicht-authentisches Hotel mit einfachen blauen Fensterläden. Doch wer benötigt schon ein opulenteres Interieur, wenn er einen Balkon mit atemberaubendem Blick aufs Libysche Meer hat? Auf der Hotelterrasse wird genau die bodenständige Küche serviert, die man sich an solch einem Ort wünscht. Der Fisch ist selbst gefangen, und der Käse stammt von den haus-eigenen Ziegen- und Schafherden. Siesta hält man übrigens am besten am Kiesstrand, à deux unterm Sonnenschirm und weit entfernt vom Trubel der restlichen 999 Küstenkilometer.

La Crète a plus de 1 000 kilomètres de côtes, mais c'est dans le sud de l'île que se trouvent les plus spectaculaires. Les falaises y sont escar-pées et des canyons se frayent un passage à travers les Montagnes Blanches, comme les très touristiques gorges de Samaria.

En revanche, la baie de Finix toute proche n'est accessible que par bateau. Elle abrite The Old Phoenix, un hôtel authentique et simple avec des volets bleus. Car est-il besoin de disposer d'un intérieur plus opulent quand on la chance d'avoir un balcon qui offre une vue à couper le souffle sur la mer de Libye ? Sur la terrasse de l'hôtel, on sert une cuisine de terroir en har-monie avec le lieu. Le poisson est pêché sur place et le fromage provient des troupeaux de chèvres et de brebis de la maison. Il ne reste plus qu'à faire la sieste, de préférence sur la plage de galets, à deux sous un parasol, loin de l'agitation des 999 kilomètres de côtes restants.

LOCATION
Travel by car to Hora Sfakion (75 km/47 miles from Chania airport, 160 km/99 miles from Heraklion), then it's a 15- to 20-minute ferry ride to Loutro; the hotel is a 15-minute walk from there

RATES
Doubles from $48, four-bed rooms from $57

ROOMS
28 en suite rooms in three different buildings

STYLE
Unpretentious beachfront hideaway

FOOD
The Old Phoenix uses mainly local produce (fish, tomatoes, yogurt) for its traditional Mediterranean dishes

X FACTOR
With sea views all around, it's easy to overlook the enchanting little church just above the hotel—once discovered, though, it's sure to become a favorite spot

BOOK TO PACK
"Zorba the Greek" by Nikos Kazantzakis

LAGE
Erst mit dem Auto nach Hora Sfakion (75 km vom Flughafen Chania, 160 km vom Flughafen Heraklion entfernt), dann in 15 bis 20 Minuten mit der Fähre nach Loutro übersetzen; aus dem Ort geht man 15 Minuten zum Hotel

PREISE
Doppelzimmer ab 35 €, Viererzimmer ab 42 €

ZIMMER
28 Zimmer mit Bad, verteilt auf 3 Gebäude

STIL
Unprätentiöses Strandversteck

KÜCHE
Fisch, Tomaten, Joghurt: Für die traditionellen mediterranen Gerichte im Old Phoenix werden hauptsächlich lokale Produkte verwendet

X-FAKTOR
Ist vor lauter Meerblick leicht zu übersehen: Die zauberhafte kleine Kirche gleich oberhalb des Hotels hat das Zeug zum absoluten Ferien-Lieblingsplatz

BUCH ZUM ORT
„Alexis Sorbas" von Nikos Kazantzakis

SITUATION
Trajet en voiture jusqu'à Hora Skafion (à 75 km de l'aéroport de Chania et à 160 km de celui d'Héraklion), traversée en bateau de 15–20 minutes en direction de Loutro, puis 15 minutes de marche jusqu'à l'hôtel

PRIX
Chambres doubles à partir de 35 €, chambres quadruples à partir de 42 €

CHAMBRES
28 chambres dans 3 bâtiments

STYLE
Refuge balnéaire sans prétention

RESTAURATION
Poisson, tomates et yaourt donnent le ton : cuisine méditerranéenne traditionnelle à base de produits régionaux

LE « PETIT PLUS »
La ravissante petite église surplombant l'hôtel, qui pourrait presque être éclipsée par la vue sur la mer et qui confère au lieu un charme fou

LIVRE À EMPORTER
« Alexís Zorba » de Níkos Kazantzákis

233

ANANDA IN THE HIMALAYAS
INDIA

The Palace Estate, Narendranagar ~ Tehri Garhwal ~ Uttarakhand ~ 249175 ~ India
Telephone +91 124 451 6650 ~ Fax +91 137 822 7550
sales@anandaspa.com
www.anandaspa.com

It's always a privilege to stay in a beautiful hotel, but to reside in the palace of a maharaja is a rare pleasure indeed. This estate with views over the Ganges valley in Rishikesh and the Himalayan foothills was built in 1895 for the maharaja of Tehri Garhwal. Just more than a century later, it became home to one of the best spas in the world, a spa where the focus is firmly on traditional Indian rituals.

Here, guests can enjoy Ayurvedic treatments, yoga, and meditation in a fairy-tale atmosphere, and draw on the harmony and energy of this special place. And when not meditating, you can simply let go in your lavishly decorated room or lose yourself reading outdoors in the stunning surroundings. A retreat in the best and truest sense of the word.

Schöne Hotels sind immer ein Privileg, aber im Palast eines Maharadschas residieren zu dürfen, das ist doch eine ziemlich einmalige Gelegenheit. 1895 wurde dieses Anwesen mit Blick über das Ganges-Tal, Rishikesh und die Vorberge des Himalajas erbaut, als Wohnsitz des Herrschers von Tehri Garhwal.

Gute 100 Jahre später eröffnete hier eines der Top-Spas der Welt, das ganz im Einklang mit den traditionellen indischen Pflege-Ritualen steht. In märchenhaftem Ambiente sorgen seither Ayurveda-Anwendungen, Yoga-Kurse und Meditationsübungen dafür, dass jeder Gast an der Harmonie und Kraft des Ortes teilhaben kann. Wer genug meditiert hat, findet dank der verschwenderischen Ausstattung der Räume oder beim Lesen in der beeindruckenden Natur auch andere Möglichkeiten, die Bodenhaftung zu verlieren. Ein *Retreat* im wahrsten und besten Sinne des Wortes.

Fréquenter les beaux hôtels est toujours un privilège, mais résider dans le palais d'un maharadja est une expérience unique. Cette ancienne résidence du souverain de Tehrî-Garhwâl, avec vue sur la vallée du Gange, Rishikesh et les contreforts de l'Himalaya, a été édifiée en 1895.

Cent ans plus tard, on aménagea dans cette propriété l'un des meilleurs spas du monde, proposant des soins traditionnels indiens. Dans une atmosphère magique, les hôtes bénéficient de soins ayurvédiques et suivent des cours de yoga et de méditation, permettant à chacun de s'imprégner de l'harmonie et de l'énergie du lieu. Après avoir suffisamment médité, on peut encore chercher à s'échapper du réel en visitant ce palais somptueux ou en s'adonnant à la lecture dans la très belle nature environnante. Un lieu de retraite dans le meilleur sens du terme.

LOCATION
In Uttarakhand, 260 km/162 miles northeast of Delhi; 6–7 hours by car, or domestic flight to Dehradun then a 1-hour drive

RATES
Doubles from $610, suites from $945, participation in a variety of yoga and meditation classes included

ROOMS
70 rooms, 5 suites, and 3 pool villas

STYLE
Princely interiors with British flair and all the comfort of a high-end resort

FOOD
Gourmet East-meets-West fusion food. The Ananda Spa Cuisine can be tailored to each of the three Ayurveda body types

X FACTOR
The view across the Ganges valley. Plus the tea lounge with its signed photographs from the colonial era

BOOK TO PACK
"A Fine Balance" by Rohinton Mistry

LAGE
260 km nordöstlich von Delhi in Uttarakhand, Fahrzeit mit dem Auto 6 bis 7 Stunden oder ein Inlandsflug nach Dehradun und 1 Stunde Fahrt

PREISE
Doppelzimmer ab 465 €, Suiten ab 720 €, inklusive Teilnahme an verschiedenen Yoga- und Meditationskursen

ZIMMER
70 Zimmer, 5 Suiten und 3 Poolvillen

STIL
Königliche Ausstattung mit britischem Flair trifft auf Resort-Komfort

KÜCHE
West-östliche Gerichte auf Gourmet-Niveau. Die Ananda Spa Cuisine kann auf die drei Ayurveda-Körpertypen abgestimmt werden

X-FAKTOR
Der Blick übers Ganges-Tal. Und die Tea Lounge mit signierten Fotografien der Kolonialzeit

BUCH ZUM ORT
„Das Gleichgewicht der Welt" von Rohinton Mistry

SITUATION
Dans l'État d'Uttarakhand, à 260 km au nord-ouest de Delhi; 6 à 7 heures de voiture ou vol vers Dehradun, puis 1 heure de transfert

PRIX
Chambres doubles à partir de 465 €, suites à partir de 720 €, incluant la participation à divers cours de yoga et de méditation

CHAMBRES
70 chambres, 5 suites et 3 villas avec piscine

STYLE
Aménagement royal un tantinet british qui s'unit au confort d'un grand hôtel

RESTAURATION
Cuisine gastronomique occidento-orientale. La cuisine de l'établissement peut être adaptée aux trois types physiques ayurvédiques

LE « PETIT PLUS »
La vue sur la vallée du Gange et le « Tea Lounge » avec des photographies datant de l'époque coloniale

LIVRE À EMPORTER
« L'Équilibre du monde » de Rohinton Mistry

"If ever there was an escape from the heat and dust,
the noise and the teeming cities of India, this is surely it."

CELIA W. DUGGER, *THE NEW YORK TIMES*

„Wer der Hitze und dem Staub, dem Lärm und dem Gewusel indischer Städte
entkommen will, ist hier am richtigen Ort."

«Qui veut échapper à la touffeur, à la poussière, au bruit et au tumulte des villes indiennes,
est ici à la bonne adresse.»

PASHAN GARH
INDIA

Panna National Park ~ Amanganj Road ~ Panna, Madhya Pradesh 488001 ~ India
Telephone +91 895 990 4701 ~ Fax +91 112 688 3324
pashangarh.panna@tajsafaris.com
www.tajhotels.com

Welcome to sloth bear country: Panna National Park in the Indian highlands. The 12 romantic hilltop cottages of Pashan Garh–built in the local tradition with dry-packed walls and tiled roofs and situated close to a watering hole frequented by antelopes and other animals–blend beautifully with the jungle landscape.

Inside the lodge, the interiors, by South African firm Nicholas Plewman Architects, offer surprising contrasts, their rustically modernist look combining slate tiles, leather furniture, and block-printed natural fabrics—although it's unlikely guests will spend much time admiring the decor. After all, there are twice-daily excursions into the national park, not to mention an attractive infinity pool to enjoy, as well as British-style picnic lunches on the veranda or on the grounds.

Zu Gast im Reich des Lippenbären: Zwölf romantische Cottages, erbaut nach dem Vorbild indischer Steinhäuser, laden in den Panna-Nationalpark im indischen Hochland ein. Die Häuser bilden mit ihrem Trockenmauerwerk und dem Ziegeldach eine schöne Symbiose mit der Landschaft, in der sie stehen: auf einem Hügel und nahe einer Wasserstelle, die regelmäßig von Antilope & Co. besucht wird.

Im Inneren bietet diese Dschungel-Lodge überraschende Kontraste, die Designer des südafrikanischen Architekturbüros Nicholas Plewman haben hier eine rustikale Moderne aus Schieferplatten, Ledermobiliar und modelbedruckten Naturstoffen inszeniert. Viel Zeit wird man damit aber kaum verbringen, denn zweimal täglich stehen Ausfahrten in den Nationalpark an. Wer von der exotischen Fauna genug hat, für den gibt es einen überaus lohnenswerten Infinity-Pool. Oder wie wäre es mit Picknick nach bewährter britischer Art?

Inspirés des maisons de pierre indiennes, 12 cottages romantiques s'ouvrent sur le parc national de Panna situé sur un haut plateau, royaume des ours lippus. Avec leurs murs de pierres sèches et leurs toits de tuiles, ces maisons s'accordent merveilleusement avec le paysage vallonné et le plan d'eau où les antilopes et d'autres animaux viennent s'abreuver.

À l'intérieur, les contrastes surprenants créés par les designers de l'agence d'architecture sud-africaine Nicholas Plewman confèrent au lodge un style rustico-moderne avec ses dallages en ardoise, ses meubles en cuir et ses étoffes naturelles imprimées. Mais on passe davantage de temps à l'extérieur, pour profiter des deux excursions quotidiennes dans le parc national. Ceux qui ont eu leur compte de faune exotique pourront profiter de la superbe piscine à débordement ou s'adonner à un pique-nique dans la plus pure tradition britannique.

LOCATION

On a 185-acre private estate in the Vindhya mountains. Guests can fly from Delhi to Khajuraho (370 miles south) then be picked up and taken to the lodge (1-hour drive)

RATES

Cottage for two from $800, full board included

ROOMS

12 cottages with spacious bathrooms

STYLE

Intriguing chic meets colonial interiors with picture windows

FOOD

The restaurant serves fine Indian food and can also arrange alfresco bush dinners on a rustic ox cart

X FACTOR

The ox cart dinners, of course! Something to tell the grandchildren or, at least, one's envious friends

BOOK TO PACK

"Midnight's Children" by Salman Rushdie

LAGE

Auf einem 75 ha großen Privatgelände im Vindhya-Gebirge gelegen. Man fliegt von Delhi nach Khajuraho (600 km südlich) und wird in 60 Minuten zur Lodge gefahren

PREISE

Cottage für zwei ab 610 €, inklusive Vollpension

ZIMMER

12 Cottages mit großzügigen Bädern

STIL

Urban-koloniale Zuflucht mit Panoramafenstern und spannendem Interiordesign

KÜCHE

Das Restaurant serviert feine indische Speisen und arrangiert auf Wunsch für seine Gäste auch ein rustikales Buschdinner auf einem alten Ochsenkarren

X-FAKTOR

Natürlich das Essen auf dem Ochsenkarren! Davon kann man noch seinen Enkeln erzählen, oder zumindest neidischen Freunden

BUCH ZUM ORT

„Mitternachtskinder" von Salman Rushdie

SITUATION

Dans un domaine privé de 75 hectares sur les collines de Vindhya. Vol intérieur de Delhi à Khajuraho (à 600 km au sud), puis 1 heure de transfert jusqu'au lodge

PRIX

Cottage à partir de 610 € par jour (pour 2 personnes) en pension complète

CHAMBRES

12 cottages avec de grandes salles de bains

STYLE

Refuge «colonial chic» avec des baies panoramiques et un intéressant design intérieur

RESTAURATION

Le restaurant propose une cuisine indienne raffinée et organise des dîners dans la brousse sur un ancien char à bœufs

LE «PETIT PLUS»

Évidemment, le dîner sur le char à bœufs! Un souvenir à partager avec ses petits-enfants ou à des amis qui vous envieront

LIVRE À EMPORTER

«Les Enfants de minuit» de Salman Rushdie

BELLEVUE SYRENE
ITALY

Piazza della Vittoria 5 ~ 80067 Sorrento ~ Italy
Telephone +39 081 878 1024 ~ Fax +39 081 878 3963
info@bellevue.it
www.bellevue.it

No one can say for sure whether Capri, Amalfi, or Sorrento is the birthplace of limoncello. What we do know, though, is that the raw ingredient for some of the finest examples of this legendary drink come from the area around Sorrento, from lemon groves almost as famous as the dark tuff cliffs with Vesuvius views that are the bedrock of the town.

The Bellevue Syrene, with its majestic seafront location above the old quarter, is the perfect place from which to enjoy all of Sorrento's attractions. It stands on a site once occupied by a villa belonging to Emperor Augustus (then later by a hotel whose guests included Ludwig II of Bavaria) and the current hotel's interiors maintain the link to antiquity. The Roman influence, though, is leavened by contemporary furniture and sumptuous colors, the walls deftly mixing shades of turquoise, lime green, and lilac. What's more, each room has a balcony from which guests can admire the picture-post-card views—while sipping the odd limoncello.

Wenn es ein Getränk gibt, das die Sonne perfekt transportiert, dann ist das der Limoncello. Ob das erste Glas des legendären Zitronenlikörs auf Capri, in Amalfi oder in Sorrent getrunken wurde, ist nicht überliefert. Fest steht: Die Zitrusplantagen rund um Sorrent liefern heute die Grundlage für einige der besten Limoncellos. Ihre Baumreihen sind fast ebenso berühmt wie die dunklen Tuffsteinfelsen, auf denen der Ort mit Blick auf den Vesuv erbaut wurde.

Sämtliche Attraktionen im Blick hat man vom Bellevue Syrene, das direkt an der Küste über der Altstadt thront. Früher stand an dieser Stelle eine Villa des römischen Kaisers Augustus, später ein Hotel, in dem Gäste wie Bayerns Märchenkönig Ludwig II. residierten. Die Antike ist nach wie vor ein Thema der Interiors, aufgelockert mit modernen Möbeln und Farben – die Wandtöne in Türkisblau, Lindgrün oder Flieder sind einfach perfekt gemischt. Übrigens: Alle Zimmer des Bellevue Syrene haben einen Balkon, wo ein Postkartenpanorama wartet – auf so viel Weitsicht ein Glas Limoncello!

S'il y a une boisson qui chante le soleil à la perfection, c'est bien le *limoncello*. On ignore si c'est à Capri, à Amalfi ou à Sorrente que le premier verre de cette légendaire liqueur au citron a été bu. Une chose est sûre, les citronneraies de Sorrente produisent les fruits qui permettent de fabriquer l'un des meilleurs *limoncelli*. Elles sont d'ailleurs presque aussi connues que la tufière sur laquelle est construite cette ville avec vue sur le Vésuve.

Trônant sur le promontoire de la vieille ville, le Bellevue Syrene est idéalement situé. À l'origine se dressait ici une villa romaine de l'empereur Auguste, et plus tard un hôtel où séjournèrent des hôtes aussi illustres que le roi Louis II de Bavière. Le style antique auquel les intérieurs sont restés fidèles est mâtiné de mobilier et de couleurs modernes – les tons turquoise, vert tilleul et lilas se marient parfaitement. Toutes les chambres ont un balcon d'où l'on peut admirer la vue panoramique en sirotant un verre de *limoncello*.

LOCATION
53 km/33 miles south of Naples airport

RATES
Rooms from $405

ROOMS
50 rooms, all with sea views

STYLE
Goethe's Italy meets 1950s charm—marble floors, Pompeii-esque frescoes, white linen billowing in the wind

FOOD
In summer, Mediterranean dishes can be enjoyed on the spectacular terraces of La Pergola; indoor restaurants Il Don Giovanni and Gli Archi are open through the winter

X FACTOR
The private rocky beach with sundeck. And, of course, the history of the place: The main building dates back to 1750 and has been a hotel since 1820

BOOK TO PACK
"The Roman Spring of Mrs. Stone" by Tennessee Williams

LAGE
53 km südlich des Flughafens Neapel

PREISE
Zimmer ab 300 €

ZIMMER
50 Zimmer, alle mit Meerblick

STIL
Goethes Italien mit dem Charme der Fifties – Marmorböden, Wanddekor à la Pompeji, im Wind sich bauschendes weißes Leinen ...

KÜCHE
Im Sommer genießt man mediterrane Menüs auf den Traumterrassen des Restaurants La Pergola; im Winter sind die beiden Innenlokale Il Don Giovanni und Gli Archi geöffnet

X-FAKTOR
Der private Felsenstrand mit Sonnendeck. Und natürlich die Historie dieses Hauses – das Hauptgebäude stammt aus dem Jahr 1750 und ist seit 1820 ein Hotel

BUCH ZUM ORT
„Mrs. Stone und ihr römischer Frühling" von Tennessee Williams

SITUATION
À 53 km au sud de l'aéroport de Naples

PRIX
Chambres à partir de 300 €

CHAMBRES
50 chambres, toutes avec vue sur la mer

STYLE
Italie de Goethe avec le charme des années 1950 : sols en marbre, décors muraux inspirés de Pompéi, lin blanc se gonflant au gré du vent

RESTAURATION
En été, une cuisine méditerranéenne est servie sur la splendide terrasse du restaurant La Pergola. Les restaurants Il Don Giovanni et Gli Archi sont ouverts les mois d'hiver

LE «PETIT PLUS»
La plage-ponton privée et, bien sûr, l'histoire de la maison : construit en 1750, le bâtiment principal abrite un hôtel depuis 1820

LIVRE À EMPORTER
«Le Printemps romain de Mrs Stone» de Tennessee Williams

BORGO SAN MARCO
ITALY

Contrada Sant'Angelo 33 ~ 72015 Fasano ~ Italy
Telephone & Fax +39 080 439 5757
info@borgosanmarco.it
www.borgosanmarco.it

Apulia is a wilder kind of Italy. Here, at the big boot's heel, the heat is hotter, the wine darker, and the olive trees older than anywhere else in the country. The region is also home to the chalky white *masserias*, and it's in one of these ancient fortresses that we find Borgo San Marco near Fasano.

Its small chapel and mighty watchtower, the latter dating from the 15th century, were built by Maltese knights keen to keep the Turks at bay. Much later, the complex became a *residenza agrituristica* and is now an exclusive rural retreat with Boheman flair. Vaulted ceilings, round arches, frescoes, and whitewashed stone walls are complemented by bold colors, fine linens and silks, and Oriental accessories. These days, guests are no longer expected to muck in: The stables have been turned into a bar, the fragrant citrus garden *L'Aranceto* is purely for relaxation, and the only massed ranks to be seen from the tower are those of the gnarly old olive trees.

Apulien ist das wilde Ende Italiens, hier ist die Hitze größer, der Wein dunkler und die Olivenbäume älter als irgendwo sonst auf dem Stiefel. Es ist auch das Land der kalkweißen Masserien, und genau so eine alte Trutzburg aus dem 15. Jahrhundert ist die Borgo San Marco bei Fasano. Die kleine Kapelle und den mächtigen Wachturm hatten Malteser-Ritter einst zum Schutz gegen die Türken errichtet.

Viel später entstand in diesen ehrwürdigen Mauern eine *Residenza Agrituristica*. Gewölbedecken, Rundbögen und Fresken, getünchte Wände und Mauern aus Naturstein, dazu ein Interieur in kräftigen Farben mit Leinen, Seidenstoffen und orientalischen Accessoires ermöglichen dem Bohemien einen ziemlich exklusiven Landurlaub. Mithelfen muss heute keiner mehr: Aus den ehemaligen Stallungen wurde eine Bar, der duftende Zitrusgarten *L'Aranceto* dient einzig der Entspannung, und vom Wachturm der alten Festung aus kann man höchstens noch Legionen knorriger Olivenbäume beobachten.

Située à la pointe sud de l'Italie, les Pouilles sont la région des extrêmes : il y fait plus chaud, son vin est d'un rouge plus profond et ses oliviers y sont plus vieux qu'ailleurs. C'est aussi le pays des *masserie*, vieilles fermes fortifiées blanches comme celle du Borgo San Marco, située à Fasano. Sa petite chapelle et son imposante tour de guet sont l'œuvre des chevaliers de Malte, qui cherchaient à se protéger des Turcs.

C'est beaucoup plus tard que la forteresse en ruine fut transformée en une *residenza agrituristica,* promesse d'un séjour luxueux à la campagne. Les plafonds voûtés, les arcades, les fresques et le badigeon blanc des murs de pierre rappellent l'histoire de la demeure, tandis que le lin et les soies colorées, ainsi que les accessoires orientaux confèrent une touche bohème aux intérieurs. Un bar a été aménagé dans les anciennes écuries et le jardin des citronniers, *L'Aranceto*, est réservé au repos. Du haut de la tour de guet, on observe aujourd'hui des légions d'oliviers noueux.

LOCATION
5 km/3 miles from Fasano, Brindisi airport is 40 km/25 miles away, Bari 60 km/37 miles

RATES
Suites from $160

ROOMS
18 suites

STYLE
Relaxed mix of ethnic and romantic within simple and often very, *very thick* walls

FOOD
The restaurant serves Apulian specialties made with freshly caught seafood and equally fresh produce from the nearby hills. The best of both worlds!

X FACTOR
As is so often the case in Apulia, the past is all around you at Borgo San Marco—just to the rear of the hotel you'll find a historic cave church with medieval fresco paintings of saints

BOOK TO PACK
"A Walk in the Dark" by Gianrico Carofiglio

LAGE
5 km östlich von Fasano, die Flughäfen von Brindisi und Bari sind 40 bzw. 60 km entfernt

PREISE
Suiten ab 120 €

ZIMMER
18 Suiten

STIL
Stilvolle Ethno-Romantik hinter schlichten, teils *seeeeehr* dicken Mauern

KÜCHE
Im Restaurant werden apulische Spezialitäten serviert, die sich in gleichem Maße aus dem bestücken, was das Meer und die nahen Berge liefern. *The best of both worlds!*

X-FAKTOR
Wie fast überall in Apulien ist auch hier die Geschichte zum Greifen nah: Auf der Rückseite des Hotels befindet sich eine sehenswerte Höhlen-Kirche mit mittelalterlichen Heiligenfresken

BUCH ZUM ORT
„In freiem Fall" von Gianrico Carofiglio

SITUATION
À 5 km à l'est de Fasano. Les aéroports de Brindisi et de Bari sont respectivement à 40 et 60 km

PRIX
Suites à partir de 120 €

CHAMBRES
18 suites

STYLE
Ethno-romantisme de bon goût dissimulé derrière des murs sans fard, extrêmement épais à certains endroits

RESTAURATION
Le restaurant sert des spécialités régionales à base de produits de la mer et des montagnes proches. Un mariage parfait!

LE «PETIT PLUS»
Comme presque partout dans les Pouilles, l'histoire est omniprésente. Derrière l'hôtel se dresse une très belle église rupestre aux fresques médiévales représentant des saints

LIVRE À EMPORTER
«Les Yeux fermés» de Gianrico Carofiglio

"As at all *masseria* hotels,
eating is a central part of the experience."

CHRISTOPHER PETKANAS, *TRAVEL + LEISURE*

„Wie in allen Masseria-Hotels ist das Essen hier ein zentraler
Bestandteil des Erlebnisses."

«Comme dans toutes les *masserie* transformées en hôtels, le repas est
une composante essentielle du séjour.»

BRIOL
ITALY

39040 Barbian-Dreikirchen/Barbiano-Tre Chiese ~ Eisacktal/Val d'Isarco ~ Italy
Telephone & Fax +39 047 165 0125
info@briol.it
www.briol.it

There's more than one route to property ownership. Johanna Settari, for instance, the great-grandmother of pension Briol's owners, was granted a piece of land for every child she bore. Over the years, she produced a brood of 15, thus earning her possession of a whole chunk of the Isarco Valley. Since then, this South Tyrolean property has been handed down from generation to generation, and every effort made to preserve the mountain landscape.

Pension Briol is run in the same spirit. Erected as a shelter in 1898, the building was completely redesigned in 1928, gaining large windows and an Alpine-meets-Bauhaus aesthetic that it retains to this day (even the crockery and washbowls are original). It is a place of simple luxury: There are no en suite bathrooms or in-room TVs here; instead, guests can watch the firewood flickering in the stove, enjoy first-class Alpine cuisine, and experience the sense of space and tranquillity that soon makes the distractions of modern life seem very far away.

So kann man sich Grundbesitz auch verdienen: Johanna Settari, die Urgroßmutter der heutigen Briol-Besitzerin, bekam zur Geburt jedes Kindes ein Grundstück geschenkt. Und da sie 15 Kinder zur Welt brachte, eroberte sich die tüchtige Mutter aus dem Wochenbett heraus fast ganz Dreikirchen im Eisacktal. Dieser Besitz wird bis heute in der Familie weitergegeben, und alles soll dabei im Sinne des Berges erhalten bleiben. Das gilt auch für das 1898 als Schutzhaus errichtete Briol. Seine jetzige Form erhielt es 1928; in alpiner Bauhaus-Manier eingerichtet und mit großen Fenstern, ist es als Gesamtkunstwerk bis heute erhalten – inklusive originalen Geschirrs und Waschschüsseln.

Es ist ein puristischer Luxus, der den Gast in dieser Pension erwartet, mit Etagenbädern und natürlich ohne Zimmer-TV. Dafür knistert im Ofen das Holz, auf den Tisch kommt eine ausgezeichnete Bergkost und sonntags ein Germzopf. Der Rest ist die Erfahrung von Stille und Weite, die sich hier fernab aller neuzeitlichen Verführungen überraschend schnell einstellt.

Johanna Settari, l'arrière-grand-mère de l'actuelle propriétaire du Briol reçut en cadeau une parcelle de terrain à la naissance de chacun de ses enfants. Comme elle mit au monde quinze enfants, cette mère courageuse finit par se retrouver à la tête d'un domaine de taille respectable à Barbiano, dans la vallée de l'Isarco, lequel est toujours entre les mains de la famille. Cela vaut aussi pour le gîte Briol, construit en 1898, dont la décoration et le mobilier actuels datent de 1928. Aménagé dans le style Bauhaus alpin, avec de grandes fenêtres, l'ensemble, y compris la vaisselle et les bassines de toilette d'origine, est une œuvre d'art globale.

Dans cette pension, c'est un luxe minimaliste qui est proposé aux hôtes, avec des salles de bains à l'étage et des chambres sans téléviseur. On entend le feu crépiter dans le poêle à bois et on se régale de l'excellente cuisine montagnarde et du *Germzopf*, sorte de brioche tressée servie le dimanche. On vit ici au calme, oubliant étonnamment vite les distractions modernes.

LOCATION
25 km/16 miles north of Bolzano at an altitude of 4,300 feet. From the village of Barbiano, access is by 4x4 taxi only (or on foot)

RATES
From $120 per person and night, half board and a salad buffet lunch included

ROOMS
13 rooms (with two shared bathrooms) in the guesthouse, 4 rooms in the nearby annex

STYLE
Authentic 1920s South Tyrolean retreat

FOOD
The wonderful recipes derive from the current owner's aunt, who learned her trade in high-class households in Rome and Paris

X FACTOR
For those refreshing morning dips, the house's designer Hubert Lanzinger created a circular outdoor pool, fed by mountain springs, that offers glorious views of the Dolomites

BOOK TO PACK
"Klausen" by Andreas Maier

LAGE
25 km nördlich von Bozen auf 1310 m Höhe gelegen. Vom Dorf Barbian/Barbiano aus nur mit dem Jeep-Taxi (oder zu Fuß) erreichbar

PREISE
Ab 90 € pro Person im Doppelzimmer, inklusive Halbpension und Salatbuffet am Mittag

ZIMMER
13 Zimmer (mit 2 Gemeinschaftsbädern) in der Pension, 4 Zimmer in der nahen Dependance

STIL
Stilreines Südtiroler Berghaus der 1920er

KÜCHE
Die grandiosen Rezepte gehen auf eine Tante der heutigen Besitzerin zurück, die einst in noblen Haushalten in Rom und Paris lernte

X-FAKTOR
Für die morgendliche Erfrischung schuf Hubert Lanzinger 1928 ein von Bergquellen gespeistes rundes Freibecken, genannt „Auge Gottes", das einen herrlichen Blick in die Dolomiten bietet

BUCH ZUM ORT
„Sommerfrische" von Jörg Plath

SITUATION
À 25 km au nord de Bolzano, à 1310 m d'altitude; accessible en taxi-jeep ou à pied depuis le village de Barbiano

PRIX
À partir de 90 € par personne en chambre double et en demi-pension avec buffet le midi

CHAMBRES
13 chambres (avec 2 salles de bains communes) dans la pension; 4 chambres dans l'annexe

STYLE
Chalet style Haut-Adige des années 1920

RESTAURATION
La propriétaire reprend les recettes grandioses d'une tante qui fut formée autrefois dans des maisons réputées à Paris et à Rome

LE «PETIT PLUS»
Pour le rafraîchissement du matin, Hubert Lanzinger créa en 1928 une piscine ovale, l'«Œil de Dieu», alimentée à l'eau de source. Elle offre une vue superbe sur les Dolomites

LIVRE À EMPORTER
«Eva dort» de Francesca Melandri

CAPRI SUITE
ITALY

Via Finestrale 9 ~ 80071 Anacapri ~ Isola di Capri ~ Italy
Telephone +39 0366 368 3927
booking@caprisuite.it
www.caprisuite.it

The best things in life are scarce, as this little hideaway proves once more. It has just two suites—the Blue Room and the Yellow Room— but each is beautifully decorated, with modern design classics set against what remains of the ancient original paintwork, plus sunny colors for a typically Capri touch. The hotel is situated away from the hustle and bustle of the ferry terminals down in the town, and is best reached via rented Vespa, also the most authentic mode of travel for exploring Anacapri village and visiting the lighthouse of Punta Carena.

The hotel itself offers a relaxing, intimate atmosphere in either lemon yellow or azure blue. The only meal provided is breakfast; that, though, is available all day. The best time to enjoy the island is after the last ferry load of day-trippers has left. Then you can watch the sun set in peace, breathe in the scent of wet rock and wild thyme that blows in from the cliffs, and fall in love with Capri all over again.

Die besten Dinge sind leider knapp, das bestätigt dieses kleine Hoteljuwel einmal mehr. Bloß zwei Suiten stehen hier zur Verfügung – der Blue Room und der Yellow Room. Beide eint die überaus gelungene Einrichtung, in der uralte Reste der ursprünglichen Wandbemalung und moderne Designklassiker zusammengebracht wurden und sonnige Farben für das typische Capri-Gefühl sorgen. Weit abseits vom Trubel der Fähranleger unten in Capri wird der Gast mit Zitronengelb und Azurblau empfangen. Als Transportmittel zum Haus empfiehlt sich eine Miet-Vespa, mit der sich im Anschluss auch stilgerecht das Dorf Anacapri und der Leuchtturm von Punta Carena erkunden lassen.

Das Hotel bietet entspannten Urlaub, schließlich geht es familiär zu. Es gibt nur Frühstück, das dafür den ganzen Tag. Die schönste Zeit auf der Insel ist nach wie vor dann, wenn die letzte Fähre die Tagestouristen mitgenommen hat. Dann versinkt die Sonne langsam, vom Meer her weht ein Geruch nach nassem Fels und wildem Thymian – ach, Capri eben.

Les chose les plus agréables ont malheureusement toujours une fin. Un séjour dans l'une des deux uniques suites magnifiquement aménagées de ce superbe petit hôtel – la «Blue Room» et la «Yellow Room» – confirme l'adage une fois de plus. Les vestiges de peintures murales très anciennes s'harmonisent parfaitement avec le design classique, et les couleurs lumineuses reflètent bien l'esprit de Capri. Loin de l'agitation des débarcadères de l'île, le jaune citron et le bleu azur du Capri Suite enveloppent les hôtes. Sur place, on peut louer une vespa pour aller visiter le joli petit village d'Anacapri et le phare de Punta Carena.

Cet hôtel très accueillant propose des vacances reposantes. Il sert uniquement le petit déjeuner, mais ce à toute heure de la journée. Après le départ du dernier bac d'excursionnistes, on profite enfin du meilleur moment sur l'île en assistant au lent coucher du soleil. Une odeur de roche mouillée et de thym sauvage s'élève de la mer. Ah, la beauté de Capri...

LOCATION
In the old heart of Anacapri in the middle of the island. Guests can be picked up from the ferry terminal or can rent a Vespa from there

RATES
Yellow Room $235, Blue Room $300, breakfast included

ROOMS
Yellow Room and Blue Room

STYLE
Sparingly but beautifully furnished; island summer lightness with a contemporary feel

FOOD
Light Mediterranean cuisine

X FACTOR
The Capri Suite concept: It's like staying at the home of a very trusting acquaintance (Flos Snoopy lamp in the Blue Room!) surrounded by citrus trees

BOOK TO PACK
"Siren Land: A Celebration of Life in Southern Italy" by Norman Douglas

LAGE
In der Altstadt von Anacapri im Herzen der Insel gelegen. Vom Fähranleger lässt man sich abholen oder mietet gleich eine Vespa

PREISE
Yellow Room ab 180 €, Blue Room ab 230 €, inklusive Frühstück

ZIMMER
Yellow Room und Blue Room

STIL
Wenig, das aber schön; federleichter Inselsommer und zeitgenössische Stilschule

KÜCHE
Leichte mediterrane Inselküche

X-FAKTOR
Das Konzept der Capri-Suiten: Ein Aufenthalt fühlt sich an, als bewohnte man ein privates Zimmer bei vertrauensvollen (Snoopy-Leuchte von Flos!) Bekannten mitten im Zitronengarten

BUCH ZUM ORT
„Der Arzt von San Michele: Axel Munthe und die Kunst, dem Leben einen Sinn zu geben" von Thomas Steinfeld

SITUATION
Dans la vieille ville d'Anacapri, au cœur de l'île de Capri; au débarcadère, une voiture attend les hôtes sur demande (possibilité de louer une vespa)

PRIX
Yellow Room à partir de 180 €, Blue Room à partir de 230 €, petit déjeuner inclus

CHAMBRES
Yellow Room et Blue Room

STYLE
Sobre mais beau; charme envoûtant des résidences insulaires et style contemporain

RESTAURATION
Cuisine méditerranéenne insulaire légère

LE «PETIT PLUS»
Le concept des suites: on a l'impression d'occuper une chambre chez des amis (la lampe Snoopy de Flos!), au milieu d'une citronneraie

LIVRE À EMPORTER
«La Légende de Capri» de Pamela Fiori

CASTEL FRAGSBURG
ITALY

Via Fragsburg 3 ~ 39012 Meran ~ South Tyrol ~ Italy
Telephone +39 0473 244 071 ~ Fax +39 0473 244 493
info@fragsburg.com
www.fragsburg.com

One of the smallest luxury hotels in the Alps, this former hunting lodge from the year 1620 sits perched on a rock above the rooftops of Merano and is reached via a winding country road guaranteed to fill every cabriolet driver with joy. Castel Fragsburg has just 20 rooms, each furnished with antiques from the region and decorated with steadfastly old-school taste (the bedding, for instance, has prancing-deer motifs).

For more than 50 years, the hotel has been in the hands of the Ortner family, who set great store by the civilized and distinctly South Tyrolean atmosphere of both hotel and grounds. A garden of fruit trees and grapevines surrounds the hotel, while the glass veranda that overlooks the steep drop down to the valley serves gourmet cuisine and, at night, offers glorious views of the lights of Merano.

Auf einem Felsen über den Dächern Merans liegt eines der kleinsten Luxushotels der Alpen. Das Castel Fragsburg ist ein ehemaliges Jagdschlösschen aus dem Jahr 1620, und schon die Anfahrt über eine Panoramastraße erfreut den Cabrio-Lenker. 20 Zimmer gibt es hier, jedes einzelne mit Antiquitäten aus der Region und solidem Sommerfrische-Geschmack ausgestattet, etwa in Form von Bettwäsche mit springenden Hirschen.

Seit über 50 Jahren wird das Haus von der Familie Ortner geführt, die besonderen Wert auf ein gepflegtes Südtirol-Erlebnis ihrer Gäste legt. Es beginnt gleich im Garten, Obstbäume und Weinstöcke rahmen das Hotel ein. Ein besonderes Highlight wartet auf der Talseite dieses exponierten Platzes: In der verglasten Veranda wird nicht nur Sterne-Küche serviert – bei Nacht hat man dazu einen tollen Blick über das reizvoll erleuchtete Meran.

Surplombant les toits de Merano sur un promontoire rocheux, cet ancien pavillon de chasse datant de 1650 est l'un des plus petits hôtels de luxe des Alpes. Il est situé au sommet d'une route panoramique qui réjouit les conducteurs de cabriolet. L'hôtel abrite vingt chambres, chacune décorée avec des antiquités régionales dans un style villégiature grand teint, notamment avec des parures de lit représentant des cerfs bondissant.

Depuis plus de cinquante ans, la direction de la maison est assurée par la famille Ortner, qui met tout en œuvre pour que ses hôtes découvrent le Haut-Adige sous son meilleur jour. Les arbres fruitiers et les vignes du jardin entourent la maison. Côté vallée, la vue est véritablement imprenable. De la véranda vitrée, on profite la nuit d'une vue plongeante sur les lumières scintillantes de Merano tout en dégustant les plats savoureux du chef étoilé.

LOCATION
Perched on a rock overlooking Merano and surrounded by fruit trees and grapevines

RATES
Doubles from $200, suites from $270, breakfast and gourmet dinner included

ROOMS
20 rooms and suites

STYLE
Idyllic hunting lodge decorated

FOOD
Michelin-starred chef Luis Haller serves up traditional South Tyrolean cuisine with distinctly Mediterranean influences

X FACTOR
For regulars, apple-blossom season is a must; the lodge is then surrounded by a sea of light-pink petals. When booking, ask the staff about the next opportunity to see this glorious sight

BOOK TO PACK
"A Thread of Grace" by Mary Doria Russell

LAGE
Zwischen Obst- und Weingärten auf einem Felsvorsprung über Meran thronend

PREISE
Doppelzimmer ab 155 €, Suite ab 200 €, inklusive Frühstück und Gourmet-Dinner

ZIMMER
20 Zimmer und Suiten

STIL
Idyllisches Jagdschloss, waghalsig positioniert

KÜCHE
Traditionelle Südtiroler Küche mit durchaus schon mediterranen Einflüssen, auf den Teller gebracht vom Sterne-Koch Luis Haller

X-FAKTOR
Pflichttermin für Stammgäste ist die Apfelblüte, dann umgibt das Schloss ein Meer aus Zartrosa. Also beim Buchen erkundigen, wann es wohl als Nächstes so weit ist!

BUCH ZUM ORT
„Wie du mir so er dir: Südtirol-Krimi" von Ralph Neubauer

SITUATION
Perché sur un promontoire rocheux au-dessus de Merano, entre des vignes et des vergers

PRIX
Chambres doubles à partir de 155 €, suites à partir de 200 €, petit déjeuner et dîner gastronomique inclus

CHAMBRES
20 chambres et suites

STYLE
Pavillon de chasse idyllique audacieusement implanté

RESTAURATION
Cuisine traditionnelle du Haut-Adige avec des influences méditerranéennes que l'on doit au chef étoilé Luis Haller

LE «PETIT PLUS»
Ne manquez pas la floraison des pommiers : le château flotte au milieu d'une mer rose. Renseignez-vous avant de réserver !

LIVRE À EMPORTER
«Les Gens de Chinsa» d'Andreas Maier

CASTELLO DI VICARELLO
ITALY

58044 Poggi del Sasso ~ Cinigiano ~ Italy
Telephone +39 056 499 0447 ~ Fax +39 056 499 0718
info@vicarello.it
www.vicarello.it

Away from the rolling hills, picturesque villages, and famous cities of art, there is a different, less eye-catching but more authentic Tuscany: the wild and romantic region of Maremma.

Few visitors venture here, but those who do often fall in love with the area's raw charm—as Carlo and Aurora Baccheschi Berti did. In the province of Grosseto, they discovered the then-ruined Castello di Vicarello and threw themselves into its sensitive restoration. The result of their efforts is a hotel that has all the rustic charm of the region while also exuding an urbane atmosphere. It is run like a private home, and dinners often bring guests of all kinds together at the long table, united by their shared appreciation of a beauty not everyone sees. In such a convivial atmosphere, the lack of in-room televisions barely even registers.

Die Maremma ist bis heute ein wildromantisches Geheimnis, das sich die Toskana bewahrt hat. Abseits der sanften Hügel, der pittoresken Dörfer und berühmten Kunststädte gibt sie sich hier unspektakulär und ursprünglich.

Wer diese Ästhetik mag, verliebt sich leicht in die spröde Landschaft – so ging es auch Carlo und Aurora Baccheschi Berti. In der Provinz Grosseto entdeckten sie eine verfallene Burg und restaurierten das Castello di Vicarello mit ebenso viel Energie wie Stilgespür. Am Ende der Mühen stand ein Hotel, das dem rustikalen Charme der Region huldigt und zugleich eine gewisse Weltläufigkeit verströmt. Es wird wie ein Privathaus geführt, und so findet man sich an dem langen Esstisch oft in einer familiären Gästerunde wieder, mit ganz unterschiedlichen Menschen, die doch eines eint: die Vorliebe für Schönheit, die nicht jeder gleich erkennt. Bei solch guter Gesellschaft fällt gar nicht auf, dass die Zimmer keinen Fernseher haben, wetten?

La Maremme est d'un romantisme sauvage dont la Toscane a bien gardé le secret. À l'écart des douces collines, des villages pittoresques et des villes au riche patrimoine artistique, elle est moins spectaculaire et plus authentique.

Les amateurs de ce type de paysage en tombent facilement amoureux. C'est ce qui est arrivé à Carlo et Aurora Baccheschi, lorsqu'ils découvrirent un château en ruine dans la province de Grosseto. Avec autant d'énergie que de feeling pour le style, ils firent du Castello di Vicarello un hôtel empreint du charme rustique de la région, mais aussi un caractère cosmopolite. Il est dirigé comme une pension de famille et, autour de sa grande table conviviale, se retrouvent des hôtes tous différents, mais unis par leur amour du beau, qui ne revêt pas les mêmes formes pour chacun. En si bonne compagnie, il est à parier que personne ne remarquera que les chambres ne sont pas équipées de téléviseurs.

LOCATION
In southern Tuscany, 10 km/6 miles from the village of Cinigiano; Siena, Pisa, and Florence airports are all between approximately 60 and 90 minutes away by car

RATES
Rooms from $950, suites from $1,220, villa from $4,335, breakfast included

ROOMS
1 double and 6 suites plus Villa Chiesina

STYLE
Rustic but never ordinary luxury

FOOD
Fruit and vegetables are from the hotel garden, the game is locally sourced; Aurora Baccheschi Berti also runs cooking courses

X FACTOR
Guests can try the hotel's best recipes at home thanks to the cookbook "My Tuscan Kitchen" and even help out with the olive harvest during their stay

BOOK TO PACK
"The English Patient" by Michael Ondaatje

LAGE
In der südlichen Toskana, 10 km außerhalb des Dorfes Cinigiano. Die Flughäfen von Siena, Pisa und Florenz sind zwischen 60 und 90 Minuten Autofahrt entfernt

PREISE
Zimmer ab 700 €, Suiten ab 900 €, Villa ab 3200 €, inklusive Frühstück

ZIMMER
1 Zimmer, 6 Suiten und die Villa Chiesina

STIL
Rustikaler, nie banaler Luxus

KÜCHE
Obst und Gemüse gedeihen im eigenen Garten, Wild ist selbst gejagt. Ihre besten Rezepte verrät Aurora Baccheschi Berti in Kochkursen

X-FAKTOR
Man kann nicht nur die Hotelküche in Form des Kochbuchs „My Tuscan Kitchen" mit nach Hause nehmen, sondern vorher auch schon bei der Olivenernte helfen

BUCH ZUM ORT
„Der englische Patient" von Michael Ondaatje

SITUATION
Sud de la Toscane, à 10 km du village de Cinigiano; les aéroports de Sienne, Pise et Florence sont à 60–90 minutes en voiture

PRIX
Chambre double à partir de 700 €, suites à partir de 900 €, villa à partir de 3200 €, petit déjeuner inclus

CHAMBRES
1 chambre, 6 suites et villa Chiesina

STYLE
Luxe rustique sans jamais être banal

RESTAURATION
Fruits et légumes du jardin, gibier chassé sur place. Aurora Baccheschi Berti révèle ses meilleures recettes dans des cours de cuisine

LE «PETIT PLUS»
Non seulement on peut emporter chez soi le livre «My Tuscan Kitchen» avec les recettes de l'hôtel, mais on peut aussi participer sur place à la cueillette des olives

LIVRE À EMPORTER
«Le Patient anglais» de Michael Ondaatje

EDEN HOTEL BORMIO
ITALY

Via Funivia 3 ~ 23032 Bormio (SO) ~ Italy
Telephone +39 0342 911 669 ~ Fax +39 0342 919 984
info@edenbormio.it
www.edenbormio.it

Even before you set foot inside, you can tell that this relatively new mountain retreat is something special. The shingle roof, the fence made of untreated chestnut wood staves, and the timber-clad yet contemporary façade add up to a fresh and natural look, reflecting the desire of Antonio Citterio's design team to ensure the architecture would be in harmony with this ski and spa resort's mountain landscape.

Inside, too, the hotel boasts clean lines and features only naturally finished materials. The welcoming larch wood used in the rooms is apparently even proven to have calming properties. In summer, the garden suites with their traditional Alpine gardens are a particular highlight, and, in winter, when the only thing growing is the ice crystals on the windows, guests can enjoy some après-ski R&R in the small wellness area.

Schon von außen erkennt man den besonderen Charakter dieses jungen Berghotels. Das Schindeldach, der Zaun aus naturbelassenen Kastanienstaketen, die Holzverkleidung in moderner Silhouette – das alles ergibt einen frischen und irgendwie biodynamischen Look.

Den Designern rund um Antonio Citterio war es wichtig, dass sich die Architektur so harmonisch wie möglich in die Bergwelt des lombardischen Ski- und Sommerfrische-Ortes einfügt. So vereinen sich auch drinnen klare Linien und nur natürlich gefinishte Materialien zu einem nachhaltigen Wohngefühl. Das freundliche Lärchenholz, das in den Zimmern verbaut wurde, soll sogar nachweislich beruhigende Wirkung haben. Im Sommer locken die Gartensuiten mit einem traditionellen Bauerngarten, und wenn im Winter nur Eisblumen an den Fenstern wachsen, steht für die Après-Ski-Entspannung ein kleiner Wellnessbereich zur Verfügung.

Au premier abord, on est frappé par le charme particulier de cet hôtel montagnard récent. Le toit en bardeaux de bois, la clôture à lattis en marronnier, l'habillage de bois moderne, tout cela confère au lieu un look jeune et en quelque sorte biodynamique.

Antonio Citterio et son équipe de créatifs ont fait en sorte que son architecture s'intègre le mieux possible dans l'univers montagnard de cette station de sports d'hiver agréable toute l'année. À l'intérieur, les lignes sont épurées et les matériaux ont reçu une finition naturelle. Le bois de mélèze employé dans les chambres aurait même une action apaisante reconnue. En été, les suites avec leur petit jardin traditionnel privé font le bonheur des hôtes. En hiver, quand les fenêtres sont couvertes de fleurs de givre, le petit espace de remise en forme permet de se détendre après le ski.

LOCATION
Almost 4,000 feet above sea level, not far from winter-sport resort Bormio, a venue for the annual Alpine Ski World Cup

RATES
Doubles from $260, suites from $325, breakfast included

ROOMS
6 singles and doubles, plus 21 suites

STYLE
Perfectly thought-out Shaker-inspired eco-luxury —the wood paneling is a veritable hand magnet

FOOD
The hotel restaurant, breakfast buffet, and bar all offer Italian cuisine with international influences

X FACTOR
Unusually for Alpine architecture, the focal point here is large, modern windows that bring mountain vistas into the rooms

BOOK TO PACK
"The Day of the Owl" by Leonardo Sciascia

LAGE
Auf 1200 m Höhe unweit des Zentrums des Wintersportortes Bormio, in dem jedes Jahr der alpine Skiweltcup gastiert

PREISE
Doppelzimmer ab 200 €, Suiten ab 250 €, inklusive Frühstück

ZIMMER
6 Einzel- und Doppelzimmer nebst 21 Suiten

STIL
Rundum durchdachter Bio-Luxus, der sich von den Shakern inspirieren ließ – die Holzpaneele sind wahre Magnete für die Handflächen

KÜCHE
Italienische Küche mit internationalen Einflüssen wird im Restaurant, am Frühstücksbuffet und an der Hotelbar angeboten

X-FAKTOR
Ungewöhnlich für alpine Gebäude und hier Angelpunkt gelungener Architektur: Große moderne Fenster holen die Bergwelt ins Hotel

BUCH ZUM ORT
„Der Tag der Eule" von Leonardo Sciascia

SITUATION
À 1200 m d'altitude, non loin du centre de la station de Bormio, qui accueille chaque année la coupe du monde de ski alpin

PRIX
Chambres doubles à partir de 200 €, suites à partir de 250 €, petit déjeuner inclus

CHAMBRES
6 chambres simples et doubles et 21 suites

STYLE
Luxe bio bien pensé, inspiré des Shakers – les lambris ne demandent qu'à être caressés

RESTAURATION
Une cuisine italienne aux influences internationales est servie dans le restaurant, au buffet du petit déjeuner et au bar de l'hôtel

LE «PETIT PLUS»
Les grandes fenêtres modernes laissent entrer la montagne à l'intérieur de l'hôtel, ce qui constitue le point fort de cette architecture peu typique des constructions alpines

LIVRE À EMPORTER
«Le Jour de la chouette» de Leonardo Sciascia

FOUR SEASONS
HOTEL FIRENZE
ITALY

Borgo Pinti 99 ~ 50121 Florence ~ Italy
Telephone +39 055 2626 1 ~ Fax +39 055 2626 500
firenze@fourseasons.com
www.fourseasons.com

After a seven-year restoration, the Palazzo della Gherardesca and the adjacent convent opened their doors as a luxury hotel in 2008. The painstaking conversion of these two architectural gems has certainly paid off, designer Pierre-Yves Rochon even retaining original frescoes and reliefs in the rooms, some of which date back to the 15th century.

After just one night in these magnificent Renaissance surroundings, you'll feel like a Florentine aristocrat yourself. The actual noblemen of the day came here to stroll in the splendid botanical gardens that form the heart of this ensemble. These were closed to the general public for centuries but, today, locals flock here at the weekends to get a glimpse of the famous Giardino della Gherardesca. Hotel guests, meanwhile, can even enjoy breakfast or siestas in the gardens. Rarely has it felt like such a privilege to be a tourist.

Nach siebenjähriger Restaurierung wurden der Palazzo della Gherardesca und das benachbarte Kloster 2008 als Luxushotel eröffnet. Der behutsame Umbau der beiden Schmuckstücke hat sich gelohnt – Designer Pierre-Yves Rochon hat in den Räumen, die teilweise noch aus dem 15. Jahrhundert datieren, originale Fresken und Reliefs sorgfältig herausgearbeitet.

So checkt man hier als Gast in die prachtvolle Epoche der Renaissance ein und fühlt sich nach einer Nacht wie ein adeliger Florentiner. Die flanierten seinerzeit wohl auch in dem prachtvollen botanischen Garten, der den Mittelpunkt des Ensembles bildet. Jahrhundertelang war er der Öffentlichkeit verschlossen, jetzt pilgern sogar die Florentiner an den Wochenenden hierher, um einen Blick auf den Giardino della Gherardesca zu erhaschen, während Gäste des Hauses dort frühstücken und Siesta halten können – wann ist man als Tourist schon mal so privilegiert?

Après sept ans de restauration, le Palazzo della Gherardesca et le couvent tout proche, transformés en hôtel de luxe, ouvrirent leurs portes en 2008. La rénovation de ces deux lieux splendides est particulièrement réussie. Dans les pièces, dont certaines datent du XVe siècle, l'architecte d'intérieur Pierre-Yves Rochon a soigneusement mis en valeur des fresques d'origine et des bas-reliefs.

Ici, on est transporté dans la fastueuse époque de la Renaissance, et l'on peut s'imaginer faire partie des nobles florentins, qui flânaient aussi en leur temps dans le magnifique jardin botanique constituant le cœur de l'ensemble. Fermé au public pendant plusieurs siècles, c'est aujourd'hui un lieu de promenade pour les habitants qui viennent le week-end admirer le Giardino della Gherardesca, tandis que les hôtes peuvent y prendre leur petit déjeuner ou y faire la sieste. Difficile d'être plus privilégié en tant que touriste…

LOCATION
Situated in the middle of Florence's biggest
private park (11 acres), 20 minutes from the
Amerigo Vespucci Airport

RATES
Rooms from $400, suites from $1,190,
excluding breakfast

ROOMS
72 rooms and 44 suites

STYLE
Renaissance palace with fabulous gardens

FOOD
La Magnolia serves breakfast, Il Palagio has
fine Tuscan food and wine. The Atrium Bar
is the perfect place to see and be seen

X FACTOR
Even the spa takes you back in time: It uses
products by Profumo-Farmaceutica Santa
Maria Novella, one of the oldest pharmacies
in the world (established in 1612)

BOOK TO PACK
"The Agony and the Ecstasy: A Biographical
Novel of Michelangelo" by Irving Stone

LAGE
Inmitten des größten Privatparks (4,5 ha) im
Zentrum von Florenz gelegen, 20 Minuten
vom Flughafen Amerigo Vespucci entfernt

PREISE
Zimmer ab 295 €, Suite ab 700 €,
ohne Frühstück

ZIMMER
72 Zimmer und 44 Suiten

STIL
Renaissance-Palast mit herrlichem Garten

KÜCHE
La Magnolia serviert Frühstück, Il Palagio
feinste toskanische Menüs und Weine.
Die Atrium Bar ist perfekt zum Sehen und
Gesehenwerden

X-FAKTOR
Selbst das Spa führt in die Geschichte zurück:
Es verwendet Produkte von Officina Profumo-
Farmaceutica Santa Maria Novella, einer der
ältesten Apotheken der Welt (seit 1612)

BUCH ZUM ORT
„Michelangelo" von Irving Stone

SITUATION
Au cœur du plus grand parc privé (4,5 hectares)
de Florence, à 20 minutes de l'aéroport
Amerigo Vespucci

PRIX
Chambres à partir de 295 €, suites à partir
de 700 €, sans le petit déjeuner

CHAMBRES
72 chambres et 44 suites

STYLE
Palais Renaissance avec un jardin splendide

RESTAURATION
La Magnolia sert le petit déjeuner, Il Palagio
les menus toscans et les vins les plus raffinés.
L'Atrium Bar est idéal pour voir et être vu

LE « PETIT PLUS »
Même le spa évoque le passé historique en
employant des produits de l'Officina Profumo-
Farmaceutica di Santa Maria Novella, l'une des
pharmacies les plus anciennes du monde, datant
de 1612

LIVRE À EMPORTER
« La Vie ardente de Michel-Ange » d'Irving Stone

GASTHOF KRONE
ITALY

Dorfplatz/Piazza Principale 3 ~ 39040 Aldein/Aldino ~ Italy
Telephone +39 047 188 6825 ~ Fax +39 047 188 6696
info@gasthof-krone.it
www.gasthof-krone.it

The first time you set foot in Aldino's village square, you could be forgiven for thinking you'd wandered onto a movie set. After all, the rustic farmhouse facades, burbling fountain, and venerable inn, set against a backdrop of lush green Alpine slopes, could be straight out of a cinematic period piece.

Gasthof Krone has stood at this idyllic spot since 1577 and has been in the hands of the same family since 1720. Today, the Franzelins continue to maintain the South Tyrol character and charm of the old inn. The guest rooms are thus furnished with wonderful farmhouse antiques, and classic Tyrolean fare is served in the cozy wood-lined dining rooms. In addition to first-class wine and dumplings, guests can expect thick feather duvets, superb mountain air, and the priceless feeling that all this is not just the work of some smart-aleck marketing team.

Hoppla, Filmkulisse? Kommt man zum ersten Mal auf den Dorfplatz von Aldein, ist dieser Gedanke durchaus nicht abwegig. Denn die ursprünglichen Fassaden der Bauernhäuser, der plätschernde Brunnen und eben auch der ehrwürdige Gasthof Krone bilden ein uriges Ensemble wie aus einem Historienfilm, umgeben von saftig-grünen Berghängen.

Seit 1577 steht der Gasthof fest an diesem idyllischen Fleck in Südtirol. Und seit 1720 führt ihn die Familie Franzelin, die es sich zur Aufgabe gemacht hat, Charakter und Charme der Herberge zu bewahren. So sind die Gästezimmer mit wunderschönen alten Bauernmöbeln eingerichtet, und in den behaglichen holzgetäfelten Stuben wird klassische Südtiroler Küche serviert. Wein und Knödel von höchster Güte, das kann man hier erwarten, dazu dicke Daunendecken, eine herrliche Bergluft – und das unbezahlbar gute Gefühl, dass sich all das kein oberschlaues Marketingteam ausgedacht hat.

Quand on découvre pour la première fois la place du village d'Aldino, on a vraiment l'impression d'être sur le tournage d'un film. Parmi des montagnes verdoyantes, les façades d'origine des maisons paysannes, les fontaines bruissantes ainsi que le vénérable Gasthof Krone constituent un ensemble pittoresque qui semble tout droit sorti d'un film historique.

Datant de 1577 et situé dans le Haut-Adige, le Gasthof Krone est dirigé depuis 1720 par la famille Franzelin, qui s'est efforcée de conserver le caractère et le charme de cette auberge. Les chambres sont meublées dans un style campagnard magnifique, et des plats typiques de la région sont servis dans des petites salles rustiques lambrissées de bois. On peut espérer trouver ici du vin et des quenelles d'excellente qualité, ainsi que des couettes épaisses et l'air vivifiant de la montagne. Inutile de préciser qu'aucune équipe de marketing aussi créative soit-elle n'aurait pu imaginer tout cela.

LOCATION
Aldino is situated at an altitude of 3,900 feet, 35 km/22 miles south of Bolzano airport

RATES
Rooms from $95, suites from $120, breakfast included

ROOMS
12 rooms and 1 suite. The main building is ideal for a winter visit. In summer, we recommend the balconied rooms in the annex

STYLE
Charming old inn

FOOD
The kitchen uses traditional recipes and ingredients from the guesthouse's own farm. The value for money is second to none

X FACTOR
For something even more Alpine, there's the Neuhütt' Alm restaurant, run by the same family and offering the same rustic welcome

BOOK TO PACK
"Cleaver" by Tim Parks

LAGE
Aldein/Aldino liegt auf 1200 m Höhe, 35 km südlich des Flughafens Bozen

PREISE
Zimmer ab 70 €, Suite ab 90 €, inklusive Frühstück

ZIMMER
12 Zimmer und 1 Suite. Im Winter wohnt man sehr schön im Haupthaus, im Sommer sind die Räume mit Balkonen im Anbau zu empfehlen

STIL
Charmantes Wirtshaus

KÜCHE
Gekocht wird nach alten Rezepten und mit Zutaten vom eigenen Hof. Das Preis-Leistungs-Verhältnis ist erstklassig

X-FAKTOR
Wer noch mehr Berg will, kann zur Neuhütt' Alm wandern, die auch zur Familie gehört und urig bewirtschaftet wird

BUCH ZUM ORT
„Der Schmerz der Gewöhnung" von Joseph Zoderer

SITUATION
À 1200 m d'altitude, à 35 km au sud de l'aéroport de Bolzano

PRIX
Chambres à partir de 70 €, suite à partir de 90 €, petit déjeuner inclus

CHAMBRES
12 chambres et 1 suite. On logera de préférence dans le bâtiment principal en hiver et dans l'annexe pourvue de balcons en été

STYLE
Charmante auberge

RESTAURATION
Plats préparés d'après des recettes anciennes et avec des ingrédients provenant de la ferme de l'auberge. Très bon rapport qualité/prix

LE «PETIT PLUS»
Ceux qui veulent profiter de la montagne pourront faire une randonnée jusqu'à la Neuhütt' Alm, auberge typique, qui appartient aussi à la famille

LIVRE À EMPORTER
«Le Silence de Cleaver» de Tim Parks

HOTEL CARUSO
ITALY

Piazza San Giovanni del Toro 2 ~ 84010 Ravello ~ Italy
Telephone +39 089 858 801 ~ Fax +39 089 858 806
info@hotelcaruso.com
www.hotelcaruso.com

Sometimes, there's no need to shell out for a suite. The best spot at Hotel Caruso, for instance, is actually the garden, with its palms and orange trees, plantings of daisies and hydrangeas, and rose-garlanded pergola.

Be warned, though: This green Eden will have you yearning for more. For a night in the 11th-century palace, situated almost 1,000 feet above the Amalfi coast. For a few lengths in the infinity-edge pool. Or perhaps for a blast of Wagner. After all, the composer has strong links with Ravello and with Hotel Caruso in particular. Not only did he himself once rest up here while trying to shake off a creative crisis, but also, in 1953, hotelier Paolo Caruso founded an annual music festival that has since been attracting Wagnerians of all nationalities to the resort. Whether it's *Götterdämmerung* or garden heaven you're after, Ravello is the place to go.

Vielleicht muss man gar nicht gleich in eine Suite investieren. Denn das Schönste am Hotel Caruso ist eigentlich sein Garten, in dem Palmen und Orangenbäume stehen, Margeriten und Hortensien blühen und Rosen den Belvedere-Laubengang umkränzen.

Aber Vorsicht, so ein Spaziergang durch das kleine Arkadien weckt dann eben doch Lust auf mehr. Auf eine Nacht in dem Palast aus dem 11. Jahrhundert, gelegen 300 Meter hoch über der Amalfiküste. Auf ein paar Bahnen im randlosen Pool, und natürlich auf ein bisschen Wagner. Der Komponist ist schließlich fest mit Ravello und dem Hotel Caruso verbunden. Erst kurierte er hier eine Schaffenskrise aus, später und bis heute zieht seine Musik Wagnerianer aller Nationalitäten zum jährlichen Festival, das Hotelier Paolo Caruso 1953 mitbegründet hatte. Ob also Grillenzirpen oder „Götterdämmerung" – Ravello klingt immer gut.

On pensera peut-être pouvoir se passer d'une suite, car la perle de l'hôtel Caruso, c'est véritablement le jardin, planté de palmiers et d'orangers, fleuri de marguerites et d'hortensias et dont les roses ornent la charmille du belvédère.

Mais une promenade dans ce jardin d'Arcadie surplombant de 300 mètres la côte d'Amalfi fera sans doute naître des envies de séjour dans ce palais construit au XIᵉ siècle, de longueurs dans sa piscine à débordement–et de Wagner. C'est à Ravello en effet que Richard Wagner vint se ressourcer à une période où il manquait d'inspiration. Depuis, les wagnériens du monde entier se retrouvent autour de sa musique lors du festival annuel fondé par l'hôtelier Paolo Caruso en 1953. Qu'il s'agisse du chant des cigales ou du *Crépuscule des dieux*, les concerts sont toujours superbes à Ravello.

DIRECTIONS
Naples airport is 65 km/40 miles away

RATES
Rooms from $640, suites from $1,495

ROOMS
24 rooms and 26 suites

STYLE
Traditional Italian grandezza with truly dramatic scenery

FOOD
In addition to high-class Italian cuisine at Belvedere, there's also the pool restaurant in summer and a choice of two separate bars

X FACTOR
The impressive visitors' book makes for illuminating reading. It contains dedications from some of Hotel Caruso's more illustrious guests, including Humphrey Bogart, Jackie Kennedy, and Nobel Prize–winning scientist Alexander Fleming

BOOK TO PACK
"Così Fan Tutti" by Michael Dibdin

LAGE
Der Flughafen Neapel ist 65 km entfernt

PREISE
Zimmer ab 470 €, Suiten ab 1100 €

ZIMMER
24 Zimmer und 26 Suiten

STIL
Klassische Grandezza mit einer tatsächlich die Brust weitenden Aussicht

KÜCHE
Neben dem großbürgerlich italienischen Restaurant Belvedere stehen den Gästen im Sommer das schöne Poolrestaurant sowie zwei Bars zur Verfügung

X-FAKTOR
Eine durchaus erhebende Abendlektüre ist das Gästebuch des Hotel Caruso, denn darin finden sich eindrucksvolle Widmungen von über jeden Zweifel erhabenen Prominenten wie Humphrey Bogart, Jackie Kennedy oder dem Nobelpreisträger Alexander Fleming

BUCH ZUM ORT
„Così fan tutti" von Michael Dibdin

SITUATION
À 65 km de l'aéroport de Naples

PRIX
Chambres à partir de 470 €, suites à partir de 1100 €

CHAMBRES
24 chambres et 26 suites.

STYLE
Très bel hôtel classique avec une vue époustouflante

RESTAURATION
Outre le restaurant italien Belvedere proposant de la grande cuisine raffinée, il y a le beau restaurant de la piscine ouvert en été ainsi que deux bars

LE « PETIT PLUS »
Le livre d'or est une lecture du soir des plus passionnantes : on y trouve les dédicaces de grandes célébrités, comme Humphrey Bogart, Jackie Kennedy et Alexander Fleming, lauréat du prix Nobel

LIVRE À EMPORTER
« Così fan tutti » de Michael Dibdin

HOTEL DREI ZINNEN
ITALY

St.-Josef-Straße 28 ~ 39030 Sexten ~ South Tyrol ~ Italy
Telephone +39 0474 710321 ~ Fax +39 0474 710092
info@hotel-drei-zinnen.com
www.hotel-drei-zinnen.com

The village of Sesto is truly blessed. Surrounded by some of the best-known Dolomite peaks, it also has views all the way into Val Fiscalina, often cited as the most beautiful of all Alpine valleys, and is home to the legendary Drei Zinnen hotel.

Built in 1931 and run by the Watschinger family ever since, the hotel was designed by Clemens Holzmeister to be "the salon of the Dolomites." From the outside it resembles a mighty fortress guarding the imposing mountain slopes, but the interiors are anything but monumental—with their generous layouts, cozy and yet unfussy ambience, and well-preserved Alpine modernist aesthetic, they are an elegant historic antidote to pine-clad Alpine traditionalism. The Drei Zinnen even has its own ski instructor, a post once held by the famous mountaineer Heinrich Harrer. A must for those nostalgic for a lost era of winter sport!

Das Bergdorf Sexten hat es gut. Ringsherum stehen die markantesten Dolomitenfelsen, und der Blick vom Dorf geht direkt hinein ins Fischleintal, das vielen als das schönste Tal der Alpen gilt. Außerdem gibt es das Drei Zinnen, ein regelrechtes Hoteldenkmal, Inbegriff der alpinen Erschließung und seit 1931 im Besitz der Familie Watschinger. Der berühmte Heinrich Harrer war hier Skilehrer, und bis heute gehört mindestens einer fest zum Hotelpersonal.

Erbaut von Clemens Holzmeister als „Salon der Dolomiten", steht das Haus bis heute als mächtige Trutzburg am Hang. Die wuchtigen Felswände sind den Gästen immer vor Augen, innen geht es aber alles andere als wuchtig zu: Mit großzügigen Grundrissen und gemütlicher Einfachheit geplant und ganz im Geist der alpinen Moderne erhalten, lässt sich hier ein überraschend unverschnörkeltes und elegantes Stück Bergarchitektur erleben. Eine Pflichtadresse für Wintersport-Nostalgiker!

Le village montagnard de Sesto est remarquablement situé. Encerclé par les plus impressionnantes roches dolomitiques, il surplombe la vallée de Fiscalina, réputée comme étant la plus belle des Alpes. Il abrite aussi le Drei Zinnen, véritable monument de l'hôtellerie ouvert au tourisme alpin, qui appartient depuis 1931 à la famille Watschinger. Le célèbre Heinrich Harrer y fut moniteur de ski et, depuis lors, l'hôtel en compte toujours un parmi ses employés.

Semblable à une forteresse dressée à flanc de montagne, cet hôtel construit par Clemens Holzmeister tel un « salon des Dolomites » offre une vue splendide sur les monumentales parois rocheuses. L'intérieur, lui, est tout sauf imposant. Alliant la simplicité et le confort, cette architecture montagnarde sobre et élégante est conforme au style alpin moderne. L'hôtel Drei Zinnen est une adresse de choix pour les nostalgiques des sports d'hiver !

318

LOCATION
In the spectacular Dolomite landscape of Val de Sesto, South Tyrol's most easterly valley; nearest airports are Bolzano and Innsbruck

RATES
Rooms from $95, including half board

ROOMS
35 rooms, all with different furnishings

STYLE
As well preserved an example of Tyrolean modernism as you'll find. Even the "card dance" murals in the games room are original

FOOD
Head chef Hannes Gatterer's kitchen is committed to delivering an honest culinary experience using local ingredients

X FACTOR
Simple and smart: The hotel's sleek new spa facility is a joy for all those yearning for a frill-free approach to wellness

BOOK TO PACK
"Mountaineers: Great Tales of Bravery and Conquest" by Ed Douglas

LAGE
Mit prachtvollem Blick auf die Sexter Dolomiten im östlichsten Tal von Südtirol gelegen, nächste Flughäfen sind Bozen und Innsbruck

PREISE
Ab 75 € pro Person und Nacht mit Halbpension

ZIMMER
35 Zimmer, alle verschieden eingerichtet

STIL
Bis hin zu den „Kartentanz"-Wandmalereien im Spielzimmer: Tiroler Moderne, wie man sie in diesem Erhaltungszustand kaum mehr findet

KÜCHE
Die Küche unter Leitung von Hannes Gatterer konzentriert sich auf ein ehrliches Geschmackserlebnis auf Basis heimischer Zutaten

X-FAKTOR
Klar und gut: Der simple neue „Baderaum" des Hotels ist eine Wohltat für alle, die kein Spa-Geschnörkel mehr ertragen können

BUCH ZUM ORT
„Bergsteiger. Auf den Spuren großer Alpinisten" von Ed Douglas

SITUATION
Dans la vallée la plus orientale du Haut-Adige; les aéroports les plus proches sont ceux de Bolzano et d'Innsbruck

PRIX
À partir de 75 € par personne et par nuit en demi-pension

CHAMBRES
35 chambres, toutes aménagées différemment

STYLE
Style moderne tyrolien jusque dans les peintures murales représentant des cartes à jouer dans un état de conservation rare

RESTAURATION
La cuisine particulièrement savoureuse de Hannes Gatterer est à base de produits locaux

LE «PETIT PLUS»
Les nouveaux bains de l'hôtel sont une bénédiction pour toux ceux qui ne supportent plus le côté kitsch des spas

LIVRE À EMPORTER
«Les Forces de la montagne» de René Desmaison

HOTEL SPLENDIDO
ITALY

Salita Baratta 16 ~ 16034 Portofino ~ Italy
Telephone +39 0185 267 801 ~ Fax +39 0185 267 806
info@splendido.net
www.hotelsplendido.com

Portofino: The very name calls to mind glorious images—of colorful fishing boats lying upturned on the beach, of rosemary growing in terra-cotta pots, and of green hills descending steeply to the sea. Perhaps that's what makes it so popular with Hollywood: first Humphrey Bogart and Lauren Bacall, then Richard Burton and Elizabeth Taylor; now it's Barbra Streisand and George Clooney. All came to stay at Hotel Splendido, an establishment whose Arcadian hillside setting and dramatic vistas are Oscar-worthy themselves.

A sea-view room with balcony is, of course, a must; best of all are the junior suites with parquet floors, classical furniture, and unfailingly fresh flowers. The pool, meanwhile, is filled with sea water and kept at 86 degrees Fahrenheit so that guests can soak up the surroundings for hours at a time. Granted, these pleasures come at a price. But if a night here is out of reach, simply revisit those mental images. They are almost as wonderful—and entirely free.

Portofino – schon der klingende Name transportiert wunderbare Bilder: bunte Fischerboote kieloben am Strand, Rosmarin in Terrakotta-töpfen und grüne Hügel, die steil ins Meer abfallen. Vielleicht fühlt sich Hollywood deshalb hier wie zu Hause. Nach Portofino kamen einst Humphrey Bogart und Lauren Bacall, Richard Burton und Elizabeth Taylor; heute sind es Barbra Streisand und George Clooney. Sie alle wohnten oder wohnen im Hotel Splendido, das am Hang liegt und mit seiner Aussicht jeden Tag eine oscarreife Vorstellung gibt.

Ein Zimmer zum Meer und mit Balkon ist ein Muss, am schönsten sind die Junior-Suiten mit Parkett, klassischen Möbeln und stets frischen Blumen. Der Hotelpool wird mit Salzwasser gefüllt und konstant auf 30 Grad gehalten, damit man stundenlang das Panorama genießen kann. Zugegeben: All das hat seinen Preis. Doch auch wer nicht nach Portofino reisen kann oder will, sollte das Bild behalten, das einem vor Augen tritt, sobald der Ortsname fällt. Es ist zauberhaft – und kostenfrei.

Portofino, ce nom suffit à évoquer les bateaux colorés des pêcheurs avec leur quille en l'air sur la plage, le romarin planté dans des pots en terre et les collines verdoyantes qui descendent à pic vers la mer. C'est sans doute pour cela que le Tout-Hollywood s'y retrouve. Autrefois, Portofino accueillait Humphrey Bogart et Lauren Bacall, Richard Burton et Elizabeth Taylor. Aujourd'hui, ce sont Barbara Streisand et George Clooney. Tous ont séjourné à l'hôtel Splendido, construit à flanc de colline et offrant une vue véritablement cinématographique.

Ici, il faut absolument réserver une chambre avec balcon donnant sur la mer. Avec leur parquet, leurs meubles classiques et leurs fleurs toujours fraîches, les suites juniors sont les plus belles. La piscine d'eau de mer maintenue en permanence à 30 °C permet d'admirer la vue des heures durant. Toutefois, ces choses-là ont un prix. Si vous ne voulez ou ne pouvez profiter de Portofino, contentez-vous de rêver aux merveilleuses images que le nom évoque. Cela ne vous coûtera rien.

LOCATION
On a peninsula in the Ligurian Sea, 35 km/
22 miles to the southeast of Genoa airport

RATES
Rooms from $1,300, suites from $2,110

ROOMS
29 rooms and 35 suites, with interiors by
Parisian designer Michel Jouannet

STYLE
The *dolce vita* at its most glamourous—pastel
shades, piqué cotton, chic pale furnishings

FOOD
Italian cuisine at La Terrazza, or there's the more
informal Pool Restaurant

X FACTOR
The hotel is famous for its first-class service.
The "spa butler," for instance, seems to have
an almost intuitive sense of his reclining guests'
needs—he's even capable of distracting Russian tycoons from their iPhones

BOOKS TO PACK
"The Talented Mr. Ripley" by Patricia Highsmith
and "Beautiful Ruins" by Jess Walter

LAGE
Auf einer Halbinsel in der ligurischen See gelegen, 35 km südöstlich von Genua

PREISE
Doppelzimmer ab 1000 €, Suiten ab 1620 €

ZIMMER
29 Zimmer und 35 Suiten, eingerichtet vom
Pariser Interiordesigner Michel Jouannet

STIL
Glamouröses Dolce Vita – noble Pastelltöne,
Baumwollpikee, honigblondes Stilmobiliar

KÜCHE
Neben dem eleganten La Terrazza gibt es noch
das legere Pool Restaurant

X-FAKTOR
Der Service des Hauses ist zu Recht weltberühmt. Nur ein Beispiel dafür ist der Badebutler,
der seinen Gästen jeden Wunsch von der Son-
nenliege abliest – er schafft es sogar, dass
russische Tycoons ihr iPhone ignorieren

BÜCHER ZUM ORT
„Der talentierte Mr. Ripley" von Patricia Highsmith und „Schöne Ruinen" von Jess Walter

SITUATION
Sur une péninsule de la mer Ligure,
à 35 km au sud-est de Gênes

PRIX
Chambres doubles à partir de 1000 €, suites
à partir de 1620 €

CHAMBRES
29 chambres et 35 suites, aménagées par l'architecte d'intérieur parisien Michel Jouannet

STYLE
Dolce vita élégante – nobles teintes pastel,
piqué de coton, mobilier dans des tons miel

RESTAURATION
Au choix : dîner élégant à La Terrazza ou ambiance décontractée au Pool Restaurant

LE « PETIT PLUS »
Le service de la maison est très réputé – à juste
titre. Pour exemple, le majordome de la piscine
répond au moindre désir de ses hôtes et parvient
même à faire en sorte que les « tycoons » russes
se passent de leur iPhone

LIVRE À EMPORTER
« Monsieur Ripley » de Patricia Highsmith

IL PELLICANO
ITALY

Località Sbarcatello ~ 58018 Porto Ercole ~ Italy
Telephone +39 0564 858 111 ~ Fax +39 0564 833 418
info@pellicanohotel.com
www.pellicanohotel.com

Every summer tour should really include a stopover at Il Pellicano. It was built in the mid-20th century for an American jet-set couple who spotted the hedonistic potential of this corner of the rocky Monte Argentario coast, which subsequently became a regular haunt for both the Kennedys and the Agnellis. Now that the Grahams' retreat has been turned into a hotel, the less well-connected can experience the pleasures of this fabulous location too.

The best place to do so is in one of the cottages higher up the cliff (preferably in a sea-view suite). By day, guests can enjoy the dolce far niente on their terrace or go for a swim in the saltwater pool; in the evenings, they can savor a cuisine that has earned the hotel two Michelin stars. And if sun, sea, and cricket sounds are not relaxation enough, there's always the beach house spa.

Jede Reise in den Sommer sollte eigentlich am Il Pellicano Station machen. Dessen Traumplatz an der Felsenküste von Monte Argentario hatte sich Mitte des 20. Jahrhunderts ein amerikanisches Jetset-Paar ausgesucht, mit sicherem Blick für das hedonistische Potenzial des Grundstücks. Die Residenz der Grahams wurde dann auch schnell zum Anlaufpunkt für Kennedys und Agnellis. Und seit das Ferienhaus in ein Hotel umgewandelt worden ist, kann man hier auch ohne persönliche Kontakte zur Upperclass die Fensterläden aufstoßen.

Am besten eignen sich dafür die höchstgelegenen Cottages – eine Suite mit Meerblick ist hier unbedingt zu empfehlen. Tagsüber genießt man das *dolce far niente* auf den sonnigen Terrassen und den Salzwasserpool, abends Menüs, die mit zwei Michelin-Sternen gekrönt sind. Das Spa ist in einem Strandhaus untergebracht – was Sonne, Grillenzirpen und Wellenrauschen noch nicht an Entspannung geliefert haben, wird sich spätestens dort einstellen.

Tout voyage estival entrepris en Italie devrait prévoir une halte à l'hôtel Il Pellicano. C'est au milieu du 20ᵉ siècle qu'un couple américain de la jet-set acheta un terrain situé sur la falaise escarpée du Monte Argentario, offrant une vue superbe aux adeptes de l'hédonisme. La résidence des Graham accueillit bientôt les Kennedy et les Agnelli, qui s'y retrouvèrent. Depuis que cette maison de vacances a été transformée en hôtel, on peut y louer une chambre sans avoir de relations dans la haute société.

Pour profiter pleinement du lieu, il faut séjourner dans une suite avec vue sur la mer dans l'un des cottages situés en hauteur, se laisser aller au farniente sur la terrasse ensoleillée, se détendre dans la piscine d'eau de mer et savourer, le soir, les plats du restaurant couronné de deux étoiles Michelin. Si le chant des cigales, le soleil et le roulement des vagues ne suffisent pas à la détente, le spa, aménagé dans une maison en bord de mer, se chargera du reste.

DIRECTIONS
On the south coast of Monte Argentario, 150 km/93 miles from Rome Fiumicino and 160 km/99 miles from Rome Ciampino

RATES
Rooms from $570, suites from $1,040, breakfast included

ROOMS
35 rooms and 15 suites

STYLE
Charming Mediterranean refuge with good old 1960s jet-set flair

FOOD
In addition to the main restaurant there is the Pelligrill, which serves Tuscan cuisine under the open sky—highly recommended

X FACTOR
The most appropriate means of getting around this spectacular coastline is, of course, by water ski

BOOK TO BUY ON LOCATION
"Hotel Il Pellicano" with photographs by Slim Aarons, John Swope, and Juergen Teller

LAGE
An der Südostküste der Halbinsel Monte Argentario; Rom Fiumicino ist 150 km, Rom Ciampino 160 km entfernt

PREISE
Zimmer ab 420 €, Suite ab 765 €, inklusive Frühstück

ZIMMER
35 Zimmer und 15 Suiten

STIL
Charmantes Mittelmeer-Refugium mit dem Flair des guten, alten Jetsets der Sixties

KÜCHE
Neben dem Hauptrestaurant gibt es noch das sehr empfehlenswerte Pelligrill, das toskanische Spezialitäten unter freiem Himmel serviert

X-FAKTOR
Die adäquateste Art der Fortbewegung in dieser prächtigen Kulisse ist natürlich Wasserski

BUCH ZUM ORT
„Hotel Il Pellicano" mit Fotos von Slim Aarons, John Swope und Juergen Teller

SITUATION
Sur la côte sud-est du Monte Argentario, Rome Fiumicino (150 km) ou Rome Ciampino (160 km)

PRIX
Chambres à partir de 420 €, suites à partir de 765 €, petit déjeuner inclus

CHAMBRES
35 chambres et 15 suites

STYLE
Charmant refuge méditerranéen dans l'esprit de la bonne vieille jet-set des années 1960

RESTAURATION
En dehors du restaurant principal, le très recommandable Pelligrill à ciel ouvert sert des spécialités toscanes

LE «PETIT PLUS»
Le ski nautique est sans doute la meilleure façon de se déplacer pour profiter du paysage somptueux

LIVRE À ACHETER SUR PLACE
«Hotel Il Pelicano», avec des photographies de Slim Aaarons, John Swope et Juergen Teller

IL SAN PIETRO DI POSITANO
ITALY

Via Laurito 2 ~ 84017 Positano ~ Italy
Telephone +39 089 875 455 ~ Fax +39 089 811 449
reservations@ilsanpietro.it
www.ilsanpietro.it

289 feet: That's the difference in height between the San Pietro's reception and its private beach down by the Tyrrhenian Sea. Only minimal effort is required for the descent, however, thanks to the lift hotel founder Carlo Cinque personally built into the rock (although not, admittedly, on his own).

Today, this high-class hotel remains in the hands of his family and has been only very subtly adapted to the passage of time. The panorama can still be admired amid ceramic tiles painted with maritime scenes; though nowadays guests can also enjoy a superbly equipped spa. The restaurant's take on traditional Amalfi cuisine, meanwhile, is so refined, it has been awarded a Michelin star. Perhaps tackling those 289 feet under one's own steam is not such a bad idea after all—at least the views will take your mind off the calorie burning.

88 Höhenmeter: So weit ist es von der Rezeption des San Pietro bis zum Privatstrand, unten am Tyrrhenischen Meer. Bei dieser kleinen Reise ist den Gästen ein Lift behilflich, den Carlo Cinque, der Gründer des Hotels, in den 1960er-Jahren noch höchstpersönlich in den Fels schlug. Nun gut, er hatte Hilfe dabei.

Bis heute ist das erstklassige Haus in Familienhand und wurde nur äußerst behutsam den Zeitläufen angepasst. Nach wie vor kann man das Panorama in Gesellschaft szenisch bemalter Keramikfliesen genießen; unter den Zitronenbäumen gibt es jetzt aber auch ein exzellent eingerichtetes Spa. Die traditionelle Küche der Amalfiküste wird hier so gelungen auf den Teller gebracht, dass sie einen Michelin-Stern erhielt. Vielleicht sollte man also doch die 88 Meter zwischendurch auch mal zu Fuß bewältigen – die Aussicht lenkt dabei zuverlässig vom Kalorienverbrauch ab.

Une hauteur de 88 mètres sépare la réception du San Pietro de la crique privée, en bas, qui donne sur la mer Tyrrhénienne. Heureusement, un ascenseur aménagé dans la roche dans les années 1960 par le fondateur de l'hôtel en personne, Carlo Cinque, est mis à la disposition des hôtes.

Dans cette très belle maison qui est toujours entre les mains de la famille, seul l'extérieur a été modernisé au fil du temps. La terrasse panoramique a été pavée de carreaux de céramique sur lesquels sont peintes des scènes, et un excellent spa a été aménagé sous les citronniers. La cuisine traditionnelle de la côte amalfitaine, si délicieusement servie dans l'assiette, a même décroché une étoile Michelin. Et pourquoi ne pas essayer de gravir les 88 mètres de dénivelé à pied : la vue spectaculaire fait oublier à coup sûr les efforts fournis.

LOCATION
60 km/37 miles south of Naples

RATES
Rooms from $615, suites from $995, breakfast included

ROOMS
61 rooms, each with private terrace and sea views

STYLE
Luxury swallow's nest with fabulously unsubtle floor tiles and a decor against which even a Pucci dress is not too much

FOOD
The candlelight dinners at Il San Pietro are genuinely romantic. Il Carlino offers informal lunches made with produce from the garden

X FACTOR
Every morning throughout the summer, the hotel offers guests a free boat trip along the Amalfi coast—the best possible way to start the day

BOOK TO PACK
"Arturo's Island" by Elsa Morante

LAGE
60 km südlich von Neapel gelegen

PREISE
Zimmer ab 450 €, Suiten ab 730 €, inklusive Frühstück

ZIMMER
61 Zimmer, alle mit eigener Terrasse und Meerblick

STIL
Luxus-Schwalbennest mit herrlich undezenten Fliesenböden und einem Dekor, in dem das Pucci-Kleid endlich nicht mehr *too much* ist

KÜCHE
Die Candlelight-Dinner im Il San Pietro sind tatsächlich romantisch. Das legere Carlino serviert Salate aus dem hoteleigenen Garten

X-FAKTOR
Eine gute Art, in den Tag zu starten: Im Sommer wird vom Hotel jeden Morgen ein kostenloser Bootsausflug entlang der Amalfiküste angeboten

BUCH ZUM ORT
„Arturos Insel" von Elsa Morante

SITUATION
À 60 km au sud de Naples

PRIX
Chambres à partir de 450 €, suites à partir de 730 €, petit déjeuner inclus

CHAMBRES
61 chambres, toutes dotées d'une terrasse avec vue sur la mer

STYLE
Nid d'hirondelle luxueux avec un carrelage superbe et un cadre dans lequel une robe Pucci est tout à fait à sa place

RESTAURATION
Les dîners aux chandelles au Il San Pietro sont vraiment romantiques. Le Carlino sert des salades provenant du jardin de l'hôtel

LE « PETIT PLUS »
L'été, l'excursion gratuite en bateau le long de la côte amalfitaine est une bonne manière de commencer la journée

LIVRE À EMPORTER
« L'Île d'Arturo » d'Elsa Morante

"The air there smells of lemons and moves with a light breeze. I will stay at the Hotel San Pietro, with its breathtaking views of the coastal townlet of Positano."

JAMIE OLIVER, CELEBRITY CHEF

„Die Luft dort riecht nach Zitronen, und ein leichter Wind weht. Ich werde im Hotel San Pietro wohnen; der Blick über das Küstenstädtchen Positano ist atemberaubend."

« Ici, l'air fleure bon le citron, tandis que souffle une légère brise. Je descendrai au San Pietro ; la vue sur la petite ville côtière de Positano est époustouflante. »

LA POSTA VECCHIA
ITALY

Palo Laziale ~ 00055 Ladispoli ~ Italy
Telephone +39 069 949 501 ~ Fax +39 069 949 507
info@lapostavecchia.com
www.lapostavecchia.com

Besides being the richest man in the world, Jean Paul Getty (1892–1976) was also one of the most enigmatic characters of the 20th century. During a trip to Italy, the tycoon discovered an old villa on the coast of Latium that once served as a guesthouse for the aristocratic Orsini family and as a post house. He purchased the property and set about realizing an American billionaire's vision of an Old World palazzo.

Getty chose only the best of the best: furniture once owned by the Medici, Gobelin tapestries, Venetian mirrors, and oil paintings by European masters. Today, La Posta Vecchia is one of Italy's most extraordinary hotels. The rooms are all named after famous guests—or, in the case of the Getty Suite, their equally famous host. Not all, though, have sea views, perhaps due to the former owner's fear of the deep. Although, given their papal decors, not having nature competing for attention is perhaps not such a bad thing.

Jean Paul Getty (1892–1976) war bis zu seinem Tod der reichste Mann der Welt, ein Tycoon und eine der schillerndsten Persönlichkeiten des 20. Jahrhunderts. Während einer Italienreise entdeckte er an der Küste Latiums eine Villa, die einst als Gästehaus der Adelsfamilie Orsini und als Poststation gedient hatte, und machte daraus das, was sich ein US-Milliardär unter einem Palazzo der alten Welt vorstellte.

Mr. Getty nahm nur das Beste: Möbel aus dem Besitz der Medici, französische Gobelins, venezianische Spiegel und Ölbilder europäischer Meister. Heute ist La Posta Vecchia eines der extravagantesten Hotels Italiens. Alle Zimmer sind nach berühmten Gästen benannt – wer dem ehemaligen Hausherrn so nahe wie möglich kommen will, reserviert die Getty-Suite. Vielleicht weil ihrem Namensgeber die See nie ganz geheuer war, spielt Meerblick nicht in allen Räumen die Hauptrolle – doch deren päpstliche Interieurs vertrügen Natur-Konkurrenz ohnehin nur schlecht.

Jusqu'à sa mort, Jean Paul Getty (1892–1976) fut l'homme le plus riche du monde et l'une des personnalités les plus brillantes du 20e siècle. Lors d'un voyage en Italie, il découvrit sur la côte du Latium une villa qui avait jadis appartenu à la famille des princes Orsini avant de servir de relais postal. Il la transforma en un palais de l'Ancien Monde, tel que l'imagine un milliardaire américain.

Getty le décora de meubles ayant appartenu aux Médicis, de tapisseries françaises, de miroirs vénitiens et de tableaux de grands maîtres européens. Aujourd'hui, La Posta Vecchia est l'un des hôtels les plus extravagants d'Italie. Toutes les chambres portent le nom de clients célèbres. Si vous désirez vous glisser dans la peau de l'ancien propriétaire, vous pourrez louer la suite Getty. Peut-être parce que celui-ci n'avait pas le pied marin, la vue sur la mer n'y joue pas un rôle clé dans toutes les chambres, encore que les somptueux intérieurs peuvent largement rivaliser avec le paysage.

DIRECTIONS
Located on the coast to the north of Rome, 30 km/19 miles from Rome Fiumicino airport; below the hotel is a narrow beach

RATES
Rooms from $420, suites from $920

ROOMS
19 rooms and suites

STYLE
Jean Paul Getty's splendid European legacy

FOOD
From risotto to ricotta creme with caramelized pears: The Cesar Restaurant with sea-view terrace has a Michelin star and serves gourmet cuisine with a regional touch

X FACTOR
The history lesson—Getty discovered ruins of two Roman villas on the grounds, a museum in the hotel basement now presents the finds

BOOKS TO PACK
"How to Be Rich" by Jean Paul Getty and "The Portrait of a Lady" by Henry James

LAGE
An der Küste nördlich von Rom gelegen, 30 km vom Flughafen Rom Fiumicino entfernt. Unterhalb des Hotels befindet sich ein schmaler Strand

PREISE
Zimmer ab 320 €, Suiten ab 700 €

ZIMMER
19 Zimmer und Suiten

STIL
Jean Paul Gettys prunkvolles Vermächtnis

KÜCHE
Das Cesar Restaurant mit Terrasse zum Meer hat einen Michelin-Stern und serviert Gourmetküche mit regionaler Note, von Risotto bis Ricotta-Creme mit karamellisierten Birnen

X-FAKTOR
Bildungsbonus: Getty entdeckte auf dem Grundstück die Ruinen zweier römischer Villen, ein Museum im Keller zeigt noch Fundstücke

BÜCHER ZUM ORT
„Wie wird man reich" von Jean Paul Getty und „Bildnis einer Dame" von Henry James

SITUATION
Sur la côte au nord de Rome, à 30 km de l'aéroport de Fiumicino; une plage étroite se trouve en contrebas de l'hôtel

PRIX
Chambres à partir de 320 €, suites à partir de 700 €

CHAMBRES
19 chambres et suites

STYLE
Fastueux héritage de Jean Paul Getty

RESTAURATION
Le Cesar Restaurant, avec terrasse sur la mer, a une étoile au Michelin et sert une cuisine gastronomique aux touches locales: risotto, crème à la ricotta et poires caramélisées, etc.

LE « PETIT PLUS »
Sur la propriété, Getty a découvert deux villas romaines. Leurs vestiges sont visibles dans le musée aménagé dans la cave de la maison

LES LIVRES À EMPORTER
« Devenir riche » de Jean Paul Getty et « Portrait de femme » de Henry James

RELAIS SAN MAURIZIO
ITALY

Località San Maurizio 39 ~ 12058 Santo Stefano Belbo ~ Italy
Telephone +39 014 184 1900 ~ Fax +39 014 184 3833
info@relaissanmaurizio.it
www.relaissanmaurizio.it

It may not be obvious at first sight, but the Langhe in northern Italy is a land of plenty. The sides of its hills produce the Nebbiolo grapes that make Barolo and Barbaresco, and the soils of its woods are home to *Tuber magnatum pico*, the white Alba truffle that Cicero once so enthused about and whose seductive aromas transform even the simplest dish into a delicacy. Connoisseurs from around the world will pay astronomical prices for this "white gold," but the best (and cheapest) way to sample it is in one of the region's restaurants—that of the Relais San Maurizio, for example, an old Franciscan monastery-turned-hotel.

Here, the fine food is served in a vaulted basement, while the accommodation itself is in the onetime monks' cells. Despite the modern-day luxury, something of the monastic character remains. Guests can walk beneath ancient trees on the grounds, gaze across vineyards while relaxing in the pool, and let their thoughts wander even further: to the next culinary high point.

Man sieht es nicht gleich, aber die Langhe sind eigentlich das Schlaraffenland Norditaliens. Auf ihren Hügeln wachsen die Nebbiolo-Trauben, aus denen Barolo und Barbaresco gekeltert werden, und in ihren Wäldern versteckt sich die *Tuber magnatum Pico*, die weiße Alba-Trüffel, von der schon Cicero schwärmte und die Kraft ihres Aromas selbst die schlichtesten Speisen in Delikatessen verwandelt. Damit erzielt man Liebhaberpreise auf der ganzen Welt, doch am besten (und günstigsten) lässt sich das weiße Gold vor Ort genießen: zum Beispiel im Restaurant des Relais San Maurizio, eines ehemaligen Franziskanerklosters.

Hier werden Köstlichkeiten im Gewölbekeller serviert – passend zu den Zimmern, die aus den einstigen Mönchszellen entstanden sind. Bei allem Komfort hat sich das Anwesen auch etwas von seiner Klösterlichkeit bewahrt. Im Park wandelt man unter uralten Bäumen, und vom Pool aus schweifen die Blicke über die Weinberge und die Gedanken noch weiter: in Richtung der nächsten kulinarischen Gipfel.

La région des Langhe est sans aucun doute pour certains le cœur gastronomique de l'Italie du Nord. Sur ses collines pousse le nebbiolo, un cépage qui compose le barolo et le barbaresco et, dans ses forêts, se cache le *Tuber magnatum pico*, la truffe blanche du Piémont, dont Cicéron chantait déjà les louanges et qui transforme les plats les plus simples en mets exquis. Comme la truffe, l'«or blanc» des Piémontais, atteint des prix astronomiques sur les marchés mondiaux, il est préférable de la goûter sur place, à un prix plus abordable, par exemple au restaurant du Relais San Maurizio, un ancien monastère franciscain.

Ici, on sert des plats succulents dans la cave voûtée. Son cadre est aussi impressionnant que celui des chambres, les anciennes cellules des moines. En dépit du confort proposé, le lieu a conservé un peu de son côté monacal. Le parc abrite de très vieux arbres et, de la piscine, le regard se perd dans les vignes, tandis que les pensées vagabondent vers la prochaine dégustation culinaire.

LOCATION
In the province of Cuneo, less than 2 hours from Milan, Genoa, and Turin

RATES
Rooms from $370, suites from $530, excluding breakfast

ROOMS
31 rooms and suites

STYLE
Tasteful style mix within monastery walls

FOOD
Da Guido has a Michelin star, while the hotel's Hemingway bar pays tribute to the writer, who loved life's simple but irresistible pleasures

X FACTOR
Accompanying a *trifolau* or truffle hunter as he scours the woods for this prized fungus is a treat for any foodie—and excellent exercise to boot. Ask at the hotel about joining such a hunt

BOOK TO PACK
"The Moon and the Bonfires" by Cesare Pavese

LAGE
In der Provinz Cuneo; von Mailand, Genua oder Turin in unter 2 Stunden erreichbar

PREISE
Zimmer ab 280 €, Suite ab 400 €, ohne Frühstück

ZIMMER
31 Zimmer und Suiten

STIL
Gediegener Stilmix hinter Klostermauern

KÜCHE
Das Restaurant Da Guido hat einen Michelin-Stern; die Hemingway-Bar des Hotels ist eine Hommage an den Schriftsteller, der simple und dabei exquisite Genüsse liebte

X-FAKTOR
Abenteuer für Feinschmecker und ein guter Workout dazu: einmal einen *trifolau* (Trüffel-experten) bei seiner Suche nach den Edelknol-len begleiten. Erkundigen Sie sich im Hotel nach einer Exkursion!

BUCH ZUM ORT
„Junger Mond" von Cesare Pavese

SITUATION
Province de Cuneo; à moins de 2 heures de Milan, de Gênes et de Turin

PRIX
Chambres à partir de 280 €, suites à partir de 400 €, petit déjeuner non compris

CHAMBRES
31 chambres et suites

STYLE
Les murs du monastère abritent un mélange cossu de styles

RESTAURATION
Le restaurant Da Guido a une étoile au Michelin; le bar Hemingway rend hommage à l'écrivain, amateur de plaisirs simples et gourmands

LE «PETIT PLUS»
Un temps fort pour les gourmets, avec en prime la chasse à la truffe aux côtés d'un *trifolau* qui connaît les gisements de ce tubercule noble. Renseignez-vous à l'hôtel!

LIVRE À EMPORTER
«La Lune et les feux» de Cesare Pavese

CREDITS / IMPRINT

008–017 all photos supplied by the hotel 018–023 all photos supplied by the hotel 024–031 Mirjam Bleeker, www.mirjambleeker.nl 032–039 all photos supplied by the hotel 040–045 all photos supplied by the hotel 046–053 all photos supplied by the hotel 054–061 Christian Redtenbacher, www.redtenbacher.net 062–067 Eliophot, all photos supplied by the hotel 068–075 all photos supplied by the Coppola Family of Destination 076–085 all photos supplied by the hotel 086–093 all photos supplied by David Crookes and UASC 094–099 all photos supplied by the Great Plains Conservation 100–105 all photos supplied by the hotel 107, 109, 110, 111 (below left) all photos supplied by Tuca Reinés/TASCHEN 108, 111 (above, below right) all photos supplied by the hotel 112–117 Cookie Kinkead, www.cookiekinkead.com, all photos supplied by the hotel 118–123 all photos supplied by the hotel 124–129 all photos supplied by the hotel 130–135 all photos supplied by the hotel 136–145 all photos by Tuca Reinés 146–153 all photos by Tuca Reinés 154–159 all photos supplied by the hotel 160–167 all photos supplied by the hotel 168–175 all photos supplied by the hotel 176–181 Gilles Martin-Raget, all photos supplied by the hotel 182–189 Guillaume de Laubier, www.guillaumedelaubier.com 190–197 Daniel Schäfer/TASCHEN GmbH, www.danielschaeferphoto.com 198–203 all photos supplied by the hotel 204–209 all photos supplied by the hotel 210–217 Günter Standl, all photos supplied by the hotel 218–223 all photos supplied by the hotel 224–229 all photos supplied by the hotel (p. 225, p. 229 by William Abranowicz; p. 226, p. 228 [below left] by Timos Tsoukalas) 230–235 Ricardo Labougle/ TASCHEN GmbH, www.ricardolabougle.com 236–243 all photos supplied by the hotel 244–249 all photos supplied by Taj Hotels Resorts and Palaces 250–255 all photos supplied by Patrizia Mussa, www.livio.it 256–263 all photos supplied by the hotel 264–271 Mathias Michel, all photos supplied by the hotel 272–279 Gianni Franchellucci, all photos supplied by the hotel 280–285 all photos supplied by the hotel 286–291 all photos supplied by Mads Mogensen, styling by Martina Hunglinger, www.madsmogensen.com 292–297 Gionata Xerra, all photos supplied by the hotel 298–305 Peter Vitale, all photos supplied by the hotel 306–311 all photos supplied by the hotel 312–315, 317 Gianni Basso/TASCHEN GmbH, www.vegamg.it 316 Genivs Loci, all photos supplied by the hotel 318–323 all photos supplied by the hotel 324–331 Patrizia Mussa/TASCHEN GmbH, www.livio.it 332–337 Gianni Basso/TASCHEN GmbH, www.vegamg.it 338–345 all photos supplied by the hotel 346–351 all photos are supplied by the hotel 352–357 all photos supplied by Mads Mogensen, styling by Martina Hunglinger, www.madsmogensen.com

To stay informed about upcoming TASCHEN titles, please subscribe to our free Magazine at www.taschen.com/magazine, find our Magazine app for iPad on iTunes, follow us on Twitter and Facebook, or e-mail us for a sample copy at contact@taschen.com. Delve in and enjoy!

© 2014 TASCHEN GmbH
Hohenzollernring 53
50672 Köln
www.taschen.com

© 2014 Eames Office, Venice, CA, www.eamesoffice.com, for the works of Charles and Ray Eames

EDITOR
Margit J. Mayer

ART DIRECTION & DESIGN
Diane Bergmann, Berlin

TEXT
Max Scharnigg, Munich; with contributions by Eliza Apperly; Christiane Reiter, Paris; Kristin Rübesamen, Berlin; Julia Strauß, Munich

PROJECT MANAGEMENT
Stephanie Paas

EDITORIAL ASSISTANT
Falkmar K. Finke

ENGLISH TRANSLATION
Iain Reynolds, Berlin

FRENCH TRANSLATION
Sabine Boccador, Saint-Maur-des-Fossés

PRODUCTION
Frauke Kaiser

PRINTED IN CHINA
ISBN 978-3-8365-4397-2

100

GETAWAYS

100 GETAWAYS

RUND UM DIE WELT · AROUND THE WORLD · AUTOUR DU MONDE

I–Z

TASCHEN

CONTENTS
A–I

CONTENTS
I–Z

LE SIRENUSE
ITALY

Via Cristoforo Colombo 30 ~ 84017 Positano ~ Italy
Telephone +39 089 875 066 ~ Fax +39 089 811 798
info@sirenuse.it
www.sirenuse.it

The Sirenusas off the Amalfi Coast are, legend has it, home to bewitching sirens, and certainly the mere sight of these islands from the hotel Le Sirenuse terrace is enough to make any guest fall in love. What's more, this magnificent Positano villa not only offers captivating views of the sea and of the houses clinging to the slopes, but it's also the epitome of a Mediterranean residence with its whitewashed walls, little balconies, and hand-painted floor tiles.

The rooms boast antiques and artworks from the region, the poolside terrace is surrounded by lemon trees, scents of rose and frangipani fill the air, and the hotel's old wooden boat lies in the harbor, waiting to take guests on excursions along the coast. Be sure to return by dark, though—not to avoid the sirens, but to enjoy a glass of prosecco while admiring the lights of Positano reflected picturesquely in the sea.

Die Sirenuse-Inseln vor der Amalfiküste sind der Mythologie zufolge die Heimat der betörenden Sirenen. Wenn man ihre Silhouette von der Terrasse des Hotels Le Sirenuse aus sieht, ist man ihrem Ruf mit Sicherheit längst erlegen. Denn die herrschaftliche Villa bietet nicht nur einen privilegierten Logenblick auf das Meer und das in den Hang gebaute Positano: Mit ihren weiß gekalkten Wänden, kleinen Balkonen und handgemachten Bodenfliesen ist sie der Inbegriff der perfekten Mittelmeer-Residenz.

In den Zimmern warten Antiquitäten und Kunstwerke aus der Region auf die Gäste, die Poolterrasse ist von Zitronenbäumen umgeben, überall duften Rosen und Frangipani, und im Hafen dümpelt das hoteleigene alte Holzboot *Sant'Antonio*. Wenn es dunkel wird, sollte man aber unbedingt wieder an Land sein – nicht wegen der Sirenen, sondern um bei einem Glas Prosecco die Lichter des pittoresken Ortes im Meer glitzern zu sehen.

Selon la mythologie, les Sirénuses, îlots situés au large de la côte amalfitaine, étaient le foyer des envoûtantes Sirènes de l'Odyssée. Quand on découvre leurs silhouettes depuis la terrasse de l'hôtel Le Sirenuse, on a déjà certainement succombé à leur chant : cette villa majestueuse offrant une vue privilégiée sur la mer et sur Positano à flanc de falaise incarne, avec ses murs blanchis à la chaux, ses petits balcons et son carrelage artisanal, la résidence méditerranéenne par excellence.

Les chambres sont ornées d'antiquités et d'œuvres d'art de la région, la terrasse de la piscine est bordée de citronniers, et les roses et les frangipaniers embaument. Dans le port tangue le *Sant'Antonio,* le vieux bateau en bois de l'hôtel. Il faut absolument regagner la terre ferme avant la tombée de la nuit, non pas à cause des Sirènes, mais pour voir scintiller sur l'eau les lumières de ce pittoresque village en savourant un verre de Prosecco.

LOCATION

Le Sirenuse lies in the heart of Positano, 230 feet above the sea. Naples airport is 55 km/34 miles away

RATES

Rooms from $520, suites from $1,485

ROOMS

58 rooms and suites

STYLE

High-class summer residence from the 18th century, renovated in the 1990s

FOOD

La Sponda serves fine Neapolitan cuisine. The champagne-and-oyster bar on the terrace is also recommended

X FACTOR

As a souvenir of the enchanting Amalfi Coast, guests can take the scent of Le Sirenuse home with them: *Eau D'Italie* is a light cologne with citrusy notes

BOOK TO PACK

"Positano" by John Steinbeck

LAGE

Le Sirenuse liegt im Herzen von Positano, 70 m über dem Meer. Der Flughafen von Neapel ist 55 km entfernt

PREISE

Zimmer ab 385 €, Suiten ab 1100 €

ZIMMER

58 Zimmer und Suiten

STIL

Vornehme Sommerresidenz aus dem 18. Jahrhundert, renoviert in den 1990ern

KÜCHE

La Sponda serviert feine neapolitanische Küche. Zu empfehlen ist auch die Champagner- und Austernbar auf der Terrasse

X-FAKTOR

Als Erinnerung an den Zauber der Amalfiküste können Gäste den Le-Sirenuse-Duft mit nach Hause nehmen: *Eau D'Italie*, einem leichten Eau de Cologne mit Zitrusnoten

BUCH ZUM ORT

„Positano. Geschichten aus einer Stadt am Meer" von Stefan Andres

SITUATION

Au centre de Positano, à 70 mètres au-dessus du niveau de la mer et à 55 km de l'aéroport de Naples

PRIX

Chambres à partir de 385 €, suites à partir de 1 100 €

CHAMBRES

58 chambres et suites

STYLE

Élégante résidence d'été datant du 18e siècle, rénovée dans les années 1990

RESTAURATION

La Sponda sert une cuisine napolitaine raffinée. Également à recommander : le bar à huîtres et à champagne sur la terrasse

LE « PETIT PLUS »

En souvenir du charme de la côte amalfitaine, les hôtes peuvent rapporter chez eux le parfum du Sirenuse baptisé *Eau d'Italie,* une eau de toilette légère avec une note d'agrumes

LIVRE À EMPORTER

« L'Odyssée » d'Homère

"Every room ... looks out over the blue sea
to the islands of the sirens
from which those ladies sang so sweetly."

JOHN STEINBECK, "POSITANO," 1953

„Jedes Zimmer (...) bietet Ausblick auf das blaue Meer bis hin zu
den Inseln der Sirenen, von wo aus diese Damen so verführerisch sangen."

«Chaque chambre offre une vue sur la mer azur et les îlots des Sirènes,
où ces dames entonnaient leurs chants si envoûtants.»

SEXTANTIO
ALBERGO DIFFUSO
ITALY

Via Principe Umberto ~ 67020 Santo Stefano di Sessanio ~ Italy
Telephone+39 086 289 9112 ~ Fax +39 086 289 9656
reservation@sextantio.it
www.sextantio.it

Having gotten lost on his motorbike in the mountains of Abruzzo, Daniele Kihlgren decided to stop near Santo Stefano di Sessanio—a decision that led to the project of his life. So fascinated was he by this medieval shepherds' village that Kihlgren, the son of an industrialist, used his inheritance to buy up some of the run-down dwellings and transform them into one of Italy's most unusual hotels.

His *albergo diffuso* (scattered hotel) comprises 27 rooms spread across various houses. Restored with the aid of archaeologists in a suitably historic style, the spaces have soot-blackened walls, heavy ceiling beams, open fireplaces, and sheep's-wool mattresses. Despite concessions to modern-day comfort, such as under-floor heating and Philippe Starck bathrooms, both of which will be well appreciated after a long fall walk, this is an Italian retreat of the most authentic kind.

Daniele Kihlgren hatte sich in den Abruzzen verfahren und legte in der Nähe von Santo Stefano di Sessanio einen Stopp ein. Aus der kurzen Pause wurde das Projekt seines Lebens: Der Industriellensohn war von der einstigen mittelalterlichen Hirtensiedlung so fasziniert, dass er sein Erbe in einen Teil davon investierte, um daraus eines der ungewöhnlichsten Hotels von Italien zu machen.

Kihlgrens *albergo diffuso* (verstreutes Hotel) umfasst 27 Zimmer in mehreren Häusern, die mit Beratung von Archäologen authentisch archaisch renoviert wurden, von den schweren Deckenbalken und rußgeschwärzten Mauern bis hin zu offenen Kaminen und Bauernbetten mit Schafwollmatratzen. Als Tribut an die Neuzeit gibt es nun auch Fußbodenheizung und Philippe-Starck-Bäder, über die man sich nach einem langen Herbstspaziergang ganz neu freuen kann. Ein Ort für alle, die Italien mal ganz ursprünglich erleben wollen.

Un jour, alors qu'il s'était égaré dans les Abruzzes, Daniele Kihlgren, fils d'un industriel milanais, fit une halte dans les environs de Santo Stefano di Sessanio. De cette étape naquit le projet de sa vie : fasciné par cet ancien village de bergers médiéval, il a investit son héritage dans le village, dont il acheta une partie pour la transformer en l'un des hôtels les plus insolites d'Italie.

Son *albergo diffuso* (hôtel disséminé) comprend 27 chambres réparties entre plusieurs maisons, toutes restaurées de manière authentiquement archaïque grâce aux conseils d'archéologues, avec des poutres massives, des murs noircis de suie, des cheminées et des lits rustiques garnis de matelas en laine de mouton. Seuls sacrifices à la modernité, le chauffage par le sol et les salles de bains Philippe Starck, que l'on se plaît à retrouver après une longue promenade automnale. Un lieu où il fait bon vivre l'Italie dans toute son authenticité.

S. STEFANO
AI PRODI FIGLI
CHE DIEDERO LA VITA
PER LA GRANDEZZA E LE INTEGRE RIVENDICAZIONI
DELL'ALMA MADRE

CAP.LE CHIARELLI BERNARDO
D'ALOISIO GIUSEPPE
TATONE AMABILE
SOLD. CHIARELLI GREGORIO
CHIARELLI NICOLA
CICCI ONORATO
GIUSTIZIA GIOVANNI
IANNACCI GIOVANNI
IANNARELLI FRANCESCO

SOLD. LEONE EMIDIO
LEONE GIACOMO
MARINI SABATINO
MECOLI ORESTE
NECCA PASQUALE
RUSCITTI BASILIO
RUSCITTI PASQUALE
RUSCIOLELLI POMPEO
SANTARELLI DOMENICO

OTTOBRE 26 1919

IL POPOLO
DI S. STEFANO DI SESSANIO
RICORDA
I SUOI FIGLI MIGLIORI
CADUTI PER LA PATRIA
NELLA SECONDA GUERRA MONDIALE

1 Serg. M. SETACCI   SABATO
2 Cap.   BATTISTONE   GIUSEPPE
       PANDOLFI   MARIO
3   TATONE   GIUSEPPE
4 Sold. CALDARELLI   AURELIO
5   CALDARELLI   OSVALDO
6   CHIARELLI   BERNARDO
7   GALANTE   LUIGI
8   LEONE   AURELIO
9   LEONE   GIACINTO
10   SANTARELLI   MAURIZIO
11   TATONE   OSVALDO
12 Partig. RUSCITTI   DINO

14 Sold. CARDELLI   ORLANDO
15   CALDARELLI   MICHELE

LOCATION
Up in the mountains of Abruzzo, to the north-east of Rome; 30 km/19 miles from L'Aquila

RATES
Rooms from $295, breakfast included

ROOMS
27 rooms in 7 houses

STYLE
Time traveling for individualists who want to live like Boccaccio without sacrificing modern-day hygiene

FOOD
The restaurant serves rustic food made with typical medieval ingredients, such as lentils, chickpeas, roasted chestnuts, and bacon; there is also a wine bar and a tearoom

X FACTOR
The medieval village is not only remarkably well preserved, but also at 4,100 feet above sea level, it is also one of the highest settlements in the land. A refreshingly different Italy

BOOK TO PACK
"Love and War in the Apennines" by Eric Newby

LAGE
Auf 1250 m Höhe in den Abruzzen, 30 km von L'Aquila und 150 km nordöstlich von Rom

PREISE
Zimmer ab 220 €, inklusive Frühstück

ZIMMER
27 Zimmer in 7 Häusern

STIL
Zeitreise für Individualisten, die sich einmal wie Boccaccio fühlen wollen, ohne dabei auf zeitgenössische Körperpflege zu verzichten

KÜCHE
Das Restaurant serviert Rustikales mit typisch mittelalterlichen Zutaten wie Linsen, Speck, Kichererbsen und Röstkastanien; daneben gibt es eine Weinbar und einen Tea Room

X-FAKTOR
Das Dorf ist nicht nur mittelalterlich erhalten, sondern mit 1250 m über dem Meer auch einer der höchstgelegenen Orte des Landes. Ein ganz anderes, belebend frisches Italiengefühl

BUCH ZUM ORT
„Die letzte Welt" von Christoph Ransmayr

SITUATION
À 1 250 mètres d'altitude dans les Abruzzes, à 30 km de L'Aquila et à 150 km au nord-est de Rome

PRIX
Chambres à partir de 220 €, petit déjeuner compris

CHAMBRES
27 chambres réparties entre 7 maisons

STYLE
Un voyage dans le temps pour les individualistes qui veulent vivre à la façon de Boccace sans renoncer à l'hygiène corporelle moderne

RESTAURATION
Le restaurant sert des plats rustiques à base d'aliments médiévaux : lentilles, lard, pois chiches et châtaignes grillées. Il y a aussi un bar à vin et une *tisaneria*

LE «PETIT PLUS»
La *dolce vita* autrement : perché au-dessus de la mer, ce village est l'un des plus hauts du pays

LIVRE À EMPORTER
«Le Dernier des mondes» de Christoph Ransmayr

TORRE DI
BELLOSGUARDO
ITALY

Via Roti Michelozzi 2 ~ 50124 Florence ~ Italy
Telephone +39 055 229 8145 ~ Fax +39 055 229 008
info@torrebellosguardo.com
www.torrebellosguardo.com

Nowhere is the old continent more aesthetic than in Florence, one of the cradles of European culture. To evade tourist hordes, however, you have to head to the hills, which offer sensational views of the city's domes and roofs.

The best of these vistas can be admired from Bellosguardo, a hill to the south of the Arno that has long been a favorite spot for postcard photographers and painters, not to mention thinkers in search of inspiration, Galileo Galilei included. To join the ranks of these enlightened visitors, book a room at the Torre di Bellosguardo. Its 13th-century tower was built as a hunting lodge by an acquaintance of Dante; during the Renaissance, a villa was added by the aristocratic Roti Michelozzi family.

Today, the place retains an air of nobility and Bohemian sophistication: Guests are greeted by a Pietro Francavilla statue, while frescoes by Bernardino Poccetti adorn the hall-like lobby. The interiors, though, shouldn't distract you from the main attraction: the Florentine cityscape laid out in the valley below.

Die Wiege des alten Europa, nirgends schaukelt sie schöner als in Florenz. Um dem Touristentrubel zu entkommen, bleibt einem hier nur die Flucht auf die Hügel, die außerdem eine grandiose Sicht über Dom und Dächer eröffnen.

Eine Anhöhe im Süden des Arno gilt als besonders pittoresk: Vom Bellosguardo aus wurden die schönsten Postkartenmotive fotografiert, Maler verewigten das Panorama der Stadt, Denker fanden hier Inspiration – unter ihnen Galileo Galilei. Wer sich in solch illustrer Nachbarschaft wohlfühlt, sollte hier unbedingt reservieren. Ein Freund Dantes ließ den Turm im 13. Jahrhundert als Jagdschloss errichten, die Marchesi Roti Michelozzi fügten in der Renaissance eine Villa hinzu. Bis heute atmet das Torre ein Flair von Noblesse und gebildeter Boheme; eine Statue von Pietro Francavilla heißt die Besucher willkommen, und die hallenartige Lobby schmücken Fresken von Bernardino Poccetti. Bei aller Begeisterung fürs Interieur gilt es jedoch auch hinauszuschauen und Florenz zu bewundern, das einem hier zu Füßen liegt.

Pour admirer la beauté de Florence, ce berceau de la vieille Europe, en échappant aux hordes de touristes, il faut faire une excursion sur ses collines qui offrent une vue grandiose sur le Duomo et les toits de la ville.

C'est de la colline de Bellosguardo, située au sud de l'Arno, que les plus beaux motifs de cartes postales ont été photographiés; des peintres ont immortalisé le site sur la toile, des penseurs, parmi lesquels Galilée, y ont trouvé l'inspiration. Si ces illustres personnalités vous séduisent, n'hésitez surtout pas à réserver une chambre au Torre di Bellosguardo. Au XIIIᵉ siècle, un ami de Dante a fait ériger une tour qui servait de pavillon de chasse et, à la Renaissance, les marquis Roti Michelozzi y ont adjoint une villa. Le Torre baigne toujours dans une atmosphère aristocratique et bohème. Une statue de Pietro Francavilla accueille les hôtes, et le hall est orné de fresques de Bernardino Poccetti. La splendide vue sur Florence, qui s'étend au pied de la colline, n'a toutefois rien à envier aux intérieurs de l'établissement.

LOCATION
Walking distance from the pulsating city center, yet a Bernard Berenson-esque world apart; 10 km/6 miles from Florence airport

RATES
Doubles from $390, suites from $460, exclusive of breakfast

ROOMS
16 rooms and suites, all individually furnished with antiques

STYLE
Florentine treasure trove

FOOD
Normally the hotel only serves breakfast. Amateur chefs can, however, also take part in first-class cooking courses

X FACTOR
Did Dante swim? Either way, the pool in the hotel's romantic grounds is the polar opposite of his Inferno and worth a trip to Torre di Bellosguardo on its own

BOOK TO PACK
"Where Angels Fear to Tread" by E. M. Forster

LAGE
In Spaziernähe zum pulsierenden Stadtkern in einer ganz eigenen Welt à la Bernard Berenson, 10 km vom Flughafen Florenz

PREISE
Doppelzimmer ab 290 €, Suiten ab 340 €, jeweils ohne Frühstück

ZIMMER
16 Zimmer und Suiten, alle individuell mit Antiquitäten eingerichtet

STIL
Florentinische Schatzkiste

KÜCHE
Regulär gibt es im Hotel nur Frühstück. Interessierte Gäste können aber an ausgezeichneten Kochkursen teilnehmen

X-FAKTOR
Hatte Dante eigentlich eine Badehose? Der Pool im romantischen Park ist jedenfalls das exakte Gegenteil seines Inferno und allein einen Besuch im Torre di Bellosguardo wert

BUCH ZUM ORT
„Engel und Narren" von E. M. Forster

SITUATION
Non loin du cœur battant de la ville, dans un univers du goût de Bernard Berenson, à 10 km de l'aéroport de Florence

PRIX
Chambres doubles à partir de 290 €, suites à partir de 340 €, petit déjeuner non compris

CHAMBRES
16 chambres et suites meublées en ancien, chacune différemment

STYLE
Coffre à trésors florentins

RESTAURATION
On ne sert généralement que le petit déjeuner, mais ceux qui le souhaitent peuvent suivre d'excellents cours de cuisine

LE «PETIT PLUS»
Au fait, Dante se baignait-il? La piscine dans le parc romantique est en tout cas le contraire exact de son Enfer. À elle seule, elle justifie un détour par cet hôtel

LIVRE À EMPORTER
«Montenario» de E. M. Forster

"No words are adequate to express what we feel about Bellosguardo and this entirely magical *vacanza*."

ACTRESS EMMA THOMPSON IN THE HOTEL'S GUEST BOOK

„Mir fehlen die Worte, um unsere Dankbarkeit auszudrücken für Bellosguardo und die absolut zauberhaften Ferien, die wir hier hatten."

« Je ne trouve pas les mots pour exprimer ma gratitude envers le Bellosguardo pour les vacances absolument merveilleuses que nous y avons passées. »

VILLA CENCI
ITALY

Strada Provinciale per Ceglie Messapica
72014 Cisternino ~ Italy
Telephone +39 080 444 8208
info@villacenci.it
www.villacenci.it

A form of housing born out of necessity, the distinctive conical *trulli* of Apulia are now heritage monuments and, despite mostly lacking windows of any kind and having only dry-stone walls, have become highly desirable properties. They are, after all, surely the coziest form of accommodation in all southern Italy.

At Villa Cenci, the *trulli* are home to nine guest suites in which the architecture is the only reminder of past austerity, with sun sails, four-poster beds, TVs, and air-conditioning ensuring guests don't want for 21st-century comforts. The sensitively restored ensemble is surrounded by 13 hectares of beautiful grounds, across which the pool affords fabulous views. The nearby countryside, meanwhile, supplies fresh fruit and vegetables for the fine organic dishes that guests can enjoy at the hotel restaurant or, should you prefer, from the comfort of your dry-stone wigwam.

Früher eine Behausung, die aus der Not geboren war, heute Nationaldenkmal: Die markanten *Trulli* in Apulien sind mittlerweile begehrte Immobilien, und das, obwohl die meisten nicht mal Fenster haben und nur aus losen Feldsteinen aufgeschichtet sind. Trotzdem gibt es in Süditalien kein innigeres Wohnerlebnis als eine Nacht unter diesen trutzigen Steinkegeln.

Die Villa Cenci bietet gleich neun *Trulli*-Suiten, an die karge Vergangenheit erinnert dabei nur noch die Form der Häuser. Ansonsten sind mit Sonnensegel, Himmelbett, TV und Klimaanlage die modernen Zeiten eingezogen. Rund um das sensibel restaurierte Landgut dehnen sich 13 Hektar herrlichste Natur aus, über die man vom Pool aus einen wunderschönen Blick hat. Das Obst und Gemüse, das in diesen Weiten gedeiht, ist Basis für die feine Bio-Küche des Hotels, die im Restaurant serviert wird – oder direkt vor der Tür der steinernen Wigwams.

Naguère habitations de fortune, les *trulli* des Pouilles sont devenus de véritables monuments historiques très courus, alors que la plupart n'ont même pas de fenêtre et qu'ils sont construits en pierre sèche. Pourtant, une nuit passée dans l'une de ces fières coupoles en pierres du sud de l'Italie reste une expérience absolument incomparable.

Dans la villa Cenci, seule la forme des *trulli*, qui abritent neuf suites, évoque le dénuement des habitants d'autrefois. Les voiles d'ombrage, les lits à baldaquins, les téléviseurs et la climatisation sont, quant à eux, tout à fait modernes. Autour de ce domaine restauré s'étendent 13 hectares de nature, sur laquelle on jouit d'une vue splendide depuis la piscine. La cuisine bio raffinée, servie au restaurant ou dans le confort de votre « tipi » en pierre, est préparée avec les fruits et légumes qui poussent dans les grands espaces alentour.

LOCATION
In Valle d'Itria, 10 km/6 miles from the sea and 90 km/56 miles from Bari airport

RATES
Rooms from $215, suites from $340, breakfast included

ROOMS
9 rooms in *trulli*, 3 in the *masseria*, and 8 in stone houses

STYLE
Ancient whitewashed stone houses with surprisingly light and vibrant interiors

FOOD
The alfresco breakfast is legendary; for lunch and dinner, there's traditional Apulian cuisine

X FACTOR
Not something you often see in Apulia: The hotel boasts a small spa and hammam. The greatest pleasure for guests of all ages, however, are the houses themselves

BOOK TO PACK
"I'm Not Scared" by Niccolò Ammaniti

LAGE
90 km vom Flughafen Bari im Valle d'Itria gelegen, die Distanz zum Meer beträgt 10 km

PREISE
Zimmer ab 160 €, Suiten ab 250 €, inklusive Frühstück

ZIMMER
9 Zimmer in den Trulli, 3 in der *Masseria* und 8 Zimmer in den Steinhäusern

STIL
Archaische Steinhäuser, weiß getüncht und mit überraschend frischem, hellem Innenleben

KÜCHE
Das Frühstück unter freiem Himmel ist legendär; mittags und abends wird nach traditionellen apulischen Rezepten gekocht

X-FAKTOR
In Apulien eher selten: Das Hotel bietet seinen Gästen auch ein kleines Spa mit Sauna und Hamam. Das größte Privileg aber ist – nicht nur für Kinder – der Aufenthalt in den Trulli

BUCH ZUM ORT
„Die Herren des Hügels" von Niccolò Ammaniti

SITUATION
Dans la Vallée d'Itria, à 10 km de la mer et à 90 km de l'aéroport de Bari

PRIX
Chambres à partir de 160 €, suites à partir de 250 €, petit déjeuner compris

CHAMBRES
9 chambres dans les *trulli*, 3 dans la *masseria* et 8 dans les maisonnettes en pierre

STYLE
Maisons de pierre archaïques badigeonnées de blanc aux intérieurs étonnamment frais et clairs

RESTAURATION
Le petit déjeuner en plein air est légendaire; midi et soir, des recettes locales traditionnelles sont proposées

LE «PETIT PLUS»
Rare dans les Pouilles: l'hôtel dispose d'un petit spa avec sauna et hammam. Le plus grand privilège reste, et pas seulement pour les enfants, de pouvoir séjourner dans les *trulli*

LIVRE À EMPORTER
« Je n'ai pas peur » de Niccolò Ammaniti

400

"Breakfast was incredible, with freshly squeezed orange juice, homemade cake, local cheese, and bread with tomato and mozzarella."

A GOURMET GUEST FROM BELGIUM

„Das Frühstück war unglaublich – frisch gepresster Orangensaft, hausgemachter Kuchen, Käse aus der Umgebung und Brot mit Tomate und Mozzarella."

« Le petit déjeuner était fantastique : orange pressée, gâteau maison, fromage de la région et pain avec tomate et mozzarella. »

VILLA D'ESTE
ITALY

Via Regina 40 ~ 22012 Cernobbio ~ Italy
Telephone +39 031 3481
info@villadeste.it
www.villadeste.it

It's a long-held view that Lake Como is the most romantic spot in northern Italy, a view that has led many of its more ardent admirers to build themselves spectacular properties along its shores. One such is Villa d'Este, which since the 16th century has been owned by cardinals, artists, and even royalty.

Now one of the country's most luxurious hotels, the villa thankfully retains much of the rich patina of these associations. The rooms are furnished with antiques and rustling silks from nearby Como, and no two are the same (those in the Queen's Pavilion wing with its enchanting trompe l'oeil are particularly fine). And if you find yourself in one without a balcony, simply admire the lake while strolling the grounds, lounging on the floating pool deck, or having dinner on the terrace. Whatever your vantage point, you'll notice that the spirit of this place has survived unchanged—its popularity with the rich and famous, after all, is just as evident today.

Neu ist es nicht, den Comer See für das romantischste Fleckchen Norditaliens zu halten. Eine lange Geschichte begehrlicher Bewunderung hat seinen Ufern einzigartige Bauten beschert, darunter die Villa d'Este, die seit dem 16. Jahrhundert Kardinäle, Könige und Künstler als Eigentümer aufzuweisen hatte.

Die prachtvolle Patina dieser Persönlichkeiten ist dem Anwesen zum Glück erhalten geblieben, auch nach dessen Wandlung zu einem der luxuriösesten Hotels des Landes. Alle Zimmer wurden mit Antiquitäten und raschelnder Seide aus dem nahen Como ausgestattet. Kein Raum gleicht dem anderen, und besonders schön wohnt man im Flügel Queen's Pavilion mit seinen zauberhaften Trompe-l'œils. Wer kein Zimmer mit Balkon bekommen hat, bewundert den See eben vom schwimmenden Pooldeck aus oder beim Dinner auf der Terrasse. Wie lebendig die Tradition des Ortes noch ist, lässt sich dort oder beim Spaziergang durch den Park feststellen, denn an berühmten Gästen mangelt es der Villa d'Este bis heute nicht.

C'est un poncif que d'affirmer que le lac de Côme est l'endroit le plus romantique de l'Italie du Nord. Au fil d'une longue histoire admirable, on a élevé sur ses berges des édifices d'exception, notamment la Villa d'Este qui, depuis le XVIe siècle, a eu pour propriétaires des cardinaux, des rois et des artistes.

Dans la propriété, l'empreinte somptueuse de ces personnalités a heureusement été préservée, même après sa transformation en l'un des hôtels les plus luxueux du pays. Les chambres ont été meublées d'antiquités et de soieries bruissantes provenant de Côme. Les chambres sont toutes différentes, et il est particulièrement agréable de séjourner dans le pavillon de la Reine décoré de fabuleux trompe-l'œil. Ceux qui n'auront pas eu la chance de réserver une chambre avec balcon pourront admirer le lac depuis la piscine flottante ou la terrasse du dîner. Ici ou dans les allées du parc, on constate que la Villa d'Este est restée fidèle à la tradition du lieu, tant les hôtes de marque continuent d'y défiler.

LOCATION
At the southernmost tip of Lake Como,
35 km/22 miles from Lugano airport and
65 km/40 miles from Milan's Malpensa airport

RATES
Rooms from $890, suites from $1,930,
breakfast included

ROOMS
125 rooms in Cardinal's Building, 27 rooms in
Queen's Pavilion, and 2 private villas

STYLE
The opulence of bygone days

FOOD
The Veranda is famous for its irresistible risotto;
the Grill serves regional cuisine

X FACTOR
The echoes of history: Villa d'Este was built
by Pellegrino Pellegrini in 1568 and has been
a hotel since 1873. It is a magnet for the
moneyed and the cultured alike

BOOK TO PACK
"Leonardo's Swans" by Karen Essex

LAGE
Am südwestlichen Zipfel des Comer Sees gele-
gen, 35 km vom Flughafen Lugano, 65 km vom
Flughafen Mailand-Malpensa entfernt

PREISE
Zimmer ab 660 €, Suiten ab 1430 €,
inklusive Frühstück

ZIMMER
125 Zimmer im Cardinal's Building, 27 Zimmer
im Queen's Pavilion und 2 private Villen

STIL
Opulenz vergangener Tage

KÜCHE
Das Veranda ist für unwiderstehlichen Risotto
berühmt, das Grill serviert Regionales

X-FAKTOR
Das Raunen der Geschichte: Die Villa d'Este
wurde 1568 von Pellegrino Pellegrini erbaut und
ist immerhin seit 1873 ein Hotel, das Geld wie
Kultur magnetisch anzieht

BUCH ZUM ORT
„Leonardo und die Principessa" von Karen
Essex

SITUATION
Sur la branche sud-ouest du lac de Côme,
à 35 km de l'aéroport de Lugano et à 65 km
de celui de Milan-Malpensa

PRIX
Chambres à partir de 660 €, suites à partir
de 1 430 €, petit déjeuner compris

CHAMBRES
125 chambres dans le bâtiment du Cardinal,
27 chambres dans le pavillon de la Reine
et 2 villas privées

STYLE
Opulence d'une époque révolue

RESTAURATION
Irrésistible risotto au restaurant Veranda
et plats régionaux au Grill

LE «PETIT PLUS»
La présence de l'histoire : construite en
1568 par Pellegrino Pellegrini, la Villa d'Este
est depuis 1873 un hôtel qui attire comme
un aimant argent et culture

LIVRE À EMPORTER
«Deux sœurs pour Léonard» de Karen Essex

VILLA FELTRINELLI
ITALY

Via Rimembranza 38–40 ~ 25084 Gargnano ~ Italy
Telephone +39 036 579 8000 ~ Fax +39 036 579 8001
booking@villafeltrinelli.com
www.villafeltrinelli.com

The ancient olive trees at Villa Feltrinelli have seen a lot over the years, and not all of it as salubrious as their Lake Garda location. After all, this waterfront mansion property, built as a summerhouse for a publishing dynasty, also had a two-year stint as Benito Mussolini's private residence. Decades later, the property was turned into a hotel, one that continues to strike the perfect balance between elegant refinement and informality.

That is chiefly thanks to the restoration led by hotel impresario Robert H. Burns, who availed himself of the extensive local resources, namely the region's history, architecture, and art. As a result, the rooms boast Venetian mirrors, high fireplaces, and handblown glass chandeliers; seven of them even have 19th-century ceiling frescoes by the Lieti brothers. At the bar, meanwhile, aperitifs are served in 1950s glasses, the perfect precursor to dinner at the Michelin-starred hotel restaurant. It seems the only dictator at work here today is good taste.

Die uralten Olivenbäume der Villa Feltrinelli haben schon viel gesehen, und nicht alles davon war so glitzernd wie die kleinen Wellen des Gardasees nebenan. Schließlich diente der einstige Sommersitz der legendären Verlegerdynastie zwei Jahre lang auch Benito Mussolini als privates Quartier. Später entstand aus dem Anwesen ein Hotel, das bis heute Eleganz und familiäre Atmosphäre in idealer Balance hält. Zu verdanken ist das der Restaurierung durch Hotel-Impresario Robert H. Burns, der dabei auf reichlich vorhandene lokale Ressourcen setzen konnte: Geschichte, Architektur und Kunst.

Für die Gäste bedeutet das einen Aufenthalt zwischen venezianischen Spiegeln, hohen Kaminen und mundgeblasenen Glaslüstern; sieben Zimmer zeigen sogar Deckenfresken der Brüder Lieti aus dem vorletzten Jahrhundert. Der Aperitif an der Bar wird in Gläsern aus den 1950er-Jahren serviert und bereitet derart auf ein Abendessen im hoteleigenen Sternerestaurant vor. Offensichtlich ist guter Stil heute der einzige Diktator hier.

Les oliviers centenaires de la villa Feltrinelli ont été les témoins de nombreux événements, qui n'ont pas toujours été aussi paisibles que les petites vagues du lac de Garde tout proche. Cette ancienne résidence d'été de la légendaire dynastie d'éditeurs a en effet accueilli Benito Mussolini pendant deux ans. Transformée plus tard en hôtel, elle maintient un juste équilibre entre élégance et convivialité. On doit sa restauration au magnat de l'hôtellerie Robert H. Burns, qui a su tirer parti du riche patrimoine historique, architectural et artistique local.

On trouve ici des miroirs vénitiens, de hautes cheminées et des lustres en verre soufflé ; sept chambres ont même des plafonds ornés de fresques delete du XIX\e siècle réalisées par les frères Lieti. Au bar, on prend l'apéritif dans des verres années 1950 avant d'aller dîner au restaurant étoilé de l'hôtel. Le bon goût est aujourd'hui la seule dictature qui règne dans ce lieu.

LOCATION
On the western shore of Lake Garda,
90 km/56 miles from Verona airport

RATES
Rooms from $1,420 with a minimum stay
of 2 nights, breakfast included

ROOMS
21 rooms and suites

STYLE
Lakeside villa from 1892 that, thanks to
a fabulous renovation, has become a place
of pilgrimage for Russian oligarchs and rich
nostalgia-seekers

FOOD
The Dining Room offers gourmet cuisine, but
the Venetian-style restaurant La Pergola is even
more atmospheric

X FACTOR
From the moment you go down for breakfast,
you feel like you're on the set of an Anthony
Minghella adaptation of a Henry James novel

BOOK TO PACK
"Twilight in Italy" by D. H. Lawrence

LAGE
Am Westufer des Gardasees gelegen,
90 km vom Flughafen Verona entfernt

PREISE
Zimmer ab 1050 € bei 2 Nächten Mindestaufenthalt, inklusive Frühstück

ZIMMER
21 Zimmer und Suiten

STIL
Seevilla von 1892, die nach atemberaubender
Renovierung zur Pilgerstätte für reiche Nostal-
giker und russische Oligarchen wurde

KÜCHE
Noch atmosphärischer als das Gourmetrestaurant The Dining Room ist das La Pergola im
venezianischen Stil

X-FAKTOR
Das Gefühl, schon auf dem Weg zum Frühstück
über den Set einer Henry-James-Verfilmung von
Anthony Minghella zu schlendern

BUCH ZUM ORT
„Italienische Dämmerung" von D. H. Lawrence

SITUATION
Sur la rive ouest du lac de Garde, à 90 km
de l'aéroport de Vérone

PRIX
Chambres à partir de 1 050 € (séjour de 2 nuits
minimum), petit déjeuner compris

CHAMBRES
21 chambres et suites

STYLE
Villa au bord de l'eau datant de 1892. Après
une somptueuse rénovation, elle est devenue
un lieu de pèlerinage pour les nostalgiques
fortunés et les oligarques russes

RESTAURATION
Le restaurant La Pergola dans le style vénitien
a encore plus de charme que le restaurant gastronomique The Dining Room

LE « PETIT PLUS »
Dès les couloirs qui mènent au petit déjeuner,
on se croit sur le tournage d'une adaptation
d'Henry James par Anthony Minghella

LIVRE À EMPORTER
« Crépuscule sur l'Italie » de D. H. Lawrence

VILLA KRUPP
ITALY

Viale Matteotti 12 ~ 80073 Capri ~ Italy
Telephone +39 081 837 7473 ~ Fax +39 081 837 6489
villakrupp.dona@alice.it
www.villakrupp.it

Among aficionados of the Mediterranean, Villa Krupp has almost cult status, a fact owing as much to its spectacular location as to the glamour of its steely sounding name. The terrace, after all, directly overlooks Capri's most famous landmark, the Faraglioni stacks.

This privileged view should not distract from the fact that the guesthouse itself is only a three-star affair: The rickety outdoor seating is made of plastic, and the rooms have kitsch decors and tile floors. But then that's all part of the charm, as is the simple breakfast for five euros. Besides, you don't need to live in luxury to enjoy Capri. There's Marina Piccola just down Via Krupp should you feel like a dip, and the welcoming Coppola family is always happy to help plan outings or suggest restaurants. Incidentally, industrialist and Capri fan Friedrich Albert Krupp never actually stayed here himself, though Maxim Gorki did, playing chess with Lenin on the terrace in 1908. Not a bad claim to fame, either.

Bei Mittelmeerfreunden hat die Villa Krupp durchaus Kultstatus. Schließlich ist ihre Lage mindestens so glamourös wie ihr nach Stahl klingender Name: Von der Terrasse der um 1900 erbauten Villa blickt man hinüber auf Capris Wahrzeichen, die Faraglioni-Felsen.

Diese privilegierte Aussicht sollte allerdings nicht darüber hinwegtäuschen, dass die Pension selbst nur ein Drei-Sterne-Haus ist, man sitzt draußen also auf wackligen Plastikstühlen und wohnt in leicht kitschigen Zimmern mit Fliesenböden. Doch das gehört hier einfach dazu, genau wie das einfache Frühstück für fünf Euro – denn man braucht keinen besonderen Luxus, um Capri genießen zu können. Zum Baden fährt man die Via Krupp hinunter zur Marina Piccola, die herzliche Familie Coppola ist ihren Gästen zudem bei der Planung von Ausflügen und Restaurantbesuchen gern behilflich. Übrigens: Der Capri-Liebhaber Friedrich Albert Krupp selbst hat hier nie gewohnt. Dafür Maxim Gorki, der 1908 auf der Terrasse mit Lenin Schach spielte. Auch nicht übel.

Pour les adeptes de la Méditerranée, la Villa Krupp est un lieu culte. Sa situation est en effet au moins aussi glamour que son nom évoquant le métal: de la terrasse de cette villa construite vers 1900 s'ouvre une vue sur les rochers Faraglioni, l'emblème de Capri.

Cette vue privilégiée ne saurait cependant masquer le fait que cette pension n'est qu'un hôtel trois étoiles, avec des chaises de jardin en plastique branlantes et des chambres un tantinet kitsch aux sols carrelés. Mais cela fait partie du charme de la villa, tout comme le petit déjeuner simple à cinq euros. Point n'est besoin de luxe pour profiter de Capri. Pour se baigner, il faut descendre la via Krupp jusqu'à la Marina Piccola, et la très sympathique famille Coppola aide volontiers ses hôtes dans l'organisation des excursions ou le choix des restaurants. Pour la petite histoire: Friedrich Albert Krupp, grand amoureux de Capri, n'a jamais vécu ici. En revanche, en 1908, Maxime Gorki a joué aux échecs avec Lénine sur la terrasse. La légende est sauve.

LOCATION
Capri is 45 to 75 minutes by boat from Naples
(depending on ferry). From the harbor, take the
funicular or a taxi to the Piazzetta—then it's a
10-minute walk to Villa Krupp

RATES
Singles from $155, doubles from $190

ROOMS
12 rooms

STYLE
Endearing *albergo* with historic flair

FOOD
Breakfast only, but the owners are happy
to recommend restaurants

X FACTOR
Marina Piccola is a wonderful place for a dip.
If Via Krupp, the road to the bay, is closed, take
a bus or a taxi from Piazza Martiri d'Ungheria

BOOKS TO PACK
"Mother" by Maxim Gorki, written at
Villa Blaesus, as it then was, and "The Skin"
by Curzio Malaparte

LAGE
Capri liegt 45 bis 75 Schiffsminuten (je nach
Fährentyp) vor Neapel. Vom Hafen fahren eine
Standseilbahn und Taxis zur Piazzetta, von dort
aus läuft man 10 Minuten zur Villa Krupp

PREISE
Einzelzimmer ab 115 €, Doppelzimmer ab 140 €

ZIMMER
12 Zimmer

STIL
Liebenswertes *Albergo* mit historischem Flair

KÜCHE
Nur Frühstück, aber die Besitzer verraten gern,
in welchen Restaurants man gut isst

X-FAKTOR
An der Marina Piccola kann man wunderbar
baden. Ist die zur Bucht führende Via Krupp
geschlossen, fahren ab der Piazza Martiri
d'Ungheria Busse und Taxis dorthin

BÜCHER ZUM ORT
Der Roman „Die Mutter", den Maxim Gorki
in der damaligen Villa Blaesus schrieb, und
„Die Haut" von Curzio Malaparte

SITUATION
De 45 à 75 minutes de bac de Naples
à Capri (selon le bateau); transfert du
port à la Piazzetta en funiculaire ou en taxi,
puis 10 minutes de marche jusqu'à l'hôtel

PRIX
Chambres single à partir de 115 €, chambres
doubles à partir de 140 €

CHAMBRES
12 chambres

STYLE
Charmant *albergo* chargé d'histoire

RESTAURATION
Petit déjeuner uniquement, mais les propriétaires ont de bonnes adresses de restaurants

LE «PETIT PLUS»
Baignades sublimes à la Marina Piccola. Si la via
Krupp menant à la baie est fermée, prendre un
bus ou un taxi à la Piazza Martiri d'Ungheria

LIVRES À EMPORTER
«La Mère» de Maxime Gorki, écrit dans
l'ancienne villa Blaesus, et «La Peau»
de Curzio Malaparte

FUJIYA INN
JAPAN

443 Shinpata Oaza Ginzan Obanazawa ~ Yamagata 999–4333 ~ Japan
Telephone +81 237 28 2141 ~ Fax +81 237 28 2140
info@fujiya-ginzan.com
www.fujiya-ginzan.com

"Blonde Madam," the locals call Jeanie Fuji, the American who has turned the Fujiya Inn into one of the best-known hotels in Japan.

Having learned the ancient art of *okami*, traditional Japanese hospitality, in the 1990s, she later went on to redesign this guesthouse at the famous hot springs of the Ginzan River. Tackling a 350-year-old institution is a sensitive task, but it's one she mastered brilliantly, ably assisted by star architect Kengo Kuma. His building is a minimalist and yet highly sensuous take on Zen aesthetics and the art of reduction. Delicate wooden partitions, bamboo screens (*sumushiko*), and shimmering green glass walls create a captivating atmosphere in which the architecture forms a suitably diaphanous backdrop to the steam of the springs.

„Blonde Madam", so nennt man Jeanie Fuji im Ort, seit sie das Fujiya Inn zu einem der bekanntesten Hotels Japans gemacht hat.

Die gebürtige Amerikanerin lernte in den 1990er-Jahren zunächst die uralte Kunst des *okami*, der japanischen Gastfreundschaft. Später gestaltete sie das 350 Jahre alte Gasthaus an den berühmten heißen Quellen des Flusses Ginzan neu. Eine heikle Aufgabe, die sie zusammen mit Stararchitekt Kengo Kuma brillant löste. Kumas Bau ist eine minimalistische und dennoch sehr sinnliche Annäherung an Zen-Ästhetik und die Kunst des Weglassens. Filigrane Holztrennwände, Bambusschirme (*sumushiko*) und grün schimmernde Glaswände schaffen in den Räumen eine faszinierende Atmosphäre. Die Gäste wandeln hier zwischen den Nebeln der heißen Quellen und einer gleichsam schwebenden Architektur.

«La Madame blonde», c'est ainsi que l'on surnomme Jeanie Fuji depuis qu'elle a fait du Fujiya Inn l'un des hôtels les plus célèbres du Japon.

Née aux États-Unis, Jeanie a d'abord appris dans les années 1990 l'art ancestral de l'hospitalité japonaise (*okami*), avant de réaménager intégralement ce *ryokan* construit il y a 350 ans près des sources chaudes de la rivière Ginzan. Une mission qu'elle a brillamment remplie avec l'architecte renommé Kengo Kuma. L'architecture de Kuma est une approche à la fois minimaliste et très chaleureuse de l'esthétique zen et de l'art du dépouillement. Les claustras de bois filtrant la lumière, les cloisons de bambou (*sumushiko*) et les parois vitrées aux reflets verts créent dans les pièces une atmosphère fascinante. Les hôtes évoluent ici entre la brume des bains chauds et une architecture pour ainsi dire flottante.

LOCATION
Situated on the Ginzan River, in the village of the same name, 35 km/22 miles north of Yamagata airport (a 1-hour flight from Tokyo)

RATES
Doubles from $610, breakfast and dinner included

ROOMS
8 rooms with 2 to 3 beds each

STYLE
Contemporary Japanese interior design and ascetic simplicity

FOOD
Traditional Japanese specialties made with ultra-fresh ingredients—a cuisine that reflects the philosophy of the hotel

X FACTOR
Everything revolves around traditional Japanese bathing rituals at the Fujiya Inn, which boasts 5 private hot springs. A word of warning, though: They are genuinely hot!

BOOK TO PACK
"In Praise of Shadows" by Jun'ichirō Tanizaki

LAGE
Direkt am Fluss Ginzan im gleichnamigen Ort gelegen, 35 km nördlich des Flughafens Yamagata (ab Tokio in 1 Flugstunde zu erreichen)

PREISE
Doppelzimmer ab 450 €, inklusive Frühstück und Abendessen

ZIMMER
8 Zimmer mit jeweils 2 bis 3 Betten

STIL
Zeitgenössisches japanisches Interiordesign und asketische Schlichtheit

KÜCHE
Auch auf dem Teller findet sich die Hausphilosophie wieder, in Form traditioneller japanischer Spezialitäten aus ultrafrischen Zutaten

X-FAKTOR
An diesem Ort dreht sich alles um klassische japanische Badefreuden, 5 heiße Privatquellen warten auf die Hotelgäste. Aber Vorsicht: Sie sind wirklich richtig heiß!

BUCH ZUM ORT
„Lob der Schatten" von Jun'ichirō Tanizaki

SITUATION
Sur la rivière Ginzan, dans la station thermale du même nom, à 35 km au nord de l'aéroport de Yamagata (à 1 heure de vol de Tokyo)

PRIX
Chambres doubles à partir de 450 €, en demi-pension

CHAMBRES
8 chambres (2–3 lits)

STYLE
Design intérieur japonais contemporain et simplicité ascétique

RESTAURATION
Le contenu des assiettes reflète la philosophie de la maison : spécialités japonaises traditionnelles à base de produits ultrafrais

LE « PETIT PLUS »
Les bains japonais classiques constituent l'attraction du lieu. Ils sont au nombre de cinq, mais attention, l'eau est vraiment très chaude !

LIVRE À EMPORTER
« Éloge de l'ombre » de Jun'ichirō Tanizaki

"When designing Fujiya Inn,
I developed the concept of layers
both in time and space."

KENGO KUMA, THE HOTEL'S ARCHITECT

„Beim Entwurf des Fujiya Inn entwickelte ich ein Schichtungsprinzip,
sowohl in der Zeit als auch im Raum."

«Pour le projet du Fujiya Inn, j'ai mis au point un principe de stratification
à la fois temporelle et spatiale.»

EVASON MA'IN HOT SPRINGS
JORDAN

P.O. Box 801 Madaba ~ 11117 Ma'In ~ Jordan
Telephone +96 25 324 5500 ~ Fax +96 25 324 5550
reservations-main@sixsenses.com
www.sixsenses.com

The location alone makes this oasis a draw—the Dead Sea is just down the road, the lights of Jerusalem are visible in the distance, and the sign reading 260 meters (853 feet) below sea level is definitely one for the photo album. The main attraction, though, is the waters, be it the healing hot springs of Ma'In or the heavy, dense saltwater of the aforementioned inland sea. If ever there were a case for packing an entire bathing wardrobe, this is it.

It's perhaps no surprise, therefore, to find the Evason Ma'In belongs to the elite fold of Six Senses spas. One of the many waterfalls cascades directly into the spa's pool, where guests can, of course, also benefit from the therapeutic properties of Dead Sea minerals (courtesy, for instance, of a Dead Sea Mud Body Wrap or an Olive Oil & Salt Scrub). And with the resort built using local materials, body and soul aren't the only things in perfect harmony here.

Die Lichter von Jerusalem in der Ferne, die salzige Luft des Toten Meers ganz nah: Schon die Lage dieser Oase fasziniert, und auf jeden Fall ein Foto wert ist das Schild, welches besagt, dass man sich hier 260 Meter unterhalb des Meeresspiegels befindet. Die heißen und heilenden Quellen von Ma'In, das Schweben im salzschweren Wasser des nahen Binnenmeeres: Wenn ein Hotel nach einer Bade-Garderobe verlangt, dann das Evason Ma'In.

Keine Überraschung also, dass sich hier die Spa-Elite in Form eines Six Senses Spa niedergelassen hat. Einer der vielen Wasserfälle rauscht direkt in den Pool der Anlage, wo man natürlich auch mit Salz aus dem Toten Meer (von *Dead Sea Mud Body Wrap* bis Olivenöl & Salz-Peeling) gepflegt wird. Das Resort selbst wurde mit regionalen Materialien erbaut, sodass einer ganzheitlichen Erholung rein gar nichts im Weg steht.

Avec les lumières de Jérusalem dans le lointain et l'air salé de la mer Morte toute proche, le cadre de cette oasis est déjà fascinant en soi. Il ne faut pas manquer de photographier le panneau indiquant que l'on se trouve ici à 260 mètres en dessous du niveau de la mer. Entre les sources thermales chaudes et la mer intérieure sur laquelle on se laisse flotter, toute une panoplie de maillots de bain est nécessaire à l'hôtel Evason Ma'In.

Rien d'étonnant donc à ce que le Six Senses Spa représente le nec plus ultra en matière de spa. L'une des nombreuses cascades dévale directement dans la piscine de l'établissement, lequel propose bien sûr aussi des soins à base de sel de la mer Morte (du peeling à la vase de la mer Morte à celui à l'huile d'olive et au sel). Le complexe hôtelier ayant été construit avec des matériaux de la région, la détente absolue est garantie.

LOCATION
30 km/19 miles southwest of the "mosaic city" of Madaba. Amman airport is 60 minutes away by car. It's a 30-minute drive to the Dead Sea and 3 hours to Petra

RATES
Rooms from $195, suites from $365, breakfast included

ROOMS
78 rooms and 19 suites

STYLE
The outside says remote fortress, the interiors call to mind Bedouin festive traditions

FOOD
Jordanian, Arabian, international—served in unusual settings such as on top of a cliff and made with homegrown organic vegetables

X FACTOR
The clifftop restaurant from which diners can enjoy far-reaching views across the rocky landscape

BOOK TO PACK
"Cities of Salt" by Abdelrahman Munif

LAGE
30 km südwestlich der „Mosaikstadt" Madaba. Die Fahrt vom Flughafen Amman dauert 60 Minuten, das Tote Meer ist 30 Minuten entfernt, bis nach Petra fährt man 3 Stunden

PREISE
Zimmer ab 145 €, Suiten ab 270 €, inklusive Frühstück

ZIMMER
78 Zimmer und 19 Suiten

STIL
Außen entlegene Festung, innen mit Anklängen an die Festkultur der Beduinen

KÜCHE
Jordanisch, arabisch und international – spektakulär inszeniert wie in einem Beduinenzelt oder mit Panoramablick; Gemüse aus dem Biogarten

X-FAKTOR
Auf Wunsch wird das Abendessen auf einer Klippe serviert, von der aus man weit über das felsige Land schauen kann

BUCH ZUM ORT
„Salzstädte" von Abdalrachman Munif

SITUATION
À 30 km au sud-ouest de Madaba, la « ville des mosaïques » ; le transfert depuis l'aéroport d'Amman dure 1 heure, la mer Morte est à 30 minutes et Petra à 3 heures de voiture

PRIX
Chambres à partir de 145 €, suites à partir de 270 €, petit déjeuner compris

CHAMBRES
78 chambres et 19 suites

STYLE
À l'extérieur, forteresse isolée ; à l'intérieur, réminiscences de la culture festive bédouine

RESTAURATION
Cuisine jordanienne, arabe et internationale, sous une tente bédouine ou avec vue panoramique sur la mer Morte ; légumes du potager bio

LE « PETIT PLUS »
Le restaurant sert le dîner sur un promontoire rocheux d'où l'on peut admirer le paysage rocailleux à perte de vue

LIVRE À EMPORTER
« Villes de sel » d'Abdul Rahman Mounif

COTTAR'S
1920s SAFARI CAMP
KENYA

Mara River ~ Masai Mara National Reserve ~ Narok ~ Kenya
Telephone +25 4770 564 911
info@cottarsafaris.com
www.cottars.com/cottars-1920s-camp

Staying at Cottar's Camp is rather like starring in a Louis Vuitton ad, thanks to interiors that put older examples of the manufacturer's suitcases to good use as furniture, pairing them with English antiques, Oriental carpets, and tribal art. It's a feeling further enhanced by a vintage charm that is entirely in keeping with the Cottar story—the family has been organizing safaris since 1919.

The camp itself comprises 10 separate tents, some featuring fireplaces and all offering romantic safari grandeur. It is located close to the Serengeti National Park and the Masai Mara reserve, both of which can be visited on the game drives that are the camp's raison d'être. After the extraordinary experiences of the day, guests can unwind in contemporary fashion with a dip in the recently added pool or take a soak in the outdoor safari bath, a canvas tub affording panoramic views of the savanna.

Als Star in einer Anzeige von Louis Vuitton fühlt man sich in diesem Safari-Camp, und das liegt nicht nur daran, dass alte Koffermodelle dieses Herstellers hier – neben englischen Antiquitäten, Orientteppichen und Stammeskunst – effektvoll als Mobiliar dienen. Es liegt allgemein am Vintage-Charme, der in Cottar's Camp so lebendig geblieben wie wohlverdient ist, schließlich werden von dieser Familie seit 1919 Safaris arrangiert.

Das Camp besteht aus zehn Zelten, einige davon mit eigenem offenem Kamin, alle mit romantischer Großwild-Grandezza eingerichtet. Der Serengeti National Park und ein Reservat der Masai, das sind die nahen Ziele für die individuellen Tagesfahrten, deretwegen man das Camp besucht. Nach diesen grandiosen Eindrücken lockt ein ziemlich neuzeitliches Vergnügen – es gibt nämlich mittlerweile auch einen Pool auf dem Gelände. Und als besonderes Angebot das Safari-Bad in einer Wanne aus Canvas, platziert mit Blick auf die Savanne.

Dans ce campement de safari, chaque hôte a l'impression d'être la vedette d'une publicité pour Louis Vuitton, non seulement parce que des malles anciennes de ce fabricant meublent les tentes aux côtés d'antiquités anglaises, de tapis d'Orient et d'objets d'art ethniques. Cela tient surtout au charme vintage que l'on a su préserver au Cottar's Camp, où la famille propriétaire organise des safaris depuis 1919.

Le campement comprend dix tentes dont certaines ont une cheminée. Toutes sont aménagées dans l'esprit des grands safaris d'autrefois. Le parc national du Serengeti et une réserve masaï sont les proches destinations des excursions personnalisées que le Cottar's Camp propose tous les jours. Après avoir fait le plein d'émotions, on peut s'adonner à un plaisir beaucoup plus moderne, car une piscine a été construite sur place. Et en prime, on peut prendre un bain « safari » dans une baignoire en toile offrant une vue sur la savane.

LOCATION
In the Serengeti, just a stone's throw from the Masai Mara reserve

RATES
Tents from $530 per person per night with full board; minimum stay of 2 nights

ROOMS
5 two-person tents, 4 tent suites for families, and 1 honeymoon tent; VIPs and large clans can rent the private house, which has 5 en suite bedrooms and more modern decors

STYLE
Uncluttered interiors with safari nostalgia

FOOD
International high-end bush cuisine

X FACTOR
For the more intrepid traveler, the most convenient way to arrive is by light aircraft—the camp has its own private airstrip, albeit a rather narrow one!

BOOKS TO PACK
"The Flame Trees of Thika" by Elspeth Huxley and "Out of Africa" by Karen Blixen

LAGE
In der Serengeti, nur einen Steinwurf vom Naturschutzgebiet Masai Mara entfernt

PREISE
Ab 405 € pro Person und Nacht, inklusive Vollpension; Mindestaufenthalt 2 Nächte

ZIMMER
5 Zwei-Personen-Zelte, 4 Zelt-Suiten für Familien und 1 Zelt für Flitterwöchner; VIPs und Clans mieten das moderner eingerichtete Private House mit 5 Schlafzimmern & Bädern

STIL
Aufgeräumte Safari-Nostalgie

KÜCHE
Internationale High-End-Buschküche

X-FAKTOR
Wer es bequem mag und furchtlos ist, kann auch mit dem Sportflugzeug anreisen – das Camp hat eine eigene (allerdings reichlich schmale!) Landepiste

BUCH ZUM ORT
„Jenseits von Afrika" von Karen Blixen

SITUATION
Dans le Serengeti, à proximité de la réserve nationale du Masai Mara

PRIX
À partir de 405 € par personne et par nuit en pension complète (séjour de 2 nuits minimum)

CHAMBRES
5 tentes 2 places, 4 tentes-suites pour les familles et 1 tente pour les jeunes mariés ; possibilité de louer en bloc la villa moderne, dotée de 5 chambres avec salle de bains

STYLE
Nostalgie des safaris empreinte de légèreté

RESTAURATION
Cuisine de brousse internationale de luxe

LE «PETIT PLUS»
Les amateurs de confort les plus hardis pourront arriver en avion de tourisme, car le campement a sa propre piste d'atterrissage (certes étroite !)

LIVRE À EMPORTER
«La Ferme africaine» de Karen Blixen

MSAMBWENI BEACH HOUSE
KENYA

P.O. Box 51 ~ 80404 Msambweni ~ Kenya
Telephone +25 420 357 7093
info@msambweni-beach-house.com
www.msambweni-beach-house.com

This luxurious, Lamu-style hideaway in Msambweni, the "land of the sable antelope," was opened in 2007 by the brothers Frederik and Filip Vanderhoeven. Its location on a clifftop above a white sandy beach is practically predestined for an infinity pool, and this one certainly lives up to its name, creating the illusion that you could simply float on out into the Indian Ocean.

Inside the hotel's suites and villas, white is the dominant theme, with Arabian influences providing characterful accents. Ornate alcoves, silk cushions set against whitewashed walls, brass lamps, and unbleached cotton recliners thus line the route to the private beach, where guests can spend cocktail hour watching the dramatic sunset. If, that is, they can tear themselves away from the recently opened spa.

In Msambweni, dem „Land der Rappenantilope", haben die Brüder Frederik und Filip Vanderhoeven 2007 dieses luxuriöse, im Lamu-Stil erbaute Hideaway eröffnet. Die Lage auf einer Klippe oberhalb des weißen Sandstrands war prädestiniert für einen Endlos-Pool, der seinem Namen wirklich gerecht wird: Man treibt scheinbar in den Indischen Ozean hinaus.

Die vornehmlich in Weiß gehaltenen Suiten und Villen setzen ihre Glanzpunkte vor allem mit den arabischen Einflüssen. Kunstvoll gemauerte Nischen, Seidenkissen auf gekalkten Mauern, Messinglaternen und Liegen aus ungebleichter Baumwolle säumen den Weg zum Privatstrand, wo man zur Cocktailstunde einen überaus eindrucksvollen Sonnenuntergang erleben kann. Sofern man nicht doch lieber im kürzlich eröffneten Spa liegt.

C'est à Msambweni, le «pays de l'hippotrague noir», que les frères Frederik et Filip Vanderhoeven ont ouvert en 2007 cette retraite luxueuse, construite dans le style de l'île de Lamu. Surplombant la plage de sable blanc, ce cadre était prédestiné pour accueillir une piscine à débordement, donnant véritablement l'impression de dériver dans l'océan Indien.

Les suites et les villas où le blanc domine sont magnifiquement ponctuées d'éléments arabes: niches superbement maçonnées, coussins de soie posés sur des murets blanchis à la chaux, suspensions en laiton et chaises longues en coton écru jalonnent le chemin qui mène à la plage privée d'où l'on peut profiter d'un impressionnant coucher de soleil à l'heure de l'apéritif. À moins que l'on préfère s'offrir une supplémentaire dans le spa récemment inauguré.

LOCATION
At the southern end of Kenya's coast, near the Tanzanian border; 60 km/37 miles south of Mombasa airport

RATES
Suites from $340, villas from $484; prices per person per night include full board

ROOMS
3 suites in the main house, 1 tent suite, and 3 villas with private pools

STYLE
Moorish villa with prime seafront location

FOOD
Belgian and French dishes are offered alongside Swahili specialties. For an even more exclusive experience, the hotel offers private lunches on the nearby sandbank

X FACTOR
The rippling waves: Be it in the spa or at the pool, the ocean is always right beside you

BOOK TO PACK
"A Grain of Wheat" by Ngũgĩ wa Thiong'o

LAGE
An der Südküste Kenias nahe der Grenze zu Tansania, 60 km südlich des Flughafens von Mombasa

PREISE
Suite ab 250 €, Villa ab 360 €, pro Person und Nacht, inklusive Vollpension

ZIMMER
3 Suiten im Haupthaus, 1 Zelt-Suite, 3 Villen mit eigenem Pool

STIL
Maurische Villa in Bestlage am Meer

KÜCHE
Neben Swahili-Spezialitäten wird hier auch belgische und französische Küche serviert. Besonders exklusiv: ein privates Dinner auf der nahegelegenen Sandbank

X-FAKTOR
Das Wellenrauschen. Ob im Spa oder am Pool, der Ozean scheint immer zum Greifen nah

BUCH ZUM ORT
„Freiheit mit gesenktem Kopf" von Ngũgĩ wa Thiong'o

SITUATION
Sur la côte sud du Kenya près de la frontière tanzanienne, à 60 km au sud de l'aéroport de Mombasa

PRIX
Suites à partir de 250 €, villas à partir de 360 €, par personne et par nuit en pension complète

CHAMBRES
3 suites dans le bâtiment principal, 1 tente-suite, 3 villas avec piscine privée

STYLE
Villa mauresque idéalement située en bord de mer

RESTAURATION
Outre des spécialités de la cuisine swahili, le restaurant propose des plats belges et français. Le fin du fin : un dîner privé sur un banc de sable

LE «PETIT PLUS»
Le roulement des vagues. Que l'on soit dans le spa ou à la piscine, l'océan Indien semble toujours tout près

LIVRE À EMPORTER
«Pétales de sang» de Ngũgĩ wa Thiong'o

CONDESA DF
MEXICO

Avenida Veracruz N. 102 ~ Colonia Condesa ~ 06700 Mexico City, D.F. ~ Mexico
Telephone +52 55 5241 2600 ~ Fax +52 55 5241 2601
contact@condesadf.com
www.condesadf.com

Situated in the heart of Mexico City is the Condesa DF, one of the metropolis's few chic hotels. Originally built in 1928 as an apartment block, this triangular building was converted into a hip hotel in 2005 by architect Javier Sanchez and star interior designer India Mahdavi of Paris.

The ethos isn't just about style, however; the hotel has identified QIPs ("Quiet Important People") as their key target group. Here, these aficionados of good but unintrusive service benefit from free Wi-Fi Internet access in surroundings entirely free from brash extravagance. At dusk, guests can enjoy the hotel's roof terrace (quietly, of course) and admire the fabulous views across the largely undesigned expanses of Mexico City.

Mitten in der lebhaften Metropole Mexico City liegt mit dem Condesa DF eines der wenigen urban-schicken Hotels der Stadt. Schon 1928 wurde dieses Gebäude mit triangelförmigem Grundriss als Apartmentblock entworfen; 2005 verwandelten es der Architekt Javier Sanchez und die Pariser Interiorgröße India Mahdavi in eine hippe Adresse.

Es geht aber nicht nur um schickes Design, schließlich hat man hier die QIPs (*Quiet Important People*) als neue Zielgruppe entdeckt. Diesen Liebhabern des diskreten guten Service soll der Aufenthalt mit so sinnvollen Einrichtungen wie freiem WiFi-Internetzugang so angenehm wie möglich gemacht werden – dümmlicher Protz bleibt draußen. Wenn es dämmert, wird die Dachterrasse zum Hotspot – dank eines wunderbaren Blicks über das komplett undesignte Mexico City. Aber nicht vergessen: *Quiet, please!*

En plein cœur de la trépidante métropole de Mexico se trouve l'un des rares hôtels de style urbain chic de la ville. Dès sa conception en 1928, ce bâtiment de forme triangulaire avait été pensé comme un immeuble collectif. En 2005, l'architecte Javier Sánchez et la décoratrice d'intérieur parisienne India Mahdavi en ont fait une adresse branchée.

Le design chic n'est pas forcément l'essentiel ici. On cible en effet une nouvelle clientèle, les QIP (Quiet Important People). Des équipements très utiles, comme le libre accès à Internet en WiFi, agrémentent au mieux le séjour de ces adeptes du service discret et de qualité – Frimeurs s'abstenir! Quand la nuit tombe, on vient bien sûr profiter du toit-terrasse (en respectant le calme exigé!), avec une vue splendide sur un Mexico resté dans son jus.

LOCATION
In the east of Mexico City, not far from Bosque de Chapultepec, the capital's largest park

RATES
Rooms from $175, suites from $245, breakfast not included

ROOMS
24 rooms and 16 suites with furniture by India Mahdavi, Patricia Urquiola, and Norman Cherner. Be sure to book a room with a balcony

STYLE
Creative hot spot in the heart of the megacity

FOOD
The patio restaurant serves innovative Mexican dishes; the rooftop bar is famed for its sushi

X FACTOR
Channel 84 of the in-house TV system shows art performances 24 hours a day

BOOK TO PACK
"Visit to Don Otavio" by Sybille Bedford

LAGE
Im Osten von Mexico City unweit des Chapultepec-Parks, dem größten der Stadt

PREISE
Zimmer ab 130 €, Suiten ab 180 €, ohne Frühstück

ZIMMER
24 Zimmer und 16 Suiten mit Möbeln von India Mahdavi, Patricia Urquiola und Norman Cherner. Man sollte unbedingt einen Raum mit Balkon buchen!

STIL
Kreativ-Biotop in der Megacity

KÜCHE
Das Restaurant im Patio serviert innovative mexikanische Gerichte, die Bar auf dem Dach stadtbekannt gutes Sushi

X-FAKTOR
Auf Kanal 84 im Hotelfernsehen laufen 24 Stunden lang Kunstperformances

BUCH ZUM ORT
„Zu Besuch bei Don Otavio" von Sybille Bedford

SITUATION
Dans les quartiers est de Mexico, non loin du parc Chapultepec, le plus grand parc de la ville

PRIX
Chambres à partir de 130 €, suites à partir de 180 €, petit déjeuner non compris

CHAMBRES
24 chambres et 16 suites meublées par India Mahdavi, Patricia Urquiola et Norman Cherner. Les chambres avec balcon sont un must!

STYLE
Biotope créatif en pleine mégapole

RESTAURATION
Le restaurant du patio sert de la cuisine mexicaine innovante, le bar sur le toit est réputé dans toute la ville pour ses sushis

LE «PETIT PLUS»
Le canal 84 de la télévision de l'hôtel diffuse des performances artistiques 24 heures sur 24

LIVRE À EMPORTER
«Visite à Don Otavio» de Sybille Bedford

ENDÉMICO
MEXICO

Carretera Tecate Ensenada Km 75, Valle de Guadalupe
Ensenada, Baja California ~ Mexico
Telephone +52 646 155 27 75
contact@hotelendemico.com
www.hotelendemico.com

Scattered loosely across the hillside as if they'd tumbled from the back of a speeding truck, the twenty cabins of Endémico in Valle de Guadalupe are raised up on stilts that make them look like individual lookout posts. The prospects thus afforded to guests are surprisingly attractive —the barren hills contrasting starkly with the carpet of grapevines covering the fertile valley floor.

The bottled results of the latter can be sampled on the terrace of your wooden cube—after a couple of glasses under the Mexican sun, you'll be even more taken with this experimental hotel. Its steel-and-wood eco-cabins are both functional and aesthetic, the main building houses a bar and a restaurant, and there's also a glorious pool with far-reaching views. Wind and weather, it is hoped, will soon age the facades, ensuring they are even better integrated into the landscape—thus making this the perfect hideaway for travelers who like to blend in.

Als hätte ein Laster hier in den Hügeln des Valle de Guadalupe seine Ladung verloren, so verstreut stehen die 20 Holzkabinen im Gelände. Jede Kabine ist auf ihren Stelzenfüßen ein eigener Aussichtsposten, wobei der Ausblick von diesen kargen Höhen überraschend bekömmlich ist – Weinstöcke bedecken den fruchtbaren Boden des gesamten Tals.

Was da heranreift, kann gleich auf der Holzterrasse vor dem Wohnwürfel verkostet werden, und spätestens beim zweiten Glas Wein unter der Sonne Mexikos wird man zugeben müssen, dass dieses Hotelexperiment äußerst zufriedenstellend verläuft. Das Eco-Design der kleinen Häuser aus Stahl und Holz ist ebenso funktional wie ansprechend, im Hauptgebäude warten Bar und Restaurant, und einen herrlichen Pool mit Fernsicht gibt's auch. Die Betreiber hoffen, dass Wind und Wetter die Fassaden der Kabinen bald verwittern lassen, damit sie perfekt mit der Umgebung verschmelzen. Zur Freude aller, die im Urlaub nicht auffallen möchten.

À la manière d'un chargement tombé d'un camion, les vingt cabanes de bois sont éparpillées dans les collines de la vallée de Guadalupe. Montées sur pilotis, ils offrent des points d'observation uniques sur le paysage. D'ailleurs, vu des hauteurs arides, le panorama est étonnamment amène: des pieds de vigne tapissent le sol fertile de la vallée.

Ce qui mûrit ici peut être aussitôt savouré sur la terrasse en bois du logement cubique. Et au deuxième verre de vin sous le soleil du Mexique, force est de reconnaître que cette expérience hôtelière est très réussie. L'éco-conception de ces maisonnettes de bois et de métal est aussi fonctionnelle que séduisante. Le bâtiment principal abrite un bar et un restaurant; il y a aussi une superbe piscine avec vue dégagée. Les hôteliers espèrent que les intempéries patineront les façades tant et si bien qu'elles se fondront dans le paysage, pour le plaisir de ceux qui veulent passer inaperçus en vacances.

LOCATION
145 km/90 miles from San Diego; in Mexico's "Valle de Guadalupe" wine-producing region

RATES
Rooms from $185

ROOMS
20 freestanding wooden huts, each with its own sundeck and stove

STYLE
Eco-minimalism with a desperado touch: lots of wood and steel, plus an Oscar Niemeyer-esque pool and straw bales for benches

FOOD
The restaurant serves local Mexican dishes, plus wines produced in the valley

X FACTOR
Each cabin's wooden deck comes with a traditional Mexican clay stove, allowing guests to enjoy a fireside glass of wine in the open air

BOOKS TO PACK
"The Burning Plain" by Juan Rulfo and "All the Pretty Horses" by Cormac McCarthy

LAGE
Im Weinanbaugebiet Valle de Guadalupe im Norden Mexikos, 145 km südlich von San Diego

PREISE
Zimmer ab 140 €

ZIMMER
20 freistehende Holzhäuschen mit Aussichts-deck und Feuerstelle

STIL
Öko-Minimalismus mit Desperado-Note: viel Holz und Stahl, aber auch ein Pool à la Oscar Niemeyer und Strohballen als Sitzbänke

KÜCHE
Das Restaurant serviert lokale mexikanische Gerichte, dazu Wein aus dem Tal

X-FAKTOR
Jede der Wohnkabinen hat einen Freisitz mit traditionellem mexikanischem Lehmofen – für moderne Lagerfeuerstimmung bei einem Glas Wein vor dem Zubettgehen

BÜCHER ZUM ORT
„Der Llano in Flammen" von Juan Rulfo und „All die schönen Pferde" von Cormac McCarthy

SITUATION
Dans la région viticole de la vallée de Guadalupe, dans le nord du Mexique, à 145 km au sud de San Diego

PRIX
Chambres à partir de 140 €

CHAMBRES
20 cabanes de bois indépendantes, avec terrasse en bois et foyer

STYLE
Minimalisme écologique avec une note *desperado*: bois et métal, mais aussi piscine à la Oscar Niemeyer et bottes de paille en guise de bancs

RESTAURATION
Le restaurant sert des plats mexicains régionaux accompagnés de vin de la vallée

LE «PETIT PLUS»
Chaque terrasse dispose d'un foyer traditionnel mexicain en argile permettant de déguster un verre de vin au coin du feu avant d'aller au lit

LIVRES À EMPORTER
«Le Llanos en flammes» de Juan Rulfo et «De si jolis chevaux» de Cormac McCarthy

"We are here to make people understand
that creativity is good for society …
We build experiences."

CARLOS COUTURIER AND MOISES MICHA, FOUNDERS OF ENDÉMICO

„Uns geht es darum, dass die Leute verstehen, wie gut Kreativität für
die Gesellschaft ist … Wir bauen neue Erfahrungen."

«Nous tenons à faire comprendre aux gens combien la créativité est bénéfique à la société…
Nous créons de nouvelles expériences.»

VERANA
MEXICO

Yelapa, Cabo Corrientes, Jalisco ~ Mexico
Telephone +1 310 455 2425
reservations@verana.com
www.verana.com

When a stylist and a film set designer develop a new hotel, there's a good chance the results will be pretty special. In fact, in the case of the Verana, opened by Heinz Legler and Veronique Lievre in the year 2000, even the journey there is spectacular: This hotel up above the Bay of Banderas can be reached only by boat, then it's a short mule ride up from the boat launch to this outpost of paradise.

Architecture and nature combine here beautifully. All the houses have private gardens, and their interiors, which are furnished with vintage pieces and George Nelson lamps, echo the colors of their surroundings. From guest accommodation to spa and poolside restaurant, everything at this jungle retreat is arranged to perfection—it could well be the finest scene Veronique has ever designed.

Wenn sich eine Stylistin und ein Filmset-Designer zusammen ein Hotel ausdenken, darf man sicher sein, dass es richtig was hermacht. Beim Verana, das Heinz Legler und Veronique Lievre Ende 2000 eröffneten, ist schon die Anfahrt spektakulär – die Hotelanlage im Dschungel über der Bucht von Banderas ist nur per Boot zu erreichen. Vom Anleger geht es mit Gepäckmaultieren das letzte Stück bergauf, dann hat man einen Außenposten des Paradieses erreicht.

Natur und Architektur harmonieren hier wahrlich filmreif. Jedes der kleinen Häuser hat einen privaten Garten; innen wiederholen sich die Farben der Umgebung, dazu kommen Vintage-Möbel und Leuchten von George Nelson. Keine Frage, hier sitzt jedes Stück am richtigen Platz. Das gilt auch für das Spa und das Restaurant am Pool – zusammen mit der eindrucksvollen Natur bestimmt die beste Kulisse, die Veronique je gestaltet hat.

Quand une styliste et un décorateur de cinéma s'associent pour créer un hôtel, on peut s'attendre à du grand art. L'accès au Verana, ouvert par Veronique Lievre et Heinz Legler en 2000, est déjà spectaculaire en soi. Situé dans la jungle surplombant la baie de Banderas, cet hôtel n'est accessible que par bateau. Et du débarcadère, on gravit avec des mulets de bât les derniers mètres qui mènent à cette antichambre du paradis.

Ici, la nature et l'architecture s'harmonisent comme dans un décor de cinéma. Chaque maisonnette a son jardin privé. Orné de meubles vintage et de luminaires de George Nelson, l'intérieur reflète les couleurs de l'environnement. Tout est ici parfaitement à sa place, ce qui vaut aussi pour le spa et le restaurant au bord de la piscine. Implanté dans une nature impressionnante, cet hôtel est certainement le plus beau décor jamais réalisé par Veronique.

LOCATION
48 km/30 miles south of Puerto Vallarta and accessible only by boat from Boca de Tomatlán (30 minutes). From the beach, it's a short walk through the jungle to the hotel; luggage is brought up by mule

RATES
Houses from $220, transfers included Minimum stay of 5 nights

HOUSES
8 houses sleeping 2 to 4 plus the V House sleeping up to 6

STYLE
Exclusive Bohemian jungle camp

FOOD
Creative Mexican cuisine served on the veranda or by the pool

X FACTOR
As if the jungle weren't enough, guests can also go whale-watching from here

BOOK TO PACK
"Like Water for Chocolate" by Laura Esquivel

LAGE
48 km südlich von Puerto Vallarta gelegen. Ab Boca de Tomatlán nur per Boot erreichbar (30 Minuten). Vom Strand aus wandert man ein Stück durch den Dschungel bis zum Hotel, das Gepäck wird auf demselben Weg von Maultieren transportiert

PREISE
Häuser ab 160 € inklusive Transfer, bei einem Mindestaufenthalt von 5 Nächten

HÄUSER
8 Häuser (2 bis 4 Gäste) und das V House (bis zu 6 Gäste)

STIL
Exklusives Boheme-Buschcamp

KÜCHE
Kreative mexikanische Menüs, serviert auf der Veranda und am Pool

X-FAKTOR
Es geht noch größer als Palmen: Auch zum *whale watching* kann man hier rausfahren

BUCH ZUM ORT
„Bittersüße Schokolade" von Laura Esquivel

SITUATION
À 48 km au sud de Puerto Vallarta. À partir de Boca de Tomatlán, accessible uniquement par bateau (30 minutes). Depuis la plage, il faut prévoir une petite marche à travers la jungle jusqu'à l'hôtel; des mulets portent les bagages

PRIX
Maisons à partir de 160 € la nuit, transfert inclus; séjour de 5 nuits minimum

MAISONS
8 maisons (2–4 personnes) et la V House (jusqu'à 6 personnes)

STYLE
Campement luxueux dans la jungle

RESTAURATION
Menus mexicains créatifs servis sur la véranda et au bord de la piscine

LE «PETIT PLUS»
Encore plus grandioses que les palmiers: les excursions en mer pour observer les baleines

LIVRE À EMPORTER
«Chocolat amer» de Laura Esquivel

LA MAMOUNIA
MOROCCO

Avenue Bab Jdid ~ 40040 Marrakech ~ Morocco
Telephone +212 524 388 600 ~ Fax +212 524 444 044
informations@mamounia.com
www.mamounia.com

This legend of a hotel has been reborn. Thanks to Jacques Garcia's exotic historicist makeover, La Mamounia now offers a gloriously grand welcome once more. Inspired by Arabian-Andalusian traditions and Berber handicrafts, the renowned Parisian decorator created a masterful mix of colors and forms that features sumptuous, specially commissioned mosaics, metalwork, and woodwork. The renovation took into account both the hotel's 90-year history and the requirements of today's high-end travelers, the addition of an Oriental vision of a spa completing the highly sensuous experience.

The luxury of the balconied suites, the magnificent architecture, the various pools and fountains, and the extensive grounds give La Mamounia a charm that even the most seasoned of travelers will find hard to resist.

Die Hotellegende lebt: Jacques Garcias exotischer Historismus hat das La Mamounia erneut zum Glänzen gebracht. Vom arabisch-andalusischen Stil und der Handwerkskunst der Berber befeuert, entwarf der Pariser Interiorstar ein koloristisches Meisterwerk und gab dafür jede Menge filigrane Mosaik-, Metall- und Holzarbeiten in Auftrag. Auf die 90-jährige Geschichte des Hotels wurde dabei ebenso Rücksicht genommen wie auf die Ansprüche heutiger Luxusreisender; so vervollständigt nun eine Orientalismus-Fantasie von einem Spa das sinnliche Gesamterlebnis.

Der Komfort der Suiten mit Balkon, die Farben- und Formenpracht der arabischen Kultur, die vielen Wasserbecken und Springbrunnen und nicht zuletzt der große Park geben dem Mamounia heute eine Strahlkraft, der sich auch Verwöhnte nicht entziehen können.

L'hôtel La Mamounia, que Jacques Garcia a revisité avec brio et un historicisme exotique, reste une légende vivante. Enthousiasmé par le style arabo-andalou et l'artisanat d'art berbère, ce grand architecte décorateur parisien a créé un chef-d'œuvre haut en couleur, avec des mosaïques et des ouvrages en métal et en bois d'une grande finesse. Et il a su concilier les quatre-vingt-dix années d'existence de l'hôtel et l'aspiration au luxe des voyageurs d'aujourd'hui. C'est ainsi qu'un spa rappelant un tableau orientaliste vient parfaire l'expérience sensuelle que réserve un séjour dans ces lieux.

Le confort des suites avec balcon, la beauté des couleurs et des formes de la culture arabe, les nombreux bassins et fontaines, ainsi que le grand parc, confèrent désormais à La Mamounia un rayonnement auquel même ceux qui sont habitués au luxe ne peuvent rester indifférents.

LOCATION
Situated in the medina, a 15-minute drive from Marrakech airport

RATES
Rooms from $735, suites from $1,100, riads from $12,150, breakfast not included

ROOMS
136 rooms, 71 suites, and 3 riads

STYLE
Fairy-tale Oriental palace that every hotel connoisseur should visit at least once

FOOD
Four hotel restaurants serving Moroccan, French, and Italian dishes

X FACTOR
The 700 orange trees on the grounds that make for a truly fragrant backdrop. These magnificent gardens were a wedding gift from a sultan, clearly a man who wanted to leave a legacy, to his son and heir

BOOK TO PACK
"The Voices of Marrakesh" by Elias Canetti

LAGE
In der Medina, 15 Autominuten vom Flughafen Marrakesch entfernt

PREISE
Zimmer ab 540 €, Suiten ab 810 €, Riad ab 8990 €, ohne Frühstück

ZIMMER
136 Zimmer, 71 Suiten und 3 Riads

STIL
Märchenhafter Orientpalast, den jeder Hotel-liebhaber einmal besucht haben sollte

KÜCHE
Die 4 Restaurants des Hauses servieren marok-kanische, französische und italienische Speisen

X-FAKTOR
Der Park mit 700 Orangenbäumen – viel aroma-tischer als dort kann Frische-Luft-Schnappen nicht sein. Der prächtige Garten war einst das Hochzeitsgeschenk eines zukunftsbewussten Sultans an seinen Sohn

BUCH ZUM ORT
„Die Stimmen von Marrakesch" von Elias Canetti

SITUATION
Dans la médina, à 15 minutes en voiture de l'aéroport de Marrakech

PRIX
Chambres à partir de 540 €, suites à partir de 810 €, riads à partir de 8 990 €, petit déjeuner non compris

CHAMBRES
136 chambres, 71 suites et 3 riads

STYLE
Palais oriental fabuleux où tout amateur d'hôtels devrait séjourner au moins une fois

RESTAURATION
Les quatre restaurants de l'établissement pro-posent des plats marocains, français et italiens

LE « PETIT PLUS »
Le parc planté de 700 orangers (difficile de respirer ailleurs un air frais qui embaume à ce point). Le sompteux jardin est le cadeau de mariage qu'un sultan soucieux de l'avenir a offert à son fils

LIVRE À EMPORTER
« Les Voix de Marrakech » d'Elias Canetti

"When La Mamounia opened in 1923, it became
Marrakech's gold standard for luxury and debauchery
among jet-setters and heads of state."

DAVID FARLEY, *THE NEW YORK TIMES*

„Als das La Mamounia 1923 eröffnete, wurde es für Weltreisende wie Staatschefs
der Goldstandard für ausschweifendes Luxusleben."

« Quand La Mamounia a ouvert ses portes en 1923, il est devenu la référence absolue en matière
de luxe et d'excès pour les voyageurs cosmopolites et les chefs d'État. »

NORD-PINUS TANGER
MOROCCO

11, Rue du Ryad Sultan Kasbah ~ Tangier ~ Morocco
Telephone +212 661 228 140
info@nord-pinus-tanger.com
www.hotel-nord-pinus-tanger.com

For those wanting to explore the multicultural vibe of Tangier and its intellectual links to Europe, the Nord-Pinus is the ideal base. Tile, leather, bronze, marble, cedarwood—the materials exude an authentic Moroccan atmosphere of the kind that has long drawn artists to this historic place.

Here, Anne Igou, who also owns the Grand Hôtel Nord-Pinus in Arles, has created interiors that combine the antique with the modern, mix Moroccan and Indian influences, and juxtapose colorful glass with black-and-white photos by Peter Lindbergh. There are also far-reaching views of the ocean, while the fish in the restaurant is delivered fresh from the harbor.

After the meal, guests can explore the narrow streets of the medina, which is right on the hotel doorstep. It pays to be back by sundown, though—that's when the roof terrace really comes into its own.

Wer dem multikulturellen Flair Tangers und seiner intellektuellen Verknüpfung mit Europa nachspüren möchte, wird dafür keinen besseren Ausgangsort finden als das Hotel Nord-Pinus. Kacheln, Leder, Bronze, Marmor, Zedernholz – die verwendeten Werkstoffe beschwören ein ganz authentisches Marokko und erklären die Sehnsucht so vieler Künstler nach diesem Ort.

Für die Ausstattung mischte Anne Igou (ihr gehört auch das Grandhotel Nord-Pinus in Arles) Antikes und Modernes, Marokkanisches und Indisches, buntes Glas und Schwarz-Weiß-Fotos von Peter Lindbergh. Die Terrassen bieten einen weiten Blick ins Blaue, und der Fisch im Restaurant kommt direkt vom Hafen. Abends streift man durch die verwinkelten Gassen – der historische Stadtkern beginnt direkt vor der Hoteltür. Im letzten Licht des Tages sollte man aber wieder zurück sein, denn dann ist es auf der Dachterrasse des Hotels am schönsten.

Pour s'imprégner de l'atmosphère multiculturelle de Tanger et de ses liens intellectuels avec l'Europe, il n'est pas de meilleur endroit que l'hôtel Nord-Pinus. Les carrelages, le cuir, le bronze, le marbre et le bois de cèdre, tous ces matériaux lui confèrent un charme marocain authentique et justifient la nostalgie que le lieu engendre chez tant d'artistes.

Anne Igou, qui possède également le Grand Hôtel Nord-Pinus en Arles, marie ici l'ancien et le moderne, le marocain et l'indien, le verre coloré et les photos en noir et blanc de Peter Lindbergh. Vue des terrasses, l'immensité bleue est magnifique, et le poisson du restaurant vient directement du port. Le soir, on déambule dans les rues tortueuses, car l'hôtel donne sur le quartier historique de la ville, mais on ne saurait trop recommander d'être de retour à la nuit tombée pour profiter du plus beau point de vue depuis le toit-terrasse de l'hôtel.

HOTEL
NORD-PINUS
RIAD SULTAN

LOCATION
This former pasha's palace sits at the highest point of the medina, 12 km/7 miles to the east of the airport

RATES
Double rooms from $260, suites from $330, small house from $500, breakfast included

ROOMS
1 room, 4 suites, and a small house

STYLE
Restored riad with beautiful tiles and impressive French flair

FOOD
The pergola-covered restaurant serves delicious Moroccan cuisine, featuring fresh seafood, vegetables, and fruits from the kasbah

X FACTOR
The massages with exclusive oils from the Ourika Valley

BOOKS TO PACK
"The Sheltering Sky" by Paul Bowles and "For Bread Alone" by Mohamed Choukri

LAGE
Der einstige Pascha-Palast thront auf dem höchsten Punkt der Altstadt, 12 km östlich des Flughafens von Tanger

PREISE
Doppelzimmer ab 190 €, Suiten ab 240 €, kleines Haus ab 360 €, inklusive Frühstück

ZIMMER
1 Zimmer, 4 Suiten sowie 1 kleines Haus

STIL
Restauriertes Riad mit wunderbaren Fliesen und beeindruckendem französischem Flair

KÜCHE
Im Restaurant mit Pergola stehen köstliche marokkanische Gerichte auf der Karte; Meeresfrüchte, Gemüse und Obst kommen frisch vom Stadtmarkt

X-FAKTOR
Die Massagen mit exklusiven Ölen aus dem Ourika-Tal

BÜCHER ZUM ORT
„Himmel über der Wüste" von Paul Bowles und „Das nackte Brot" von Mohamed Choukri

SITUATION
L'ancienne maison du pacha domine la casbah, à 12 km à l'est de l'aéroport de Tanger

PRIX
Chambre double à partir de 190 €, suites à partir de 240 €, maisonnette à partir de 360 €, petit déjeuner compris

CHAMBRES
1 chambre, 4 suites et 1 maisonnette

STYLE
Riad restauré avec des carrelages splendides et un charme français éblouissant

RESTAURANT
Le restaurant avec pergola propose de succulents plats marocains. Les fruits de mer, les légumes et les fruits viennent tout droit du marché

LE «PETIT PLUS»
Les massages aux huiles essentielles de la vallée de l'Ourika

LIVRES À EMPORTER
«Un thé au Sahara» de Paul Bowles et «Le Pain nu» de Mohamed Choukri

SELMAN MARRAKECH
MOROCCO

Km 5 route d'Amizmiz ~ 40160 Marrakech ~ Morocco
Telephone +212 524 45 96 00 ~ Fax +212 524 38 62 03
info@selman-marrakech.com
www.selman-marrakech.com

An oasis on the edge of the Atlas Mountains, the Selman is the realization of one Moroccan couple's dream of a hotel. Saida and Abdeslam Bennani Smires had always been passionate about luxury and beautiful horses. Now, with the aid of architect and interior designer Jacques Garcia, they have combined the two to create a spectacular setting for both guest and beast.

The heart of this Moorish palace is an enormous pool that not only offers palm tree reflections along its 260-foot length but also provides an ideal catwalk for bikini models. Elsewhere, beauties of a rather different kind can be found—namely, in the paddocks of the hotel's Arabian stallions. These magnificent animals are deeply rooted in Moroccan culture—as is first-rate hospitality of the kind guests enjoy here throughout their stay.

Eine Oase am Rande des Atlas-Gebirges, so sieht der Hotel gewordene Traum eines marokkanischen Ehepaares aus. Saida und Abdeslam Bennani Smires hatten seit jeher eine Leidenschaft für Luxus und schöne Pferde; gemeinsam mit dem Architekten Jacques Garcia schufen sie deshalb mit dem Selman eine märchenhafte Anlage für Mensch und Tier.

Mittelpunkt des maurischen Palastes ist ein Pool von spektakulären Ausmaßen. Auf 80 Metern Länge spiegeln sich dort nicht nur die Palmen, das lange Becken gibt auch einen exzellenten Laufsteg für Bikini-Models ab. Schönheiten ganz anderer Art lassen sich im Park rund um die Anlage beobachten, wo majestätische Araberhengste ihren Auslauf haben. Die edlen Tiere sind fest in der marokkanischen Kultur verwurzelt – übrigens genauso wie die vortreffliche Gastfreundschaft, die man hier in vollen Zügen genießen kann.

Cet hôtel, semblable à une oasis située au pied de l'Atlas, est le rêve devenu réalité d'un couple marocain. Depuis toujours, Saida et Abdeslam Bennani Smires sont des passionnés de luxe et de beaux chevaux. Avec l'architecte Jacques Garcia, ils ont fait du Selman un lieu fabuleux réunissant hommes et chevaux.

Une piscine aux dimensions spectaculaires constitue le cœur de ce palais mauresque. Ses 80 mètres de longueur ne reflètent pas seulement les palmiers. Le long bassin offre aussi un cadre idéal pour les défilés de bikinis. Et dans le parc qui entoure l'hôtel, on peut admirer des beautés d'une autre nature : les majestueux pur-sang arabes dans leur enclos. Ces nobles animaux sont très ancrés dans la culture arabe, au même titre que le grand sens de l'hospitalité que l'on ressent d'emblée en ces lieux.

LOCATION
Within sight of the Atlas Mountains, a 10-minute drive from Marrakech airport

RATES
Rooms from $445, breakfast included

ROOMS
56 rooms and suites, plus 5 riads

STYLE
Magnificent residence with stables in the Arabian-Andalusian tradition

FOOD
In addition to the Selman Restaurant, there's Le Pavillon, the elegant Selman Bar, and a particularly lovely pool bar

X FACTOR
Besides views that will capture the heart of any horse aficionado, the main attraction is the hotel's location: Here, guests can enjoy truly peaceful nights and yet are just a few minutes' drive from the medina

BOOKS TO PACK
"White Gold" by Giles Milton and "The Sacred Night" by Tahar Ben Jelloun

LAGE
Mit Blick auf das Atlas-Gebirge, 10 Autominuten vom Flughafen Marrakech entfernt

PREISE
Zimmer ab 330 €, inklusive Frühstück

ZIMMER
56 Zimmer und Suiten sowie 5 Riads

STIL
Prachtvolles Gestüt nach arabisch-andalusi-schem Vorbild

KÜCHE
Außer dem Selman Restaurant erwarten einen Le Pavillon, die elegante Selman Bar und eine besonders schöne Pool-Bar

X-FAKTOR
Neben den paradiesischen Aussichten für Pferdeliebhaber überzeugt vor allem die Lage des Hotels: Hier schläft man in vollkommener Ruhe und residiert dennoch nur wenige Auto-minuten von der Medina

BÜCHER ZUM ORT
„Weißes Gold" von Giles Milton und „Die Nacht der Unschuld" von Tahar Ben Jelloun

SITUATION
Vue sur l'Atlas, à 10 minutes en voiture de l'aéroport de Marrakech

PRIX
Chambres à partir de 330 €, petit déjeuner compris

CHAMBRES
56 chambres et suites ainsi que 5 riads

STYLE
Haras somptueux inspiré des modèles arabo-andalous

RESTAURATION
Outre le Selman Restaurant, il y a aussi Le Pavillon, l'élégant Selman Bar et le splendide pool-bar

LE «PETIT PLUS»
Cadre paradisiaque pour les passionnés de chevaux, cet hôtel jouit avant tout d'une situation privilégiée: on y dort dans le calme absolu tout en résidant à quelques minutes en voiture de la médina

LIVRES À EMPORTER
«Captifs en Barbarie» de Giles Milton et «La Nuit sacrée» de Tahar Ben Jelloun

"This is a live installation of the most beautiful breed
of horse in the world: the Arabian thoroughbred,
which is an integral part of our history and culture."

SAIDA AND ABDESLAM BENNANI SMIRES, OWNERS

„Dies ist eine Live-Installation der schönsten Pferderasse der Welt, die Teil unserer
Geschichte und unserer Kultur ist: des Arabervollbluts."

«Ceci est une présentation vivante de la plus belle race de chevaux du monde :
le pur-sang arabe, qui fait partie de notre histoire et de notre culture. »

JUVET LANDSKAPSHOTELL
NORWAY

Alstad ~ 6210 Valldal ~ Norway
Telephone +47 9503 2010
knut@juvet.com
www.juvet.com

To offer as immediate an experience of the Norwegian countryside's raw beauty as possible—that was the aim with this landscape hotel, created on one of the oldest farms in the Sunnmøre region by architects Jensen & Skodvin. Their solution, to drop seven small suites on stilts into the middle of the woods, is as dramatic as it is discreet. The cabins are finished in natural shades to avoid distracting from the colors of the surroundings, in which birch, aspen, and pine trees combine with river-sculpted rocks to create a picture-postcard panorama.

The accommodations are furnished in a simple Scandinavian style and existing historic buildings have been carefully modernized—the old sheep pen is now a lounge with an open fire, and the cowshed serves as a dining room for up to 50 guests. There's also a spa, spectacularly situated by a cold mountain stream, at which the views alone are enough to enhance your sense of well-being.

Die raue Schönheit der norwegischen Natur so direkt wie möglich erfahrbar zu machen, mit diesem Ziel überarbeitete das Architekturbüro Jensen & Skodvin einen der ältesten Bauernhöfe im Sunnmøre-Gebiet. Unaufgeregt spektakulär ist dabei ihre Idee geraten, sieben kleine Kuben als Suiten auf Stelzen in den Wald zu stellen. Sie sind in Naturtönen eingerichtet, damit die Farben der Landschaft die ganze Aufmerksamkeit der Gäste bekommen. Birken, Espen und Kiefern, dazu vom Flusswasser abgeschliffene Felsen – wie ein Gemälde liegt die Wildnis hinter den Fenstern.

Die Einrichtung ist von skandinavischer Schlichtheit, und die vorhandene, urige Bausubstanz wurde ebenfalls behutsam modernisiert. So ist der alte Schafstall jetzt eine Lounge mit offenem Kamin, während der Kuhstall als Speisezimmer für bis zu 50 Personen fungiert. Absolut berauschend ist das Spa: Direkt am eiskalten Gebirgsbach fühlt man sich schon nach ein paar Minuten nur durch die Aussicht ganzheitlich erfrischt.

C'est avec l'objectif de permettre une approche la plus directe possible de la beauté âpre de la nature norvégienne que le bureau d'architecture Jensen & Skodvin a transformé en hôtel l'une des plus anciennes fermes de la région de Sunnmøre. Il eut ainsi l'idée discrètement spectaculaire de disposer dans la forêt sept cubes sur pilotis. Ces suites sont aménagées dans des tons naturels, de sorte que les couleurs du paysage retiennent toute l'attention des hôtes. Bouleaux, trembles, pins et rochers érodés par la rivière : la nature sauvage compose un tableau derrière les baies vitrées.

L'aménagement est empreint de simplicité scandinave, et les bâtiments authentiques existants ont été modernisés avec soin. C'est ainsi que la bergerie est devenue un salon doté d'une cheminée et que l'étable est aujourd'hui une salle à manger susceptible d'accueillir 50 personnes. Situé tout près du torrent à l'eau glaciale, le spa est à couper le souffle : il suffit de quelques minutes pour s'imprégner de la fraîcheur du paysage.

LOCATION
Near Geiranger Fjord, 100 km/62 miles from Ålesund airport, 500 km/311 miles from Oslo

RATES
Suites from $265, breakfast included. 2-night minimum stay

ROOMS
7 freestanding suites grouped around a farmhouse that sleeps 20

STYLE
Historic meets futuristic in the wilderness

FOOD
The hotel was established on one of the area's oldest farms; its former stable is now a restaurant serving rustic Norwegian fare

X FACTOR
According to legend, anyone who drinks from the St. Olav spring will have eternal youth and health, an effect surely enhanced by bathing in its waters—as guests can at the Juvet spa

BOOK TO PACK
"Sophie's World" by Jostein Gaarder

LAGE
Unweit des Geirangerfjords, 100 km südöstlich des Flughafens Ålesund und 500 km von Oslo

PREISE
Suite ab 195 €, inklusive Frühstück, bei einem Mindestaufenthalt von 2 Nächten

ZIMMER
7 freistehende Suiten gruppieren sich um ein Farmhaus mit 20 Übernachtungsbetten

STIL
Die Wildnis & ich, futuristisch oder historisch

KÜCHE
Das Hotel entstand aus einem der ältesten Bauernhöfe der Gegend. Im ehemaligen Stall des Gehöfts serviert das Restaurant rustikale norwegische Gerichte

X-FAKTOR
Der Legende nach erlangen diejenigen, die aus der St.-Olav-Quelle trinken, ewige Jugend und Gesundheit. Sicher noch effektiver: Im Spa des Juvet-Hotels badet man sogar darin!

BUCH ZUM ORT
„Sofies Welt" von Jostein Gaarder

SITUATION
Près du fjord de Geiranger, à 100 km au sud de l'aéroport d'Ålesund et à 500 km d'Oslo

PRIX
À partir de 195 €, petit déjeuner compris, séjour de 2 nuits minimum

CHAMBRES
7 suites indépendantes disposées autour d'une ferme comptant 20 lits

STYLE
La nature et moi, futuriste ou historique

RESTAURATION
L'hôtel a été créé dans les murs d'une des plus vieilles fermes de la région. Dans l'ancienne étable, on sert de la cuisine paysanne norvégienne

LE « PETIT PLUS »
D'après la légende, boire à la source Saint Olaf est gage de jeunesse éternelle et de santé. Dans le spa de l'hôtel Juvet, on s'y baigne même, ce qui est certainement encore plus efficace !

LIVRE À EMPORTER
« Le Monde de Sophie » de Jostein Gaarder

"We are guests in nature, so it's
a good idea to build hotels that can be taken
away without leaving scars."

ARCHITEKT JAN OLAV JENSEN

„Wir sind Gäste in der Natur. Deshalb finden wir es gut, wenn ein Hotel wieder daraus
entfernt werden könnte, ohne Narben zu hinterlassen."

« Nous sommes les hôtes de la nature. Nous pensons donc que c'est une bonne chose
qu'un hôtel puisse un jour en être soustrait sans laisser de cicatrice. »

HOTEL MONASTERIO
PERU

Calle Palacio 136 ~ Plazoleta Nazarenas ~ Cuzco ~ Peru
Telephone +51 84 60 4000 ~ Fax +51 84 60 4001
perures.fits@orient-express.com
www.monasteriohotel.com

When it was built by the Incas in the 15th century, Cuzco was more than just a settlement—it was the center of the Incan universe. Today, the city is a UNESCO world heritage site and a place with a fascinating history.

For those wanting to explore that past, there's no better base than Hotel Monasterio. A former monastery dating back to 1592, it has now been turned into a beautiful live-in museum in which guests can wander cloisters that seem suspended in time and explore corridors that for centuries only monks had tread. The floor plans of the latter's cells are largely unchanged, though their spartan furnishings have given way to valuable antiques, polished mirrors, and crystal chandeliers. The rooms, of which no two are the same, are even equipped with an oxygen enrichment system to counter altitude sickness. In the morning, oxygen levels thus recharged, you'll be ready to explore the enchanting streets of Cuzco or to take a trip to Machu Picchu—the lost city of the Incas is three hours away by train.

Als die Inka im 15. Jahrhundert Cuzco errichteten, gründeten sie mehr als nur eine Stadt: Cuzco war das Zentrum ihrer Welt. Heute ist der Ort UNESCO-Weltkulturerbe, und wer in seine aufregende Geschichte tauchen möchte, zieht am besten ins Hotel Monasterio.

In den Mauern eines 1592 erbauten Klosters ist dort das schönste bewohnbare Museum Perus entstanden – man wandelt zeitenthoben durch Kreuzgänge und auf Wegen, die hunderte Jahre lang nur Mönche gegangen sind. Der Grundriss der einstigen Zellen wurde kaum verändert, deren spartanische Ausstattung schon. Kein Raum gleicht dem anderen; es gibt wertvolle Antiquitäten, blitzblank geputzte Spiegel und Kristallleuchter. Die Zimmer können sogar mit Sauerstoff angereichert werden, um der Höhenkrankheit vorzubeugen. Nach einer Nacht unter der Sauerstoffdusche kann man sich von der Magie Cuzcos verzaubern lassen oder einen Ausflug nach Machu Picchu unternehmen – die verlorene Stadt der Inka liegt eine dreistündige Zugfahrt entfernt.

En construisant Cuzco au XVe siècle, les Incas ont fondé plus qu'une ville: Cuzco était le centre de leur univers. Aujourd'hui, ce site est inscrit au patrimoine mondial de l'UNESCO. Pour se plonger dans sa riche histoire, le mieux est de séjourner au Monasterio.

Dans l'enceinte d'un monastère érigé en 1592 fut aménagé le plus beau musée habitable du Pérou. Comme projeté hors du temps, on déambule à travers les cloîtres et sur les chemins que seuls les moines ont empruntés pendant des siècles. Le plan des cellules a été à peine modifié, contrairement à leur intérieur autrefois spartiate. Toutes différentes, les pièces abritent des antiquités précieuses, des miroirs impeccables et des luminaires de cristal. Les chambres peuvent même être alimentées en oxygène pour prévenir le mal des montagnes. Après une nuit sous la «douche à oxygène», on peut se laisser envoûter par la magie de Cuzco ou bien partir en excursion à Machu Picchu, la «cité perdue des Incas», à trois heures de train d'ici.

LOCATION
Located in the heart of Cuzco, 10 minutes from the airport

RATES
Rooms from $700, suites from $880, oxygen enrichment $50

ROOMS
109 doubles, 12 junior suites, 1 deluxe suite, 3 presidential suites, 2 royal suites

STYLE
Monastic architecture and classical interiors on a sacred Incan site

FOOD
Two restaurants serving Peruvian and international cuisine (the banquet dinner at El Tupay is a real experience). Deli Monasterio sells Peruvian cakes and fresh sandwiches

X FACTOR
The air all around you—athletes swear by its natural performance-enhancing properties

BOOK TO PACK
"The Condor and the Cows" by Christopher Isherwood

LAGE
Im Zentrum von Cuzco gelegen, 10 Fahrminuten vom Flughafen entfernt

PREISE
Zimmer ab 520 €, Suiten ab 650 €, Sauerstoffanreicherung 40 €

ZIMMER
109 Doppelzimmer, 12 Junior-Suiten, 1 Deluxe-Suite, 3 Präsidenten-Suiten, 2 Royal-Suiten

STIL
Klösterliche Architektur und klassischer Komfort auf den Grundmauern der Inka-Kultur

KÜCHE
2 Restaurants mit peruanischer und internationaler Küche (ein Erlebnis ist das festliche Dinner im El Tupay). Im Deli Monasterio kauft man peruanische Kuchen und Brote

X-FAKTOR
Die Höhenluft, die einem hier ständig um die Nase weht – viele Sportler schwören auf dieses natürliche Doping

BUCH ZUM ORT
„Kondor und Kühe" von Christopher Isherwood

SITUATION
Dans le centre de Cuzco, à 10 minutes en voiture de l'aéroport

PRIX
Chambres à partir de 520 €, suites à partir de 650 €, alimentation en oxygène 40 €

CHAMBRES
109 chambres doubles, 12 suites junior, 1 suite Deluxe, 3 suites présidentielles, 2 suites royales

STYLE
Architecture monastique et confort classique dans le berceau de la civilisation inca

RESTAURATION
Deux restaurants servent de la cuisine péruvienne et internationale (le dîner festif au El Tupay est inoubliable). Le Deli Monasterio vend des gâteaux péruviens et du pain

LE «PETIT PLUS»
L'air d'altitude omniprésent. Pour beaucoup de sportifs, c'est un vrai dopage naturel

LIVRE À EMPORTER
«Le Condor» de Christopher Isherwood

DEDON ISLAND
PHILIPPINES

Malinao Rd, General Luna ~ Siargo Islands, Mindanao ~ Philippines
Telephone +49 40 3070 86 690, America & Europe ~ +63 917 701 7820, Asia, Africa & Australia
home@dedonisland.com
www.dedonisland.com

The creators of Dedon Island claim that, ideally, they would never wear shoes again. Staying at one of their charming villas, it's not hard to see why. Siargao Island is part of the Philippine archipelago and is one of its most idyllic spots, offering porcelain beaches, intact mangrove forests, and first-class surfing and diving.

That wasn't enough for the friendly team behind this resort, however. They thus set about adding a variety of innovative features that make life on the island even more pleasurable, building an enchanting ocean pagoda that can be reached at low tide, creating a new wooden viewing platform, and suspending woven seating pods from the palm trees, thus enabling guests to literally hang loose as they sit listening to the rippling of the waves.

Die Erfinder des Dedon Island sagen, dass sie am liebsten nie wieder in ihrem Leben Schuhe anziehen würden. Ein Wunsch, den jeder nachvollziehen kann, der einmal Gast in einer ihrer bezaubernden Villen sein durfte. Siargao Island ist Teil des philippinischen Archipels im Pazifik und gehört zu den schönsten Exemplaren seiner Art, mit porzellanweißen Stränden und intakten Mangroven-Wäldern bis zu den erstklassigen Möglichkeiten für Surfer und Taucher.

Dieses gesegnete Umfeld war dem sympathischen Team des Resorts aber nicht genug. Mit innovativen Ideen gingen sie daran, das Inselleben für ihre Gäste noch zu optimieren. Sie bauten eine zauberhafte Pagode mitten im Meer, die man bei Ebbe zu Fuß erreicht, errichteten eine hölzerne Aussichtsplattform und installierten hängende Relax-Waben an den Palmen, in denen man, begleitet vom Wellenrauschen, dann endgültig über den Dingen schwebt.

Les créateurs du Dedon Island disent qu'ils voudraient ne plus devoir porter de chaussures de leur vie. Un souhait que peut comprendre quiconque a séjourné dans l'une de leurs splendides villas. Située dans l'archipel des Philippines, l'île de Siargao n'a pas son pareil avec ses plages immaculées, ses forêts de mangroves préservées et les expériences inouïes qu'elle offre aux surfeurs et aux plongeurs.

Ne se satisfaisant pas de ce cadre béni, la sympathique équipe de l'établissement a agrémenté la vie de ses hôtes sur l'île avec des idées innovantes. Elle a ainsi construit sur la mer une fabuleuse pagode, que l'on peut rejoindre à pied à marée basse. Il y a aussi une plate-forme panoramique de bois et, suspendus aux palmiers, des cocons de relaxation d'où l'on plane au-dessus du bas monde, accompagné par le roulement des vagues.

LOCATION
In the southeast of Siargao Island on a private bay, 1 hour by plane from Cebu

RATES
From $435 off season, from $480 in peak season, prices per person per night

ROOMS
9 villas between 1,020 and 1,615 sq. ft.

STYLE
Traditional Philippine architecture combined with contemporary eco-luxury

FOOD
The cuisine fuses Philippine and international influences, and dishes are always freshly made with either homegrown or locally sourced ingredients

X FACTOR
Incredible vistas included: From the resort's viewing platform, guests can watch fearless surfers attempting to conquer Cloud 9—perhaps the world's most famous wave

BOOK TO PACK
"Illustrado" by Miguel Syjuco

LAGE
Im Südosten von Siargao Island an der eigenen Bucht gelegen, 1 Flugstunde von Cebu

PREISE
In der Nebensaison ab 335 €, in der Hauptsaison ab 370 € pro Person und Nacht

ZIMMER
9 Villen zwischen 95 m² und 150 m²

STIL
Traditionelle philippinische Architektur trifft auf zeitgenössischen Öko-Luxus

KÜCHE
Philippinisch-internationale Küche, die entweder mit selbst angebauten oder zumindest regional besorgten Nahrungsmitteln immer ganz frisch zubereitet wird

X-FAKTOR
Spektakuläre Fernsicht ist hier inbegriffen: Cloud 9 – die vielleicht berühmteste Welle der Welt – und ihre tollkühnen Bezwinger lassen sich von der Aussichtsplattform bewundern

BUCH ZUM ORT
„Die Erleuchteten" von Miguel Syjuco

SITUATION
Crique privée dans le sud-est de l'île de Siargao, à 1 heure de vol de Cebu

PRIX
En basse saison à partir de 335 €, en haute saison à partir de 370 € par personne et par nuitée

CHAMBRES
9 villas de 95 à 150 m²

STYLE
Rencontre de l'architecture philippine traditionnelle et du luxe écologique contemporain

RESTAURATION
Cuisine philippino-internationale de toute fraîcheur préparée avec des produits cultivés sur place ou des produits régionaux

LE «PETIT PLUS»
La vue spectaculaire est incluse dans le prix: depuis la plate-forme panoramique, on peut admirer les surfeurs fous affrontant Cloud 9, la vague sans doute la plus célèbre du monde

LIVRE À EMPORTER
«Ilustrado» de Miguel Syjuco

"Our aim with Dedon Island was
to leave the natural environment
as untouched as possible."

JEAN-MARIE MASSAUD, DESIGNER

„In unseren Entwürfen für Dedon Island versuchten wir,
so wenig wie möglich in die Natur einzugreifen."

« Notre but était de toucher
le moins possible à la nature. »

FORMENTERA YOGA
SPAIN

Platja de Migjorn ~ Formentera, The Balearics ~ Spain
Telephone +34 606 117 373
jill@formenterayoga.com
www.formenterayoga.com

Whether you want to practice your poses or just relax on the beach, the Formentera Yoga Beach House is worth a visit—the retreat sits above perhaps the most beautiful stretch of coast in the Balearics. This is a place of picturesque coves and clear turquoise water, one with none of the brashness of neighboring Ibiza.

After all—as the owners of this small seafront hotel appreciate—sun, sand, and first-class yoga instructors are all anyone here really wants. That and a shady hammock for siestas, a refreshingly uncluttered room with untreated teak furniture, and a sunset smoothie enjoyed against an acoustic backdrop of rippling waves and chilled-out DJ sounds.

Auch wenn sich hier alles um Yoga dreht – das Beach House von Formentera Yoga ist auch eine wirkliche Empfehlung für alle, die einfach nur gerne am Strand sind. Der vielleicht schönste Küstenabschnitt der Baleareninsel liegt nämlich direkt unterhalb des Hotels: türkisfarbenes Wasser und malerische Buchten, sehr weit weg von der knalligen Nachbarinsel Ibiza.

Die Betreiber des kleinen Strandhotels wissen genau, dass man hier neben Sonne, Meer und ausgezeichneten Yoga-Trainern nicht viel mehr braucht: eine Hängematte im Schatten für die Siesta, erfrischend klar gestaltete Zimmer mit unbehandelten Teakholzmöbeln und abends dann ein Smoothie: Dazu einen DJ an den Plattentellern, der den Sound der Wellen nur ein bisschen verstärkt – auch eine Art Asana.

Même si tout tourne ici autour du yoga, Formentera Yoga est une excellente adresse pour tous ceux qui aspirent tout simplement à profiter de la plage. La côte, qui est probablement la plus belle des îles Baléares, est située au pied de l'hôtel : l'eau est turquoise, les criques pittoresques et la tapageuse Ibiza est bien loin.

Les propriétaires savent parfaitement que leurs hôtes ne souhaitent rien de plus que le soleil, la mer et d'excellents professeurs de yoga. Un hamac à l'ombre pour la sieste, des chambres épurées au mobilier en teck non traité et la dégustation d'un smoothie le soir, tandis qu'un DJ amplifie juste un peu le bruit des vagues sur les platines : bref, une expérience digne d'une asana.

LOCATION
18 km/11 miles south of the island of Ibiza.
Boats go from Ibiza Town to Formentera's
La Savina port; there, take a taxi to the hotel

RATES
3-, 4-, and 5-day packages from
$790 to $2,230, full board included

ROOMS
22 doubles, 5 three-bed rooms, and 2 suites,
sleeping up to 45 guests

STYLE
Beach life with an Indonesian touch

FOOD
Vegetarian; ayurvedic also offered

X FACTOR
Yoga of all kinds with a sea-view backdrop.
Plus excellent vegetarian cuisine that will have
you asking for recipes to take home

BOOKS TO PACK
"It's Here Now (Are You?)" by Bhagavan
Das and "Speaking with the Angel" edited
by Nick Hornby

LAGE
18 km südlich der Insel Ibiza. Mit dem Boot geht
es vom Ibiza Old Town Port zum La Savina Port
von Formentera und von dort aus weiter mit
dem Taxi zum Hotel

PREISE
3, 4 oder 5-Tage-Pakete zwischen
585 € und 1650 €, mit Vollpension

ZIMMER
22 Doppelzimmer, 5 Dreibettzimmer, und
2 Suiten für maximal 45 Gäste

STIL
Strandleben mit indonesischem Touch

KÜCHE
Vegetarisch-ayurvedische Küche möglich

X-FAKTOR
Yoga in allen Spielarten und mit Blick aufs
Meer. Dazu die ausgezeichnete, zum Nach-
kochen inspirierende Gemüseküche

BÜCHER ZUM ORT
„It's Here Now (Are You?)" von Bhagavan Das
und „Speaking with the Angel" von Nick
Hornby (Hrsg.)

SITUATION
À 18 km au sud de l'île d'Ibiza ; transfert en
bateau du port d'Ibiza vers La Savina, le port
de Formentera et, de là, en taxi

PRIX
Formules 3, 4 ou 5 jours entre 585 € et 1 650 €
en pension complète

CHAMBRES
22 chambres doubles, 5 chambres à 3 lits,
et 2 suites pour 45 personnes maximum

STYLE
« Les pieds dans l'eau », avec une touche
indonésienne

RESTAURATION
Cuisine végétarienne, ayurvédique sur demande

LE « PETIT PLUS »
Le yoga sous toutes ses formes, avec vue sur
la mer. La superbe cuisine mise à disposition
pour reproduire les recettes

LIVRES À EMPORTER
« La Science des émotions » de Bhagavan
Das et « Conversation avec l'ange » de Nick
Hornby (éd.)

HOSPES MARICEL
SPAIN

Carretera d'Andratx 11 ~ 07181 Cas Català (Calvià) ~ Majorca ~ Spain
Telephone +34 971 707 744 ~ Fax +34 971 707 745
reservations.maricel@hospes.com
www.hospes.com

Water is what defines an island and, at Majorca's Hospes Maricel, it features particularly prominently—not only in the hotel's name ("mar" meaning sea), but also in the spa, which has been installed in underground caves in such a way that the waves lap almost to guests' feet. Above is perhaps the island's most glamorous terrace, a sundeck so spectacular even a leopard on a leash wouldn't look out of place.

In fact, this 1940s mansion has a tradition of flamboyance, having once hosted the chicest parties on the island. It was converted into an elegant hotel in 2002 by Xavier Claramunt. Even more striking, though, are the rooms in the annex: They boast typical Majorcan stone walls that provide the perfect backdrop for clean-lined furnishings in glass, wood, and steel.

Wasser ist auf einer Insel das wichtigste Element, und in dieses Haus wurde es mit erstaunlicher Raffinesse integriert. Nicht nur im Namen des Hotels – Mar wie Meer – versteckt es sich: Dessen Spa wurde so gekonnt in vorhandene Grotten integriert, dass dort die Wellen bis direkt an die Füße der Gäste schwappen. Eine Ebene höher wartet die vielleicht schönste Sonnenterrasse Mallorcas, so extravagant, dass man darauf auch mit einem Geparden an der Leine kaum auffallen würde.

Tatsächlich fanden in diesem Palais aus den 1940ern früher die schicksten Partys statt. Xavier Claramunt verwandelte es dann 2002 in ein mondänes Hotel. Die spektakulärsten Zimmer liegen heute in den Anbauten: Sie haben typisch mallorquinische Steinwände, vor denen strenges Design aus Glas, Holz und Stahl ausgezeichnet zur Geltung kommt.

Sur une île, l'eau est l'élément le plus important. Dans cette maison, elle a été intégrée avec un grand raffinement. Elle se reflète tant dans le nom de l'hôtel («mar» comme mer) que dans son spa, si habilement aménagé dans les grottes existantes que les vagues viennent clapoter aux pieds des hôtes. Au-dessus se trouve la terrasse, sans doute la plus belle de Majorque. Elle est si extravagante que l'on pourrait s'y promener avec un guépard en laisse sans se faire remarquer.

Ce palais construit dans les années 1940 a connu les fêtes les plus chics. En 2002, Xavier Claramunt l'a transformé en un hôtel mondain. Aujourd'hui, les chambres les plus remarquables sont situées dans les annexes : leurs murs de pierre typiquement majorquins mettent superbement en valeur le design épuré où le verre, le bois et l'acier sont à l'honneur.

LOCATION
Right by the sea in Calvià to the west of Palma.
15 minutes by car from the airport

RATES
Rooms from $318, suites from $710, breakfast
not included. Minimum stay of 3 nights during
high season

ROOMS
44 rooms and 7 suites. The rooms in the annex
all have their own pools

STYLE
Mediterranean mansion with avant-garde
interiors

FOOD
The Maricel restaurant serves innovative
Mallorcan cuisine; there is also a pool bar
and a cocktail lounge

X FACTOR
It's not just the spa that exceeds all expectations—the Hospes Maricel breakfast was once
named the best in the world

BOOK TO PACK
"Winter in Majorca" by George Sand

LAGE
Direkt am Meer in Calvià, westlich von Palma.
Zum Flughafen fährt man 15 Minuten

PREISE
Zimmer ab 235 €, Suiten ab 525 €, ohne
Frühstück. 3 Nächte Mindestaufenthalt in
der Hochsaison

ZIMMER
44 Zimmer und 7 Suiten. Alle Räume in den
Nebengebäuden haben eigene Pools

STIL
Mediterraner Palast mit avantgardistischem
Innenleben

KÜCHE
Das Maricel serviert innovative mallorquinische
Gerichte; außerdem gibt es eine Pool-Bar und
eine Cocktail-Lounge

X-FAKTOR
Nicht nur das Spa erfüllt superlativische Erwartungen – das Frühstück des Hospes Maricel
wurde einmal zum besten der Welt gekürt

BUCH ZUM ORT
„Ein Winter auf Mallorca" von George Sand

SITUATION
En bord de mer à Calvià, à l'ouest de Palma,
à 15 minutes de l'aéroport

PRIX
Chambres à partir de 235 €, suites à partir
de 525 €, petit déjeuner non compris. En
haute saison, séjour de 3 nuits minimum

CHAMBRES
44 chambres et 7 suites; tous les hébergements
situés dans les annexes ont leur propre piscine

STYLE
Palais méditerranéen avec une atmosphère
avant-gardiste

RESTAURATION
Le Maricel sert des plats majorquins innovants;
il y a aussi un pool-bar et un bar à cocktails

LE «PETIT PLUS»
Le spa extraordinaire, mais également le petit
déjeuner de l'Hospes Maricel, réputé comme
le meilleur du monde

LIVRE À EMPORTER
«Un hiver à Majorque» de George Sand

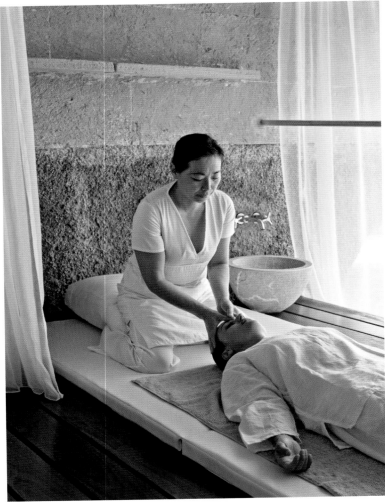

SON GENER
SPAIN

Carretera Vella Son Servera ~ Km 2.9 Derecha
07550 Son Servera, Majorca ~ Spain
Telephone +34 971 183 612 ~ +34 971 183 736
hotel@songener.com
www.songener.com

Majorca is his world. Be it a private residence or a luxury hotel, Antoni Esteva always manages to blend a traditional finca aesthetic with exciting contemporary style. The Son Gener in the east of the island is no exception. Built on the foundations of an old manor house, it is now one of Majorca's finest hotels.

With their simple wooden furniture, plain linen fabrics, and views of the surrounding sun-dappled hills, the ten suites offer a warm, uncomplicated, and authentically cozy ambience that is the ideal starting point for a restful break. This unfussiness continues elsewhere too, be it in the wine cellar, the organic vegetable garden, the stunning pool, or the meditation room—the Son Gener simply excels at providing everything a guest needs for a relaxing vacation. It's not so much the air of laid-back luxury that gives the hotel such an intimate atmosphere, however, as the harmonious way it taps into the spirit of this special place.

Antoni Esteva ist sein Name, und Mallorca ist seine Insel. Egal ob Privathaus oder Hotel – was der Architekt hier baut, verknüpft stets traditionelle Finca-Ästhetik mit einem aufregend zeitgenössischen Anspruch. Ganz nach dieser Philosophie entwickelte er auch das Son Gener im Osten Mallorcas auf den Grundmauern eines alten Herrenhauses zu einem der schönsten Landhotels der Insel.

Schlichte Holzmöbel und einfache Leinenstoffe sorgen in den zehn Suiten im Wechselspiel mit dem warmen Licht der sonnigen Hügellandschaft für unkomplizierte und authentische Gemütlichkeit – die beste Grundlage guter Erholung. Diese Linie verfolgt das Anwesen in allen Bereichen. Ob im Weinkeller, Bio-Gemüsegarten, traumhaften Pool oder Meditationssaal, was immer der Entspannung der Gäste dienlich ist, bietet das Son Gener in feiner Form an. Dabei ist nicht lässiger Luxus das Geheimnis der intimen Atmosphäre, sondern der Sinn für nachhaltige Harmonie, der diesen besonderen Ort geprägt hat.

Antoni Esteva est son nom et Majorque, son île. Maison individuelle ou hôtel, tout ce que cet architecte y construit allie traditionnelle de la finca et modernité vibrante. C'est dans cet esprit qu'il a créé sur le soubassement d'une vieille maison de maître l'un des plus beaux hôtels de campagne de l'île : le Son Gener.

Dans les dix suites, le mobilier rustique et le lin naturel en dialogue avec la lumière chaude baignant les collines environnantes créent une ambiance chaleureuse, détendue et authentique, on ne peut plus propice à un repos réparateur. Fidèle à ce parti pris, l'établissement joue la carte de l'élégance sur toute la ligne pour contribuer au bien-être de ses hôtes – de la cave à vins et du potager bio à la splendide piscine, en passant par le salon de méditation.

Mais le secret de cette atmosphère feutrée ne réside pas tant dans le luxe décontracté que dans le sens de l'harmonie durable dont est empreint le lieu.

LOCATION
Between the towns of Son Servera and Arta near the east coast of Majorca, approx. 60 km/37 miles from Palma

RATES
$440, breakfast included

ROOMS
10 junior suites

STYLE
Purist lines meet traditional finca ambience

FOOD
Excellent island cuisine from a kitchen that sets great store by the source and quality of its products—the vegetables are grown in the hotel's own organic garden; the meat and fish are from producers in the surrounding area

X FACTOR
The first-class homemade *sobrassada*, a traditional Majorcan sausage produced here under the watchful eye of legendary head chef Josefa

BOOK TO PACK
"Goya, or The Tortuous Road to Understanding" by Lion Feuchtwanger

LAGE
Nahe der Ostküste Mallorcas zwischen den Orten Son Servera und Arta, etwa 60 km von Palma entfernt

PREISE
325 €, inklusive Frühstück

ZIMMER
10 Juniorsuiten

STIL
Purismus im traditionellen Finca-Ambiente

KÜCHE
Exzellente Inselküche, bei der großer Wert auf Herkunft und Qualität der Produkte gelegt wird – das Gemüse kommt aus dem hoteleigenen Bio-Garten, Fisch und Fleisch von Direkterzeugern in unmittelbarer Nachbarschaft

X-FAKTOR
Die eigene *Sobrassada*, eine mallorquinische Wurstspezialität, die unter Aufsicht der legendären Köchin Josefa hier in bester Qualität produziert wird

BUCH ZUM ORT
„Goya oder Der arge Weg der Erkenntnis" von Lion Feuchtwanger

SITUATION
À proximité de la côte est de Majorque, entre les localités de Son Servera et Arta, à environ 60 km de Palma

PRIX
325 €, petit déjeuner compris

CHAMBRES
10 suites juniors

STYLE
Lignes épurées dans une ambiance finca traditionnelle

RESTAURATION
Excellente cuisine insulaire qui privilégie les produits locaux et de qualité : les légumes proviennent du propre potager bio de l'hôtel, la viande et le poisson de producteurs du voisinage immédiat

LE « PETIT PLUS »
La *sobrassada* maison, une saucisse majorquine de très grande qualité confectionnée sous la houlette de la légendaire chef Josefa

LIVRE À EMPORTER
« Le Roman de Goya » de Lion Feuchtwanger

MOLINO DEL REY
SPAIN

Valle de Jorox ~ Alozaina-Málaga 29567 ~ Spain
Telephone +34 952 480 009
molinodelrey@hotmail.com
www.molinodelrey.com

Meditating in a rocky cave and taking a candlelit dip in a seawater pool are just two of the treats that await guests at the Molino del Rey. Here, it's all about the luxury of letting go, something with which the surroundings can only help: The old mills that house the guest accommodations are tucked away in the Andalusian hills and blessed with an air of unshakable calm, while water from the source of a tributary of the Rio Grande flows through the retreat.

Over the years, this place of simple pleasures has become a hit with guests from around the world, who appreciate not only the great yoga courses but also the many other possibilities: Day trips to Granada, Seville, or Córdoba, walks in the avocado groves and surrounding conservation area, hot-stone massages in the shade—the only difficulty is deciding what to do first.

In einer Höhle im Fels meditieren oder im See-wasserpool bei Kerzenlicht schwimmen – das sind die Spielarten des Luxus, die im Molino del Rey zu erwarten sind. Es geht hier also um die Besinnung auf das Wesentliche, und das wird vom Ambiente bestens unterstützt: Die alten Mühlen, in denen man logiert, sind ein-gebettet in das andalusische Hügelland und strahlen eine eherne Ruhe aus. Gespeist werden die Mühlen übrigens aus der Quelle eines Seitenflusses des Rio Grande.

Mit seiner Freude am Einfachen zieht dieses Retreat seit Jahren ein begeistertes Publikum aus der ganzen Welt an, das die Qual der Wahl schätzt. Zwischen den Yogastunden nach Gra-nada, Sevilla, Córdoba? Vielleicht doch lieber eine Wanderung durch Avocadohaine und das angrenzende Naturschutzgebiet? Oder lieber eine Hot Stone Massage im Schatten? Manchmal sind gerade die einfachen Angebote ganz schön kompliziert.

Méditer au cœur d'une caverne ou se baigner à la lueur des bougies dans une piscine d'eau de lac, voici quelques-unes des activités luxueuses que propose le Molino del Rey. Il s'agit ici de faire un retour aux sources dans une atmosphère qui s'y prête idéalement : implantés au milieu des collines andalouses, les vieux moulins au calme olympien qui accueillent les hôtes sont alimentés par la source d'un affluent du Rio Grande.

Avec son sens des plaisirs simples, cette retraite attire depuis des années un public enthousiaste venu du monde entier qui n'a ici que l'embarras du choix : séances de yoga, excursions à Grenade, Séville ou Cordoue, balades parmi les avocatiers ou dans le parc naturel à proximité. À moins que l'on ne préfère profiter d'un massage aux pierres chaudes à l'ombre. Parfois les activités les plus simples peuvent s'avérer bien compliquées à choisir.

LOCATION
50 km/31 miles west of Malaga airport

RATES
$110 per person and day, half board included

ROOMS
Total of 22 beds—10 doubles and 2 singles.
All en suite with air-conditioning and
tea-making facilities

STYLE
Simple Andalusian retreat for individualists

FOOD
Vegetarian, with specialties ranging from
paella and Spanish tortillas to muffins

X FACTOR
Expert workouts and meditation: Some of the
best yoga instructors in the world come here
to lead courses

BOOKS TO PACK
"Health, Healing & Beyond: Yoga and the
Living Tradition of Krishnamacharya" by T. K. V.
Desikachar and "Raquel, the Jewess of Toledo"
by Lion Feuchtwanger

LAGE
50 km westlich vom Flughafen Málaga

PREISE
80 € pro Person und Tag, inkl. Halbpension

ZIMMER
Insgesamt 22 Betten, verteilt auf 10 Doppel-
zimmer und 2 Einzelzimmer, jeweils mit Bad,
Klimaanlage und Teekocher

STIL
Andalusisch-schlichter Rückzugsort für
Hotelindividualisten

KÜCHE
Vegetarisch mit so diversen Spezialitäten
wie Paella, Tortilla und Schokoladenmuffins

X-FAKTOR
Meditation und Körperschule auf Profi-
Niveau: Einige der besten Yoga-Gastlehrer
der Welt machen hier gern Station

BÜCHER ZUM ORT
„Yoga – Gesundheit von Körper und Geist:
Leben und Lehren Krishnamacharyas"
von T. K. V. Desikachar und „Die Jüdin von
Toledo" von Lion Feuchtwanger

SITUATION
À 50 km à l'ouest de l'aéroport de Malaga

PRIX
80 € par personne et par jour en demi-pension

CHAMBRES
22 lits répartis dans 10 chambres doubles
et 2 chambres single, chacune avec salle de
bains, climatisation et bouilloire électrique

STYLE
Retraite andalouse au style dépouillé pour
individualistes

RESTAURATION
Cuisine végétarienne autour de spécialités
diverses: paëlla, tortillas, muffins au chocolat

LE «PETIT PLUS»
Méditation et école du corps de niveau professionnel: certains des meilleurs professeurs de
yoga du monde entier apprécient le lieu

LIVRES À EMPORTER
«Le Yoga du yogi – L'héritage de T. Krishnamacharya» de Kausthub Desikachar et «La Juive
de Tolède» de Lion Feuchtwanger

FABRIKEN FURILLEN
SWEDEN

62458 Lärbro ~ Gotland ~ Sweden
Telephone +46 498 223 040 ~ Fax +46 498 203 041
fabriken@furillen.com
www.furillen.com

There's something almost apocalyptic about the approach to this small Swedish hotel. Where, a minute ago, you were passing through pleasant forests and small Gotland fishing villages, you suddenly find yourself amid the waste heaps of a huge limestone quarry.

It's here, in the middle of this deserted industrial landscape (the quarry was abandoned in the 1970s), that Fabriken Furillen has opened its doors. Apart from the unusual location, the hotel offers tasteful, clean-lined Scandinavian interiors, a large slice of industrial chic, and instant access to the Baltic. On sunny days, the pale piles of limestone and the blue sea beyond form an intriguing contrast that is entirely in keeping with the hotel's eccentric character. Further evidence of the latter can be seen in such unorthodox forms of accommodation as an isolated wooden cabin and an Airstream trailer. Wherever you choose to stay, you'll have plenty of time for reading and taking pictures at Furillen—and plenty to talk about back home.

Bei der Anfahrt zum Furillen kommt Endzeitstimmung auf. Eben noch ging es vorbei an lieblichen schwedischen Wäldern und den kleinen Fischerdörfern Gotlands. Dann aber steht man in den Halden des gigantischen Kalksteinbruchs, der hier in den 1970er-Jahren stillgelegt wurde. In die Überbleibsel des verwaisten Industriegeländes hat das Furillen-Hotel seine wohlgestalteten Räumlichkeiten platziert.

Vor der Tür gurgelt die Gischt der Ostsee, dahinter erfreuen skandinavisches Design von gediegener Klarheit und ein gutes Quäntchen Industrial-Chic. Der helle Kalkstein auf den Halden und das kalte blaue Meer ergeben an Sonnentagen einen unwiderstehlichen Kontrast, der gut zum exzentrischen Gesamtauftritt des Furillen passt. Letzterer äußert sich auch in Sonder-Apartments wie einer einsam gelegenen Holzhütte oder einem Airstream-Wohnwagen. Fest steht: Man wird hier viel lesen, viel fotografieren und dann auch viel erzählen, daheim.

L'arrivée à Furillen fait naître comme une sensation de fin du monde : laissant derrière soi les douces forêts suédoises et les petits villages de pêcheurs de Gotland, on se retrouve sans transition au milieu des vestiges d'une gigantesque carrière de calcaire désaffectée depuis les années 1970. C'est sur ce site industriel abandonné que l'hôtel Furillen déploie ses espaces bien conçus.

Dehors, l'air est empli des embruns de la mer Baltique, tandis que l'intérieur opère l'alliance entre le design scandinave épuré et le chic industriel. Les reflets lumineux sur les dépôts de calcaire et la mer froide et bleue forment par beau temps un paysage aux contrastes saisissants qui s'accorde avec l'aspect excentrique de l'hôtel. Ce dernier se manifeste notamment dans l'originalité des modes d'hébergement proposés, comme une cabane en bois isolée ou une caravane Airstream. Une chose est sûre : ce lieu invite à lire beaucoup, photographier beaucoup, puis raconter beaucoup au retour.

LOCATION
The peninsula of Furillen on the north coast of Gotland. The nearest village is Lärbro, 40 km/25 miles northeast of Visby airport

RATES
Rooms from $300, breakfast included

ROOMS
18 rooms

STYLE
Pared-down Scandinavian style meets industrial chic, all in a bizarre landscape of limestone, pine trees, and coastline

FOOD
Swedish specialties made from local, seasonal produce and whatever the fishermen catch

X FACTOR
The truffle safaris: During the season, you can go hunting for Swedish truffles (found only on Gotland). There's also a good chance of coming across a fossil or two

BOOK TO PACK
"The Girl with the Dragon Tattoo" by Stieg Larsson

LAGE
Auf der Insel Furillen an Gotlands Nordostküste gelegen. Der nächste Ort ist Lärbro, 40 km nordöstlich des Flughafens Visby

PREISE
Zimmer ab 220 €, inklusive Frühstück

ZIMMER
18 Zimmer

STIL
Skandinavisch-industrieller Purismus, originell eingebettet in eine extreme Landschaft aus Wasser, Stein und Kiefern

KÜCHE
Interessante schwedische Spezialitäten, zubereitet aus den saisonalen Produkten der Region und den Fängen der Fischer

X-FAKTOR
Augen auf: Wer zur richtigen Zeit da ist, kann nach der schwedischen Trüffel suchen, die es nur auf Gotland gibt. Wer noch mehr Glück hat, findet vielleicht sogar Fossilabdrücke

BUCH ZUM ORT
„Verblendung" von Stieg Larsson

SITUATION
Sur l'île de Furillen, accolée à la côte nord-est de Gotland; la localité la plus proche est Lärbro, à 40 km au nord-est de l'aéroport de Visby

PRIX
Chambres à partir de 220 €, petit déjeuner compris

CHAMBRES
18 chambres

STYLE
Purisme scandinavo-industriel et paysage extrême fait d'eau, de pierres et de pins

RESTAURATION
Savoureuses spécialités suédoises préparées avec les produits de saison régionaux et les prises des pêcheurs

LE «PETIT PLUS»
En saison, la chasse aux truffes suédoises, endémiques de Gotland. Les plus chanceux dénicheront des fossiles

LIVRE À EMPORTER
«Les Hommes qui n'aimaient pas les femmes» de Stieg Larsson

TREEHOTEL
SWEDEN

Edeforsvägen 2a ~ 96024 Harads ~ Sweden
Telephone +46 928 104 03
info@treehotel.se
www.treehotel.se

When industry newcomers decide to open a hotel, the results are often highly unconventional. That's certainly the case with Britta and Kent's Treehotel, situated about 30 miles from Luleå in northern Sweden, the idea for which came to the couple after watching "The Tree Lover," a movie celebrating the importance of trees to human history and culture. Thus inspired, they built a group of structures that are up to six meters off the ground, each one designed by a different Scandinavian architect.

The lighting and furniture were custom-made and, in conjunction with the majestic pines outside the windows, offer guests a truly unique experience that combines closeness to nature with a purist aesthetic. No trees were harmed in the making of the hotel, and everything is designed to be as environmentally friendly as possible. Whether you're fulfilling a childhood dream or simply communing with nature, staying at Treehotel feels like a genuine adventure, though probably one best avoided by those with no head for heights.

Wenn Quereinsteiger ins Hotelfach wechseln, entstehen oft besonders unkonventionelle Häuser. So war es auch beim Treehotel, 50 Kilometer vom nordschwedischen Luleå entfernt. Die Inspiration dazu kam den Gastgebern Britta und Kent durch den Film „The Tree Lover", in dem die historische und kulturelle Bedeutung der Bäume für den Menschen gewürdigt wurde. Mit diesem Impuls errichteten sie ein Camp, bis zu sechs Meter über dem Boden, und ließen jedes der fünf Baumzimmer von einem anderen skandinavischen Architekten gestalten.

Beleuchtung und Möblierung wurden speziell für das Treehotel angefertigt und ergeben zwischen den Kiefern ein einzigartiges Wohngefühl: viel Natur, aber auch puristisches Design. Kein Baum wurde dafür beschädigt, und alles erfüllt höchste ökologische Ansprüche. Als Gast erlebt man ein echtes Abenteuer, ganz egal, ob man sich dort oben einen Kindheitstraum erfüllt oder an der stillen Kraft der Bäume teilhaben möchte. Nur ein bisschen schwindelfrei sollte man sein.

Quand on se lance dans l'hôtellerie en venant d'une autre filière, il en résulte souvent des constructions très peu conventionnelles. C'est le cas du Treehotel, situé à 50 km de Luleå, dans le nord de la Suède, dont l'idée est venue à Britta et Kent après avoir vu le film « The Tree Lover », hommage à l'importance historique et culturelle des arbres pour les hommes. Ils ont ainsi imaginé un campement à six mètres au-dessus du sol et fait appel à un architecte scandinave différent pour chacune des cinq cabanes dans les arbres.

Les luminaires et le mobilier ont été spécialement conçus pour le Treehotel. La nature environnante dominée par les pins côtoie le design épuré, ce qui rend l'expérience unique. Aucun arbre n'a été endommagé, le respect absolu de l'environnement étant la priorité en toute chose. Que l'on veuille réaliser tout là-haut un rêve d'enfance ou que l'on souhaite s'imprégner de l'énergie silencieuse des arbres, on vit ici une véritable aventure. Mais il vaut mieux ne pas avoir le vertige.

LOCATION

On the edge of the northern Swedish hamlet of Harads, surrounded by nothing but nature. One hour by car from Luleå airport

RATES

Tree house for two from $690 per night, breakfast included

ROOMS

Five very different tree houses up to 6 meters off the ground, with river or forest views

STYLE

Contemporary Scandinavian architecture

FOOD

Meals are served at Britta's Pensionat in the 1930s/'50s main building

X FACTOR

Located amid the tall pines, the tree sauna offers guests an encounter with all four elements—fertile earth, burning fire, fresh air, and clean water

BOOK TO PACK

"The Native Trees of Canada" by Leanne Shapton

LAGE

In Nordschweden, 1 Stunde von Luleå Airport entfernt am Rande des Dörfchens Harads – und drum herum nichts als Natur

PREISE

Baumhaus für 2 ab 510 € pro Nacht, inklusive Frühstück

ZIMMER

5 sehr verschiedene Baumhäuser in bis zu 6 m Höhe, mit Fluss- oder Waldblick

STIL

Aktuelle skandinavische Architektur

KÜCHE

Gegessen wird in Britta's Pensionat, dem Zentralgebäude aus den 1930er/50er-Jahren

X-FAKTOR

In der Baumsauna zwischen uralten Kiefern trifft man die 4 Elemente: Fruchtbare Erde, brennendes Feuer, frische Luft und reines Trinkwasser sind hier vereint

BUCH ZUM ORT

„The Native Trees of Canada" von Leanne Shapton

SITUATION

Dans le nord de la Suède, en pleine nature, à la lisière du petit village d'Harads et à une heure de l'aéroport de Luleå

PRIX

Cabane dans les arbres pour 2 personnes à partir de 510 € la nuit, petit déjeuner compris

CHAMBRES

Cinq cabanes dans les arbres toutes très différentes, construites jusqu'à 6 mètres de hauteur, avec vue sur la rivière et la forêt

STYLE

Architecture scandinave contemporaine

RESTAURATION

Les repas sont servis au Britta's Pensionat, situé dans le bâtiment central qui date des années 1930 à 1950

LE«PETIT PLUS»

Sauna perché dans les arbres : on yretrouve les quatre éléments réunis : la terre fertile, le feu ardent, l'air frais et l'eau pure

LIVRE À EMPORTER

« Le Signe de jadis » de Kerstin Ekman

"While we want to have our hotel
in the middle of nature,
we want to do it on nature's terms."

KENT LINDVALL AND BRITTA JONSSON LINDVALL, TREEHOTEL'S FOUNDERS

„Wir wollen unser Hotel mitten in der Natur haben,
aber wir wollen es nach deren Regeln errichten."

«Nous voulons que notre hôtel soit au milieu de la nature,
et nous souhaitons le construire selon les règles qu'elle impose.»

THE ALPINA GSTAAD
SWITZERLAND

Alpinastrasse 23 ~ 3780 Gstaad ~ Switzerland
Telephone +41 33 888 9888 ~ Fax +41 33 888 9889
info@thealpinagstaad.ch
www.thealpinagstaad.ch

The opening of Gstaad's first new grand hotel in a century inevitably engenders high expectations. After all, this winter resort is a magnet for the rich, the super-rich, and the famous.

With its carefully thought-out interpretation of high-end luxury, the Alpina looks well equipped to meet the needs of this demanding clientele. The many tons of wood salvaged from old chalets ensure the suites have the requisite alpine atmosphere. Fine antiques are scattered around the building. Boulders from the local mountain stream give the bel étage fireplace an authentically regional character. And every corner of the hotel is atmospherically lit. It's just a short walk to Gstaad's pedestrian precinct, but, with three restaurants, an in-house cinema, and a spa area featuring a kids' slide, the hotel itself offers manifold diversions—not to mention superior mountain vistas from its private balconies.

Wenn nach 100 Jahren zum ersten Mal wieder ein Grandhotel in Gstaad eröffnet, sind die Erwartungen hoch. Schließlich geben sich die Reichen, Superreichen und Berühmten hier gern ein winterliches Stelldichein.

Das Alpina ist auf diese ungnädige Klientel gut vorbereitet und glänzt mit einer durchdachten Interpretation von Superluxus. Da sind die vielen Tonnen echtes Chalet-Altholz, die in jeder Suite Alm-Stimmung erzeugen. Da sind standesgemäße Details wie die ansehnliche Antiquitätensammlung, die über das Haus verteilt ist, oder die großen Steine aus dem nahen Gebirgsbach, die dem mächtigen Kamin in der Beletage ein regionales Gesicht geben. Da sind weiters ein stimmungsvolles Beleuchtungskonzept, das jeden Winkel des Hauses erfasst, und eine Spa-Landschaft inklusive Wasserrutsche für die Kleinen. In die Gstaader Fußgängerzone ist es nur ein kurzer Spaziergang; das Hotel bietet mit drei Restaurants und einem eigenen Kino aber auch eigene Zerstreuung – und den Bergen ist man vom Balkon aus sowieso näher.

Quand, au bout de cent ans, un nouvel hôtel de luxe ouvre ses portes à Gstaad, les attentes sont grandes. Le club des riches, des très riches et des célébrités ne se donnent-ils pas rendez-vous dans cette station huppée en hiver?

Paré pour affronter cette clientèle difficile, l'Alpina brille par son interprétation très étudiée du grand luxe. Ici, des tonnes de vieux bois de chalet authentique créent une ambiance alpine dans chaque suite; là, on joue la carte du standing avec une riche collection d'antiquités disséminées dans l'hôtel ou les blocs de pierre provenant du proche torrent qui donnent une physionomie régionale à l'imposante cheminée. Par ailleurs, un éclairage d'ambiance se diffuse jusque dans les moindres recoins, et l'espace spa comprend un toboggan aquatique pour les enfants. Le quartier piétonnier, situé à deux pas, invite à la flânerie, à moins qu'on ne préfère s'attarder dans l'un des trois restaurants ou profiter de la salle de cinéma privée de l'Alpina. Et depuis balcons, la montagne est toute proche.

LOCATION
5-minute walk from the center of Gstaad, on a rise affording views across the Sarine valley

RATES
Rooms from $935, suites from $1,600, including $100/day restaurant and bar vouchers

ROOMS
25 rooms and 31 suites, all with private balconies and stunning alpine vistas

STYLE
No-expenses-spared new-build grand hotel

FOOD
The three elegant hotel restaurants offer a choice of gourmet international cuisine, Swiss specialties, and (the now almost obligatory) Japanese delicacies

X FACTOR
For smokers, there's a handsome cigar lounge with heavy leather armchairs, cognac, and walk-in humidor

MAGAZINES TO PACK
"Vanity Fair," "Tatler," "Hello!"

LAGE
5 Gehminuten vom Ortszentrum Gstaads entfernt auf einer Anhöhe mit Blick über das Saanenland

PREISE
Zimmer ab 690 €, Suiten ab 1180 €, jeweils inklusive 80 € Verzehrgutschein pro Tag

ZIMMER
25 Zimmer und 31 Suiten, jeweils mit eigenem Balkon und bestem Alpenblick

STIL
Neues Grandhotel, das keine Kosten scheut

KÜCHE
Die 3 eleganten Restaurants des Hauses bieten den Gästen internationale Sterneküche, eidgenössische Schmankerl und (ohne geht so was heute nicht) japanische Spezialitäten

X-FAKTOR
Für Raucher gibt es einen wunderschönen Smoking-Room mit schweren Ledersesseln, Cognac und begehbarem Humidor

MAGAZINE ZUM ORT
„Vanity Fair", „Bunte", „Hello!"

SITUATION
À 5 minutes à pied du centre-ville de Gstaad, sur les hauteurs avec vue sur le pays de Gessenay

PRIX
Chambres à partir de 690 €, suites à partir de 1 180 €, bon de consommation quotidien de 80 € compris

CHAMBRES
25 chambres et 31 suites, toutes avec balcon et vue imprenable sur les Alpes

STYLE
Hôtel de luxe neuf, qui ne regarde pas à la dépense

RESTAURATION
Trois élégants restaurants servent de la cuisine étoilée internationale, des plats suisses et – un must de nos jours – des spécialités japonaises

LE «PETIT PLUS»
Les fumeurs apprécieront le magnifique fumoir avec imposants fauteuils en cuir, cognac et cave à cigares

MAGAZINES À EMPORTER
«Vanity Fair», «Gala», «Point de vue»

WALDHAUS SILS
SWITZERLAND

Via da Fex 3 ~ 7514 Sils-Maria ~ Switzerland
Telephone +41 81 838 5100 ~ Fax +41 81 838 5198
mail@waldhaus-sils.ch
www.waldhaus-sils.ch

Many of Waldhaus Sils's cosmopolitan guests come year in, year out. And who can blame them? Not only does it offer a picture-book location and the best in Swiss hospitality, but it also has a unique charm. That, no doubt, is due in part to its status as an independent, family-owned grand hotel (now run by the fifth generation of Kienbergers), but it's also due to an entirely unstuffy attitude toward guests, particularly younger ones, and to an unconventional activity program that reflects a passion for high culture.

The special atmosphere shouldn't really come as a surprise, though. After all, countless European intellectual heavyweights, among them Theodor W. Adorno and Luchino Visconti, have stayed at this woodland refuge, and it remains a treat appreciated by creatives of all kinds. Perhaps a hotel with such character simply gets the guests it deserves.

Der Aufenthalt im Waldhaus ist für eine ganze Reihe von Kosmopoliten ein jährlich begangenes Fest. Schließlich bietet das Haus in seiner Bilderbuchlage nicht nur Schweizer Hotellerie vom Feinsten, sondern verfügt über einen ganz eigenen Puls. Das beginnt bei seiner Geschäftsform als unabhängiges Grandhotel, das in der fünften Generation von der Familie Kienberger geführt wird, geht über den lockeren Umgang mit allen Gästen, vor allem auch Kindern, und das Anbieten unkonventioneller Zerstreuungen bis hin zur Begeisterung, mit der hier Hochkultur thematisiert wird.

Wundern darf einen die spezielle Waldhaus-Aura nicht: Durch die Halle wandelten schon unzählige namhafte europäische Geistesgrößen, von Adorno bis Luchino Visconti, und bis heute erliegen Kreative aller Sparten dem Charme des Silser Refugiums. Es ist schon so: Ein Haus mit Charakter erzieht sich seine Gäste.

Pour toute une clientèle cosmopolite, un séjour au Waldhaus tient du pèlerinage annuel. En effet, implanté dans un site digne d'une image d'Épinal, cet hôtel ne propose pas uniquement le meilleur de l'hôtellerie suisse : son cœur bat différemment. Et ce, à commencer par son statut d'hôtel de luxe indépendant, tenu par la famille Kienberger depuis cinq générations, jusqu'à la convivialité à l'égard de tous les hôtes, en particulier des enfants, en passant par les activités peu conventionnelles qui sont proposées et par l'enthousiasme pour la culture avec un grand C.

Cette aura particulière n'a rien d'étonnant : le hall d'entrée a vu passer nombre de grandes têtes pensantes européennes, d'Adorno à Visconti, et de nos jours encore, les artistes en tout genre succombent au charme de cette retraite. Un établissement de caractère ne cultive-t-il pas sa propre clientèle ?

LOCATION
10 km/6 miles southwest of St. Moritz in the Upper Engadine, with prime views across Lake Sils

RATES
Doubles from $500, suites from $770, half board included

ROOMS
140 rooms and suites

STYLE
Comfortable alpine castle with a unique charm

FOOD
La Terrazza offers Italian cuisine; the Pool Restaurant is more informal

X FACTOR
Where else do you still find a dedicated reading room? There's no better place to browse great literature than this beautiful library, particularly if the authors were once guests themselves—as is often the case

BOOK TO PACK
"Daisy Miller" by Henry James

LAGE
10 km südwestlich von St. Moritz im Oberengadin, mit dem wohl besten Blick auf den Silsersee

PREISE
Doppelzimmer ab 375 €, Suiten ab 575 €, inklusive Halbpension

ZIMMER
140 Zimmer und Suiten

STIL
Eine gemütliche Burg in den Bergen mit außerordentlichem Charme

KÜCHE
Neben dem italienischen La Terrazza lockt das etwas legerere Pool Restaurant

X-FAKTOR
Wo gibt es denn noch einen bildschönen Lesesalon? Hier! Nirgends lässt sich besser Weltliteratur schmökern, zumal wenn die Autoren auch Gäste des Waldhauses waren – was nicht selten der Fall ist

BÜCHER ZUM ORT
„Durcheinandertal" von Friedrich Dürrenmatt und „Daisy Miller" von Henry James

SITUATION
À 10 km au sud-ouest de Saint-Moritz, en Haute-Engadine, avec vue imprenable sur le lac de Sils

PRIX
Chambres doubles à partir de 375 €, suites à partir de 575 €, en demi-pension

CHAMBRES
140 chambres et suites

STYLE
Confortable château alpin au charme hors pair

RESTAURATION
Le restaurant italien La Terrazza et le Pool Restaurant, plus décontracté

LE«PETIT PLUS»
Où trouve-t-on encore une belle bibliothèque? Ici! Nulle part ailleurs peut-on mieux savourer la littérature mondiale, surtout quand ses auteurs ont été les hôtes du Waldhaus

LIVRES À EMPORTER
« Val pagaille » de Friedrich Dürrenmatt et «Daisy Miller» de Henry James

"Theodor W. Adorno, Thomas Bernhard,
Joseph Beuys, Kathryn Bigelow,
David Bowie, Claude Chabrol … "

THUS BEGINS AN ALPHABETICAL LIST OF THE 45 MOST FAMOUS WALDHAUS GUESTS

„Theodor W. Adorno, Thomas Bernhard, Joseph Beuys, Kathryn Bigelow, David Bowie, Claude Chabrol…" –
so beginnt eine alphabetische Liste der 45 berühmtesten Gäste des Waldhaus.

«Theodor W. Adorno, Thomas Bernhard, Joseph Beuys, Kathryn Bigelow, David Bowie, Claude Chabrol…»
Ainsi commence la liste alphabétique des 45 hôtes les plus célèbres du «Waldhaus».

WHITEPOD
SWITZERLAND

1871 Les Giettes ~ Switzerland
Telephone +41 244 713 838 ~ Fax +41 244 713 955
reservations@whitepod.com
www.whitepod.com

From the outside, these matte white domes for adventure-seeking vacationers are a strange blend of Inuit's igloo, Himalayan bivouac, and space capsule destined for Mars.

Beneath that alien exterior, however, they are remarkably inviting, boasting comfortable beds with thick bedding, en suite bathrooms, and wood-burning stoves. All the same, these geodesic pods, situated almost 4,600 feet above sea level in the Swiss canton of Valais, offer a simpler kind of alpine experience, one in which guests can get closer to the landscape. They can also justifiably feel they are doing their bit to preserve it: The Whitepod camp is designed to be as low impact as possible and has already won an award for its eco-friendly approach.

Irgendwo zwischen einem Inuit-Iglu, einem Himalaja-Biwak und einer Kapsel für die nächste Mars-Mission – so muten sie an, die 15 Quartiere, die unter dem Namen Whitepod im Schweizer Wallis für abenteuerlustige Übernachtungsgäste bereitstehen.

Unter der matt-weißen Hightech-Hülle wartet ein wirklich reizendes Interieur aus gemütlichem Bett (mit dicken Decken), Bad und einem knisternden Holzofen. In diesen geodätischen Unterkünften auf 1400 Metern Höhe wird man innerhalb einer Nacht zum Komplizen der Berge – und genießt eine erfrischende Konzentration auf das Wesentliche. Gleichzeitig unterstützt man den Öko-Tourismus: Das Camp wurde als rundum naturfreundliches Projekt konzipiert und dafür bereits mit einem Umweltpreis ausgezeichnet.

Tenant à la fois de l'igloo inuit, du bivouac himalayen et de la capsule de la prochaine mission sur Mars, les 15 unités du complexe baptisé «Whitepod» accueillent dans le Valais suisse des hôtes à l'âme aventureuse.

Sous l'enveloppe high tech blanc mat se dissimule un intérieur séduisant, équipé d'un lit confortable et douillet, d'une salle de bains et d'un poêle à bois crépitant. Dans ces logements en forme de géodes perchés à 1400 mètres d'altitude, on devient, l'espace d'une nuit, complice de la montagne et on se ressource en se concentrant sur l'essentiel. Sans oublier qu'en séjournant ici, on pratique aussi le tourisme vert : ce complexe a déjà été primé pour sa conception entièrement écologique.

LOCATION
Almost 4,600 feet up in the Valais Alps, close to the village of Les Cerniers; 125 km/78 miles east of Geneva airport

RATES
Pods from $320 in summer and $400 in winter, breakfast included

ROOMS
15 pods between 280 and 430 sq. ft.

STYLE
Modern alpine domes with exceptionally cozy interiors

FOOD
Breakfast is available in the main 18th-century chalet. There are also two Swiss restaurants on site—one serving light cuisine, the other aimed at fans of heartier, more traditional fare

X FACTOR
Something practical for a change:
The camp also offers a survival course

BOOK TO PACK
"Snow Waste" by Michael E. Bemis

LAGE
Auf 1400 m Höhe in den Walliser Alpen gelegen, nahe dem Dorf Les Cerniers, 125 km östlich des Genfer Flughafens

PREISE
Pod (Kapsel) ab 240 € im Sommer, ab 300 € im Winter, inklusive Frühstück

ZIMMER
15 Pods mit je 26 bis 40 m²

STIL
Moderne Alpin-Jurten mit absoluter Wohlfühlgarantie

KÜCHE
Im zentralen Chalet aus dem 18. Jahrhundert gibt es Frühstück. Zudem gehören zwei Schweizer Restaurants zur Anlage – eines serviert leichte Küche, im anderen stärken sich Freunde des Schweizerisch-Deftigen

X-FAKTOR
Ausnahmsweise mal was Nützliches: der vom Hotel angebotene Lawinen-Hilfskurs

BUCH ZUM ORT
„Die Schneefalle" von Silvio Blatter

SITUATION
À 1 400 mètres d'altitude dans les Alpes valaisannes, près du village des Cerniers, à 125 km à l'est de l'aéroport de Genève

PRIX
«Pod» (capsule) à partir de 240 € en été et de 300 € en hiver, petit déjeuner compris

CHAMBRES
15 «pods» de 26 à 40 m²

STYLE
Yourtes alpines modernes, dans lesquelles le bien-être est garanti à 100%

RESTAURATION
Petit déjeuner dans le chalet principal datant du 18e siècle. Deux restaurants suisses, l'un proposant de la cuisine légère, l'autre s'adressant aux amateurs de plats roboratifs

LE «PETIT PLUS»
Pour une fois, on fait l'éloge de l'utile : le cours de survie en milieu montagnard (pour les groupes, cours de sécurité en avalanche)

LIVRE À EMPORTER
«Contes à pic» de Samivel

BRASSIERE COZY BEACH
THAILAND

210 Moo 5 ~ Tambol Samroiyod ~ Prachuabkirikhan 77220 ~ Thailand
Telephone +66 32 630 555 ~ Fax +66 32 630 554
brassierebeach@hotmail.com
www.brassierebeach.com

Here, guests have the beach all to themselves—a rare treat in Thailand. What's more, this small hotel not only offers privacy and isolation, being the only establishment along this stretch of coast, but it also has everything you could want from a tropical paradise: lush palm forests, soft sand, and blue sea studded with rocky isles.

Legend has it that the two islets directly opposite the hotel are the naked breasts of a fisherman's daughter to whom the locals, having taken pity on the girl, donated bras. That's how the Brassiere Cozy Beach, which opened in 2005, got its name and also its unusual theme: The simple, but charmingly decorated, rooms are named after lingerie, and Yingluck Chareonying, the hotel's designer, has even incorporated brassieres as alluring accessories.

In Thailand ist das schon ziemlich erwähnenswert – wer im Brassiere Cozy Beach absteigt, hat den Strand für sich alleine, denn es ist das einzige Hotel an diesem wunderbaren Küstenabschnitt. Dabei vereint der alles, was man sich nur wünschen kann: saftig grünen Palmenwald, weichen Sand und davor das Meer mit den typischen Felsinseln.

Der Sage nach sind die zwei Inseln direkt vor dem kleinen Hotel die nackten Brüste einer Fischerstochter, für die die Einheimischen aus Mitleid Büstenhalter (brassiere) sammelten. So kam dieses 2005 eröffnete Hotel auch zu seinem Namen und Leitmotiv: Die charmant-schlicht eingerichteten Zimmer sind nach Dessous benannt, und Yingluck Chareonying, die Designerin des Hotels, lässt hier und da sogar BHs als Accessoires aufblitzen. Wenn das keine reizenden Aussichten sind.

En Thaïlande, cela si rare que cela mérite d'être mentionné : les hôtes du Brassiere Cozy Beach ont la plage pour eux seuls, car c'est le seul hôtel sur cette portion de littoral enchanteresse. Qui plus est, il réunit tout ce dont on peut rêver : une palmeraie vert vif, du sable fin et la mer semée d'îlots rocheux.

Selon la légende, les deux îlots en face du petit hôtel sont les seins nus d'une fille de pêcheur, pour laquelle les autochtones pris de pitié ont collecté des soutiens-gorge (brassiere, en anglais). D'où le nom et le thème de cet hôtel ouvert en 2005 : les neuf chambres d'une sobriété charmante portent des noms de dessous, et Yingluck Chareonying, qui a aménagé l'hôtel, a disposé avec brio çà et là des soutiens-gorge en guise d'accessoires. De quoi faire naître des envies.

LOCATION
South of Hua Hin on the Gulf of Thailand; the drive from Bangkok airport takes just under 4 hours

RATES
Rooms from $130, breakfast included

ROOMS
9 rooms with mountain or sea views. The rooms "No's Bra" and "Pannee", each of which has its own pool, are particular highlights

STYLE
Romantic beach hideaway

FOOD
The restaurant serves simple but tasty Thai dishes

X FACTOR
In addition to canoes and bicycles, the Brassiere Cozy Beach also rents out boards for stand-up paddling, a surprisingly meditative form of water sport that every guest should try

BOOK TO PACK
"The Beach" by Alex Garland

LAGE
Südlich von Hua Hin am Golf von Thailand gelegen; knapp 4 Fahrtstunden vom Flughafen Bangkok entfernt

PREISE
Zimmer ab 95 €, inklusive Frühstück

ZIMMER
9 Zimmer mit Berg- oder Meerblick. Besonders erfreulich: die Units „No's Bra" und „Pannee" mit privaten Pools

STIL
Aussteiger-Strandromantik

KÜCHE
Das Restaurant serviert einfache, leckere Thai-Gerichte

X-FAKTOR
Das Hotel bietet nicht nur Kanus und Räder zum Ausleihen an, sondern auch Bretter für Stand-up-Paddeln. Diesen überraschend meditativen Wassersport sollte man unbedingt mal ausprobieren!

BUCH ZUM ORT
„Der Strand" von Alex Garland

SITUATION
Au sud de Hua Hin, sur le golfe de Thaïlande; à 4 petites heures de voiture de l'aéroport de Bangkok

PRIX
Chambres à partir de 95 €, petit déjeuner compris

CHAMBRES
9 chambres avec vue sur la montagne ou sur la mer. Le rêve: les chambres «No's Bra» et «Pannee» dotées de piscines privées

STYLE
Romantisme balnéaire hors des sentiers battus

RESTAURATION
Le restaurant sert des plats thaïs simples et succulents

LE «PETIT PLUS»
Outre des canoës et des vélos, on peut aussi louer à l'hôtel des planches de *stand up paddle*, un sport aquatique étonnamment méditatif à essayer au moins une fois dans sa vie!

LIVRE À EMPORTER
«La Plage» d'Alex Garland

RAYAVADEE
THAILAND

214 Moo 2 ~ Tambon Ao-Nang ~ Amphoe Muang ~ Krabi 81000 ~ Thailand
Telephone +66 75 620 740-3 ~ Fax +66 75 620 630
reservation@rayavadee.com
www.rayavadee.com

When people rave about southern Thailand, they usually mean its unspoiled fishing villages, glorious sandy beaches, crystal-clear water, and striking limestone rocks—the very scene that awaits guests at the Rayavadee Resort on the edge of the Krabi National Marine Park. Spread out along a picturesque bay popular with climbers, the impressive complex is designed in the style of a Thai village, with more than 100 pavilions and beach villas scattered amid the trees. Their interiors pay tribute to local aesthetic traditions, while the views of the Andaman Sea outside do the rest.

The beach is open to the public and hence best enjoyed in the early morning or after 6 p.m., but guests can also explore the nearby caves, go diving with exotic fish, or simply relax on one of the elegant sun loungers. All that remains is to visit the evening barbecue—lit by paper lanterns—, grab a freshly opened coconut, and accept that you too are now a staunch southern Thailand devotee.

Wenn Reisende von Südthailand schwärmen, dann meinen sie urtümliche Fischerdörfer, herrliche Sandstrände, kristallklares Wasser und markante Kalksteinfelsen. Genau in dieser Kulisse liegt das beeindruckende Rayavadee Resort am Rande des Krabi National Marine Park. Die Anlage wurde im Stil eines Thaidorfes erbaut und erstreckt sich sehr großzügig über eine malerische Bucht, die bei Kletterern berühmt ist. Über 100 Pavillons und Strandvillen sind locker zwischen den Kokospalmen verteilt, ihre Einrichtung zollt der regionalen Ästhetik Tribut. Das restliche Flair besorgt die Andamanensee vor der Tür, die man idealerweise frühmorgens oder nach 18 Uhr genießt, denn der Strand ist öffentlich.

Wer sich von den eleganten Strandliegen losreißt, kann hier Felsgrotten oder beim Schnorcheln eine bunte Fischwelt erkunden. Dann sollte man sich nur noch abends im Schein der Papierlaternen beim Barbecue eine Kokosnuss öffnen lassen, und schon ist man der Nächste, der von Südthailand schwärmt.

Les inconditionnels du sud de la Thaïlande vous chanteront les villages de pêcheurs authentiques, les magnifiques plages de sable, l'eau cristalline et les grandioses falaises de calcaire. C'est dans ce cadre qu'est situé l'impressionnant Rayavadee Resort, à la lisière du Krabi National Marine Park. Aménagé comme un village thaï, le complexe se déploie dans une baie pittoresque réputée auprès des amateurs d'escalade. Plus de 100 bungalows et villas sont disséminés entre les cocotiers. Leurs intérieurs sacrifient à l'esthétique locale, tandis que dehors, la mer d'Andaman met la touche finale au tableau idyllique. La plage étant publique, il est conseillé de se baigner à l'aube ou après 18 heures.

Qui parvient à s'arracher aux élégants transats peut visiter des grottes ou, avec masque et tuba, observer les poissons multicolores. Et si le soir venu, à la lueur des lampions, on déguste une noix de coco fraîche autour d'un barbecue, on devient soi-même un inconditionnel du sud de la Thaïlande.

LOCATION
On the Phra Nang peninsula, close to the
Krabi National Marine Park, 2 hours from Phuket

RATES
Rooms from $656, villas from $2,155, breakfast
and airport transfer included

ROOMS
98 two-story pavilions and 4 beach villas
spread across an almost-100-acre site

STYLE
Tasteful beach houses in picturesque southeast
Asian style

FOOD
Thai cuisine, be it in the elegant dining room
or the informal beach restaurant

X FACTOR
Guests can take a Thai cooking course and
sign up for an introduction to the art of flower
arranging—then try out their newly acquired
skills back home

BOOK TO PACK
"Killed at the Whim of a Hat" by Colin Cotterill

LAGE
Auf der Phra-Nang-Halbinsel am Rande des
Krabi National Marine Park, 2 Stunden Flugzeit
von Phuket entfernt

PREISE
Pavillons ab 510 €, Villen ab 1600 €, inklusive
Frühstück und Flughafen-Transfer

ZIMMER
98 zweistöckige Pavillons und 4 Strandvillen,
verteilt auf über 40 Hektar

STIL
Geschmackvolle Strandhäuser in pittoreskem
Asia-Stil

KÜCHE
Thaiküche vom eleganten Dinner drinnen bis
zum legeren Strandrestaurant

X-FAKTOR
Das Resort bietet nicht nur einen Kochkurs an,
sondern gibt auch Anleitung in der schönen
Kunst des Blumenbindens

BUCH ZUM ORT
„Der Tote trägt Hut" von Colin Cotterill

SITUATION
Sur la péninsule de Phra Nang, à la lisière
du Krabi National Marine Park, à 2 heures
d'avion de Phuket

PRIX
Bungalows à partir de 510 €, villas à partir
de 1 600 €, petit déjeuner et transfert compris

CHAMBRES
98 bungalows sur deux niveaux et 4 villas
répartis sur plus de 40 hectares

STYLE
Villas «les pieds dans l'eau» aménagées avec
goût dans le pittoresque style asiatique

RESTAURATION
Cuisine thaïe servie en toute simplicité au
restaurant de la plage ou dans le cadre raffiné
de la salle à manger

LE «PETIT PLUS»
Outre des cours de cuisine, l'établissement
propose aussi une initiation à l'art floral

LIVRE À EMPORTER
«Tué sur un coup de tête» de Colin Cotterill

"Its towering limestone cliffs and tropical foliage, and the crystal-blue waters of the Andaman Sea, make this hideaway a romantic alternative to places like Phuket."

TRAVEL + LEISURE

„Turmhohe Kalksteinfelsen und tropisches Grün, dazu das kristallblaue Wasser der Adamanensee: Dieses Hideaway ist die romantische Alternative zu Plätzen wie Phuket."

«Ses hautes falaises de calcaire, sa végétation tropicale, ainsi que les eaux bleues limpides de la mer d'Andaman, font de cette retraite une alternative romantique à des endroits comme Phuket.»

THE HOUSE HOTEL BOSPHORUS
TURKEY

Salhane Sokak No: 1 Ortaköy 34347 ~ Istanbul ~ Turkey
Telephone +90 212 327 77 87 ~ Fax +90 212 327 77 93
info.bosphorus@thehousehotel.com
www.thehousehotel.com/the-house-hotel-bosphorus/

Hip Turkish design practice Autoban has been making quite a name for itself in recent years. And with its conversion of this waterfront residence into The House Hotel Bosphorus, it has done much to establish its reputation too. The interiors skillfully combine old and new Istanbul: Behind the main building's Ottoman baroque facade are 26 rooms in which guests can admire a contemporary mix of Autoban signature materials, such as marble, brass, oak, and walnut wood—the latter two combining to form 3D-effect parquet flooring.

The House Hotel Bosporus is situated right on the river in Ortaköy, part of the lively district of Beşiktaş, and as a result boasts fabulous views of the Bosporus and Topkapi Palace. It's a location that makes this the perfect place for musing on past, present, Occident, and Orient—ideally over a drink in the hotel lounge.

Seit einigen Jahren schon macht das türkische Designteam Autoban international von sich reden. Im Falle des House Hotel Bosphorus trugen die hippen Designer mit ihrem Umbau viel zum ausgezeichneten Ruf des Hauses bei. Mit Bravour lösten sie die Aufgabe, altes wie neues Istanbul zu präsentieren: Außen glänzt das Hauptgebäude des Hotels mit einer osmanischen Barock-Fassade, und in den 26 Zimmern ist der zeitgemäße Einsatz der Autoban-Lieblingsmaterialien zu bewundern – Marmor, Messing und die Kombination von Eiche und Nussbaum zu Parkett in 3-D-Optik.

Das House Hotel liegt in erster Uferreihe in Ortaköy, einem Viertel des quirligen Stadtteils Beşiktaş, und das ist ein Glück für die Gäste, denn die Lage verspricht eine wunderbare Sicht auf den Bosporus und den Topkapi-Palast. Mit diesem Panorama ist die Lounge wie gemacht dafür, bei einem Drink über Alt und Neu, Orient und Okzident nachzusinnen.

Depuis quelques années déjà, Autoban fait parler de lui. En transformant le House Hotel Bosphorus, cette équipe de designers turcs en vogue a largement contribué à l'excellente réputation internationale de la maison. Avec brio, il a concilié le vieux et le nouvel Istanbul : le bâtiment principal arbore une façade de style baroque ottoman, tandis que dans les 26 chambres, on peut admirer l'emploi contemporain des matériaux de prédilection d'Autoban : marbre, laiton ainsi que du chêne et du noyer combinés pour créer un parquet «en trois dimensions».

Cet hôtel du quartier d'Ortaköy, dans le district animé de Beşiktaş, a été construit au premier rang sur les berges, une situation privilégiée qui promet une vue magnifique sur le Bosphore et le palais de Topkapı. Avec un tel panorama, le salon est comme fait pour la méditation sur l'ancien et le neuf, sur l'Orient et l'Occident.

LOCATION
Right by the Bosporus in Ortaköy, 35 km/
22 miles from Atatürk airport; the terrace and
balconies have views across the water to Asia

RATES
Rooms from $220 to $1,500, breakfast included

ROOMS
26 rooms spread across five floors

STYLE
Palace of cool that effortlessly blends different
influences, much like the clientele with its mix
of youngish and more mature guests

FOOD
The House Café Ortaköy serves international
and Turkish cuisine and boasts two terraces

X FACTOR
Guests can even arrive by motorboat should
they so wish—this waterfront hotel has its
own jetty

BOOK TO PACK
"Istanbul: Memories and the City"
by Orhan Pamuk

LAGE
Direkt am Bosporus in Ortaköy, 35 km vom
Atatürk-Flughafen; von der Terrasse und den
Balkonen blickt man hinüber nach Asien

PREISE
Zimmer zwischen 160 € und 1100 €, jeweils
inklusive Frühstück

ZIMMER
26 Zimmer auf 5 Stockwerken

STIL
Ein *cool palace*, der die Stilrichtungen genauso
unaufgeregt mischt wie es hier das mal junge,
mal reifere Publikum tut

KÜCHE
Internationale und türkische Gerichte im House
Café Ortaköy mit zwei Terrassen

X-FAKTOR
Wer will, kann auch mit dem Motorboot anreisen: The House hat einen eigenen Anleger

BUCH ZUM ORT
„Istanbul: Erinnerungen an eine Stadt" von
Orhan Pamuk

SITUATION
Sur les rives du Bosphore à Ortaköy, à 35 km
de l'aéroport Atatürk; de la terrasse et des
balcons, on aperçoit l'Asie

PRIX
Chambres de 160 € à 1100 €, petit déjeuner
compris

CHAMBRES
26 chambres réparties sur 5 étages

STYLE
Palace décontracté avec un mélange de styles
aussi réussi que celui des générations qui le
peuplent – jeunes et moins jeunes

RESTAURATION
Cuisine internationale et turque au House Café
Ortaköy, qui dispose de deux terrasses

LE «PETIT PLUS»
Le House Hotel possédant son propre
débarcadère, on peut s'y rendre en bateau
à moteur

LIVRE À EMPORTER
«Istanbul, souvenirs d'une ville» d'Orhan Pamuk

SANCTUARY GORILLA FOREST CAMP
UGANDA

Bwindi Impenetrable National Park ~ Uganda
Telephone +256 414 340 290
info@sanctuaryretreats.com
www.sanctuaryretreats.com

Winston Churchill once described Uganda as the pearl of Africa, and there's still something rather mystical about the place today. Not only is this central African country the source of the Nile, but it is also home to the mountain gorillas. They, of course, are the main draw at the Sanctuary Gorilla Forest Camp, the only officially recognized luxury camp within the volcanic Bwindi Impenetrable National Park, a UNESCO world heritage site.

The camp, which comprises eight en suite tents, is situated in the heart of gorilla territory on a flat ridge high up in the forest. After a long trek to track these gentle giants, a soak in the tub, which looks out onto the forest, will be much appreciated, as will the services of the butler who attends to every tent. A raised platform offers open-air dining with panoramic views, and there's traditional Bakiga guitar music around the evening campfire—a must for every guest at this unique retreat.

Winston Churchill nannte es die Perle Afrikas, und bis heute umgibt Uganda etwas Mystisches. Hier sind die Quellen des Nils, und hier ist die Heimat der Berggorillas. Das Sanctuary Gorilla Forest Camp ist das einzige offiziell anerkannte Luxuscamp innerhalb des Bwindi Impenetrable National Park, der mit seiner Vulkanlandschaft zum UNESCO-Welterbe gehört.

Mitten im Gorilla-Gebiet, auf einem flachen Grat hoch oben im Wald, liegt das Camp mit seinen acht En-suite-Zelten. Die Badewanne mit Blick hinaus in den Wald ist nach einem Wandertag auf der Suche nach den „sanften Riesen" wirklich nötig, und auch die Dienste des Butlers, der jedem Zelt zur Verfügung steht, lässt man sich dann gerne gefallen. Für das Panorama-Essen unter freiem Himmel gibt es eine leicht erhöhte Plattform, das Lagerfeuer und die Klänge der traditionellen Bakiga-Gitarre gehören an diesem einzigartigen Ort zum abendlichen Pflichtprogramm.

«Perle de l'Afrique», comme l'appelait Winston Churchill, l'Ouganda est resté enveloppé d'une aura mystique. Le Nil y naît, et c'est la patrie des gorilles de montagne. Le Sanctuary Gorilla Forest Camp est le campement de luxe officiel du parc national de la Forêt impénétrable de Bwindi, inscrit au patrimoine mondial de l'UNESCO pour son paysage volcanique.

Au cœur du fief des gorilles, sur un plateau de crête où culmine la forêt, se trouve ce campement comprenant huit tentes avec salle de bains. La baignoire avec vue sur la forêt est la bienvenue après une journée de marche à la recherche des «doux géants», de même que les services du majordome à la disposition de chaque tente. Dans ce site d'exception, les repas panoramiques en plein air ont lieu sur une terrasse légèrement exhaussée, tandis que tous les soirs crépite le feu de camp aux sons de la *bagika*, la guitare traditionnelle.

LOCATION
In southwest Uganda's Bwindi Impenetrable
National Park near Rwanda and Congo,
25 km/16 miles from the closest airstrip

RATES
From $355 per person per night in a two-person
tent, full board and laundry service included

ROOMS
8 luxury tents, each with en suite bathroom
and views of unspoiled rain forest

STYLE
Rain forest camp and occasional gorilla family
hangout

FOOD
The first-class campfire dinners served under
starry skies and against a panoramic jungle
backdrop are simply unforgettable

X FACTOR
Apes on your doorstep: What sets this place
apart from many other safaris is that, here,
the gorilla groups often come into camp

BOOK TO PACK
"Gorillas in the Mist" by Dian Fossey

LAGE
Der Bwindi Impenetrable National Park liegt im
Südwesten Ugandas nahe Ruanda und dem
Kongo, 25 km von der nächsten Landepiste

PREISE
Ab 265 € pro Person und Nacht im Zweimann-
zelt, inklusive Vollpension und Wäscheservice

ZIMMER
8 Luxus-Zelte mit jeweils eigenem Bad und
Blick in den unberührten Regenwald

STIL
Regenwald-Camp mit, so man Glück hat,
exklusivem Gorilla-Familienanschluss

KÜCHE
Unvergesslich: Beim Rundum-Blick in den
Dschungel am Lagerfeuer unter den Sternen
ein exzellentes Dinner genießen

X-FAKTOR
Näher kann man nicht rankommen: Im Gegen-
satz zu manch anderen Safaris kommen die
Gorilla-Familien hier sogar oftmals ins Camp

BUCH ZUM ORT
„Gorillas im Nebel" von Dian Fossey

SITUATION
Dans le sud-ouest de l'Ouganda, près du
Rwanda et de la RDC, le parc national de la
Forêt impénétrable de Bwindi est à 25 km
d'une piste d'atterrissage

PRIX
À partir de 265 € par personne et par nuit
sous tente deux places, pension complète
et blanchisserie comprises

CHAMBRES
8 tentes de luxe avec salle de bains privée
et vue sur la forêt pluviale préservée

STYLE
Campement dans la forêt et, avec un peu de
chance, accueil dans une famille de gorilles

RESTAURATION
Inoubliable : l'excellent dîner autour d'un feu
de camp à la belle étoile, au cœur de la forêt

LE «PETIT PLUS»
Au plus près : rare dans les safaris, les gorilles
viennent souvent jusque dans le campement

LIVRE À EMPORTER
«Gorilles dans la brume» de Dian Fossey

SEMLIKI SAFARI LODGE
UGANDA

Toro-Semliki Game Reserve ~ Tororo, Semliki Valley ~ Uganda
Telephone +256 414 251182
info@wildplacesafrica.com
www.wildplacesafrica.com/semliki-safari-lodge

At this lodge in the middle of the African wilderness, you can drift off in a muslin-draped, hand-carved four-poster bed while listening to lions and watching the campfire shadows dancing on the walls of your tent. And when you wake in the morning, you can have hot muffins and tea brought to your bedside. From the terrace, you'll enjoy an exclusive view of the savanna and the unspoiled Semliki Valley—exclusive in that this outpost of luxury and civilization is the only lodge in the whole valley.

It is run by Wild Places, a group that works to maintain the protected status of the surrounding Toro-Semliki Game Reserve, situated at the point where the grassland meets the rain forest. With its exceptional diversity of flora and fauna, Semliki Safari Lodge is a place every animal-lover, adventurer, and old-school safari aficionado will want to visit at least once in his or her lifetime.

Was für ein Erlebnis: nachts im Herzen der afrikanischen Wildnis zu liegen, in einem hand-geschnitzten Bett unter einem zarten Himmel aus Musselin, und das Brüllen der Löwen zu hören, während auf der Zeltwand die Schatten des Lagerfeuers tanzen. So ein Einschlafen bietet die Semliki Safari Lodge ihren Gästen. Und morgens bekommt man warme Muffins mit Tee ans Bett gebracht. Von der Terrasse geht der Blick sehr exklusiv auf die Savanne und das unberührte Semliki-Flusstal. Exklusiv, denn die Lodge ist die einzige im Semliki Valley, ein Außenposten der Komfortzivilisation.

Betreut wird er von der Vereinigung Wild Places, die sich für den Erhalt des Toro-Semliki-Wildreservats einsetzt. Dieses bietet eine besonders reiche Tier- und Pflanzenwelt, denn hier trifft tropischer Regenwald auf Grassavanne. Tierliebhaber, Abenteurer und Safari-Nostalgi-ker sollten die Lodge deswegen zumindest einmal im Leben auf dem Reiseplan haben.

Que diriez-vous de dormir au cœur de la savane africaine dans un lit sculpté à la main sous un baldaquin en fine mousseline, tandis que les lions rugissent au loin et que les ombres du feu de campement dansent sur la toile de la tente ? C'est ainsi que l'on s'endort au Semliki Safari Lodge. Et le matin, on vous apporte au lit des muffins encore chauds et du thé. La terrasse offre une vue exclusive sur la savane et sur la vallée préservée du Semliki. Exclusive, car le lodge est le seul dans la vallée, tel un poste avancé de la civilisation du confort.

Le lodge est géré par Wild Places, une association de défense de la réserve naturelle de Toro-Semliki. À cheval sur la forêt pluviale et la savane herbeuse, celle-ci abrite une faune et une flore particulièrement riches. Aussi, passionnés d'animaux, aventuriers et safaristes dans l'âme devraient-ils séjourner ici au moins une fois dans leur vie.

LOCATION
The only lodge in this 215-square-mile reserve, Semliki is about an hour's drive from Fort Portal and has its own grass airstrip

RATES
From $155 to $370 per person per night depending on season, full board included

ROOMS
8 tents with en suite bathrooms

STYLE
Rustic and cozy safari ambience

FOOD
Three-course evening dinners in the bush, plus excellent homemade chutneys and freshly baked bread every day

X FACTOR
The African wildlife, of course! Guests can go chimpanzee tracking with staff from the reserve's own primate-research project

BOOK TO PACK
"Don't Run, Whatever You Do: My Adventures as a Safari Guide" by Peter Allison

LAGE
Zur einzigen Lodge in dem 558-km²-Reservat ist es rund 1 Stunde Fahrt von Fort Portal im Osten des Landes; eigene Gras-Landepiste vorhanden

PREISE
Je nach Saison zwischen 115 € und 275 € pro Person und Nacht, inklusive Vollpension

ZIMMER
8 Zimmer mit jeweils eigenem Bad

STIL
Rustikale Safari-Gemütlichkeit

KÜCHE
Jeden Abend ein 3-Gänge-Menü mitten im Busch. Exzellente hausgemachte Chutneys und täglich frisch gebackenes Brot

X-FAKTOR
Natürlich Afrikas Tierwelt! Im Reservat läuft ein Primaten-Projekt, dessen Forscher man beim Schimpansen-Tracking begleiten kann

BUCH ZUM ORT
„Don't Run, Whatever You Do: My Adventures as a Safari Guide" von Peter Allison

SITUATION
Le seul lodge dans la réserve de 558 km² est à 1 heure de voiture de Fort Portal, dans l'est du pays ; piste d'atterrissage en herbe privée

PRIX
Selon la saison, de 115 € à 275 € par personne et par nuit en pension complète

CHAMBRES
8 chambres avec salle de bains individuelle

STYLE
Ambiance safari rustique

RESTAURATION
Dîner entrée-plat-dessert en pleine brousse. Délicieux chutneys maison et pain frais tous les jours

LE «PETIT PLUS»
La faune africaine, bien sûr! On peut pister les chimpanzés aux côtés de primatologues

LIVRE À EMPORTER
«Chroniques abyssiniennes» de Moses Isegawa

HOUSEBOAT AT
ST KATHARINE DOCKS
UK

50 St Katharine Way ~ London E1W 1LA ~ United Kingdom
Telephone +44 20 7702 1299
matrixisland@ymail.com
www.chicretreats.com/boutique-hotels-england/houseboat-st-katherines-dock

Creating a genuine getaway in a city as relentlessly busy as London is no mean feat. It's one the owners of this uniquely maritime urban retreat have pulled off in style, however, not least because their hotel remains something of a well-kept secret—despite being just a minute's walk from Tower Bridge.

Formerly a commercial port, the docks are now home to an elegant marina featuring renovated warehouses, wooden pontoons, and small bridges linking the various basins, one of which contains this former coal barge. On board, you'll find it hard to believe the vessel once carried anything so prosaic: Its three suites are spacious, luxurious, and adorned with pictures of historic ocean liners. The ever-present views of the Thames, meanwhile, are as inspiring as the sensation of walking barefoot across boat decking in the middle of a big city.

In einer ständig ausgebuchten Metropole wie London noch als „Getaway" durchzugehen, ist ein ziemlich schwieriges Unterfangen für ein Hotel. Das Houseboat am Dock von St Katharine meistert es vorbildlich, nicht zuletzt, weil es immer noch ein Geheimtipp ist – und das eine Minute von der Tower Bridge entfernt.

Die einstige Handelshafenanlage wurde zu einem eleganten Jachthafen umgebaut, die historischen Gebäude renoviert. Stege aus Holzplanken und kleine Brücken verbinden die Hafenbecken, und in einem davon liegt fest vertäut das Houseboat. Seine Vergangenheit als Kohlekahn ist dem Schiff nicht mehr anzusehen, die drei Suiten sind äußerst großzügig bemessen und mit Plakaten historischer Ozeandampfer dekoriert. Der allgegenwärtige Blick auf die Themse ist genauso rundum belebend wie die Möglichkeit, hier im Sommer barfuß über Planken zu wandeln und bei frisch gebackenen Scones mitten in der City ein maritimes Urlaubserlebnis zu genießen.

Dans une métropole affichant complet en permanence comme Londres, l'appellation « refuge » tient plutôt de la gageure pour un hôtel. Le bateau-hôtel mouillant aux docks de St Katharine relève le défi, notamment parce que c'est encore une adresse confidentielle, et ce à une minute de la tour de Londres!

L'ancien port de commerce a été transformé en élégant port de plaisance et les édifices anciens ont été restaurés. Des pontons en bois et des passerelles relient entre eux les bassins du port, dans l'un desquels le Houseboat est fermement amarré. Rien ne trahit le passé de péniche charbonnière de ce bateau dans ses trois suites très spacieuses décorées d'affiches représentant des paquebots anciens. L'omniprésence de la Tamise est tout aussi parfaitement rafraîchissante que la possibilité de déambuler pieds nus sur les ponts en été et de savourer des vacances sur l'eau autour de scones frais, tout en ayant largué ses amarres en plein cœur de la City.

LOCATION
With Tower Bridge right next door, St Katharine's Docks offers an unmistakably London vibe

RATES
Rooms from $460, suites from $535, breakfast included

ROOMS
5 rooms and suites, each with en suite bathrooms and individual interiors

STYLE
Casual rock star luxury combined with an honest, nautical backdrop

FOOD
Private dinners can be arranged on deck—on land there are all the culinary delights of an international capital

X FACTOR
Should you need a break from the watery views, the boat has its own cinema room

BOOK TO PACK
"I Never Knew That About London" by Christopher Winn

LAGE
Die St Katharine Docks liegen in unmittelbarer Nachbarschaft zur Tower Bridge – mehr London geht nicht

PREISE
Zimmer ab 350 €, Suiten ab 410 €, inklusive Frühstück

ZIMMER
5 Zimmer und Suiten mit En-suite-Bädern und jeweils individueller Einrichtung

STIL
Lässige Rockstar-Großzügigkeit, fest verankert in handfestem nautischem Rahmen

KÜCHE
Auf dem Deck können private Dinner ausgerichtet werden – und an Land wartet das ganze kulinarische Angebot einer echten Metropole

X-FAKTOR
Wer genug von der Aussicht aufs Wasser hat, kann sich im Movie-Room bestens unterhalten

BUCH ZUM ORT
„I Never Knew That About London" von Christopher Winn

SITUATION
Les docks de St Katharine sont à proximité immédiate de la tour de Londres, une situation on ne peut plus centrale

PRIX
Chambres à partir de 350 €, suites à partir de 410 €, petit déjeuner compris

CHAMBRES
5 chambres et suites avec salle de bains privée, toutes aménagées différemment

STYLE
Générosité décontractée digne d'une star du rock, bien ancrée dans un cadre nautique

RESTAURATION
Repas privés sur le pont du bateau. Sur la terre ferme, toute la palette culinaire d'une authentique métropole

LE «PETIT PLUS»
Qui est repu de la vue sur la Tamise se distraira on ne peut mieux dans le salon de cinéma

LIVRE À EMPORTER
«Orages ordinaires» de William Boyd

THE BATH PRIORY
UK

Weston Road ~ Bath ~ BA1 2XT ~ United Kingdom
Telephone +44 122 533 1922 ~ Fax +44 122 544 8276
info@thebathpriory.co.uk
www.thebathpriory.co.uk

With its elegant terraced houses and Roman thermal springs, Bath is one of England's most picturesque cities—and the Bath Priory, built in 1835 on land belonging to the city's abbey, is its most stylish hotel. With extensive Victorian grounds and romantic interiors by Carole Roberts, this hotel is the perfect place for an authentically British weekend break.

The rooms feature Colefax & Fowler and Pierre Frey fabrics, a heritage color scheme, and supremely comfortable beds, while the hotel's gardens are recommended by the Royal Horticultural Society. Take a seat on the elegant patio overlooking the croquet lawn, enjoy a glass of port, or the fabulous full afternoon tea (miniature sandwiches, scones, and clotted cream), and let yourself be transported back to the golden age of empire.

Mit seinen eleganten Häuserzeilen und römischen Thermen ist Bath bis heute eine der schönsten Städte Englands – und das Bath Priory ihr stilvollstes Hotel. Das Haus wurde 1835 auf dem Grundstück einer Abtei erbaut und steht mit seinem viktorianischen Park und den von Carole Roberts romantisch eingerichteten Zimmern bereit für ein hundertprozentig britisches Wochenende.

Stoffe von Colefax & Fowler und Pierre Frey, das verwendete Heritage-Farbschema und die Mitgliedschaft in der Royal Horicultural Society dürfen dabei genauso wenig fehlen wie der Schluck Portwein, bevor man in eines der exzellenten Betten fällt. Beim grandiosen *Full Afternoon Tea* (mit Mini-Sandwiches, Scones und *clotted cream*) oder auf der eleganten Sonnenterrasse mit Blick über die Krocketwiese fühlt man sich unbedingt in die goldene Zeit des Empire zurückversetzt.

Avec ses élégants alignements de maisons et ses thermes romains, Bath compte parmi les plus belles villes d'Angleterre, et le Bath Priory en est l'hôtel le plus raffiné. Édifié en 1835 sur les terres d'une abbaye, cet établissement propose un week-end «so british» dans son parc victorien et ses chambres à l'aménagement romantique signé Carole Roberts.

Les tissus Colefax & Fowler et Pierre Frey, la gamme chromatique Heritage et l'affiliation à la Royal Horticultural Society sont ici des figures imposées, tout comme le doigt de porto dégusté avant de sombrer dans un bon lit. Quand on savoure le grandiose «full afternoon tea» (goûter dinatoire avec petits sandwiches, scones et *clotted cream*) ou quand on profite de l'élégante terrasse donnant sur le terrain de croquet, on se croirait revenu à l'âge d'or de l'Empire britannique.

LOCATION
20 km/12 miles southeast of Bristol and 165 km/ 102 miles west of Heathrow airport

RATES
Rooms from $330 and suites from $1,045, breakfast included

ROOMS
27 rooms and 6 suites. The Heather and Lilac rooms are particularly picturesque, with balconies overlooking the 3-acre grounds

STYLE
Country house with gourmet cuisine and spa

FOOD
The award-winning restaurant is as excellent as it is elegant, its chef making extensive use of products from the southwest of England

X FACTOR
Events such as the horticultural tour with head gardener Jane Moore or the etiquette dinner with running commentary from a former butler

BOOK TO PACK
"The Inimitable Jeeves" by P. G. Wodehouse

LAGE
Bath liegt 20 km südöstlich von Bristol und 165 km westlich des Flughafens Heathrow

PREISE
Zimmer ab 250 €, Suiten ab 775 €, inklusive Frühstück

ZIMMER
27 Zimmer und 6 Suiten; sehr malerisch die Räume Heather und Lilac mit privaten Balkonen zum 1,2 Hektar großen Park

STIL
Country House mit Spa und Gourmet Cuisine

KÜCHE
Das mehrfach ausgezeichnete Restaurant ist so elegant wie exzellent, der Chef verwendet gern Produkte aus Englands Südwesten

X-FAKTOR
Hotel-Events wie eine Pflanzentour mit Stargärtnerin Jane Moore oder das Etikette-Dinner mit *running commentary* eines Profi-Butlers

BUCH ZUM ORT
„Der unvergleichliche Jeeves" von P. G. Wodehouse

SITUATION
Bath est à 20 km au sud-est de Bristol et à 165 km à l'ouest de l'aéroport de Heathrow

PRIX
Chambres à partir de 250 €, suites à partir de 775 €, petit déjeuner compris

CHAMBRES
27 chambres et 6 suites; les chambres Heather et Lilac, avec balcons donnant sur le parc de 1,2 hectare, sont très pittoresques

STYLE
Manoir avec spa et restaurant gastronomique

RESTAURATION
Restaurant étoilé aussi élégant qu'excellent, dont le chef travaille volontiers des produits du sud-ouest de l'Angleterre

LE «PETIT PLUS»
La balade botanique en compagnie de la star des jardins Jane Moore ou le dîner avec tout le décorum commenté en non-stop par un majordome

LIVRE À EMPORTER
«L'Inimitable Jeeves» de P. G. Wodehouse

THE GUNTON ARMS
UK

Cromer Road ~ Thorpe Market ~ Norwich NR11 8TZ ~ United Kingdom
Telephone +44 1263 832 010
office@theguntonarms.co.uk
www.theguntonarms.co.uk

Having fallen in love with the bucolic North Norfolk countryside, London art dealer Ivor Braka and his then-wife, Sarah Graham, purchased this traditional inn and subsequently poured all their creative energies into its renovation.

The result of Branka's considerable efforts is a slightly eccentric eight-bedroom country hotel where guests can enjoy the atmosphere of an old English estate—and the good taste of the owner who has breathed new life into its historic architecture via carefully selected artworks and the sensitive use of color. Set in a beautiful 1,000-acre deer park that was once a popular hunting ground for a pleasure-seeking prince (the future King Edward VII), the Gunton Arms now attracts London sophisticates drawn by the regal calm and the first-rate cuisine—highlights include game from the surrounding estate and fresh Cromer crab, a well-known local delicacy.

Bei einer Landpartie in der Grafschaft Norfolk verfiel der Londoner Kunsthändler Ivor Braka dem Charme des Anwesens Gunton Halls. Jahre später konnte er mit seiner damaligen Frau Sarah Graham ein traditionelles Pub auf dem Gelände erwerben, das Gunton Arms, und investierte seine ganze Leidenschaft in die Renovierung der historischen Gemäuer.

Am Ende dieser beachtlichen Bemühungen stand ein leicht exzentrisches Landhotel mit acht Gästezimmern, traumhaft gelegen in einem 400 Hektar großen Wildpark, einer Kulisse wie aus „Robin Hood". Hier lässt sich urenglische Sommerfrische genauso erfahren wie der *taste* des Gastgebes, der mittels Kunst und einer sensiblen Farbpalette neue Akzente setzte. Wo sich einst der spätere König Edward VII. und seine Jagdgesellschaften ergingen, freuen sich nun kultivierte Londoner an der majestätischen Ruhe und der ausgezeichneten Küche, die unter anderem auf eigenes Wild und die berühmten Cromer-Taschenkrebse setzt. *Most enjoyable!*

Au cours d'une partie de campagne dans le Norfolk, le marchand d'art londonien Ivor Braka eut le coup de foudre pour le domaine de Gunton Hall. Des années plus tard, il acheta avec son épouse d'alors, Sarah Graham, un pub traditionnel rattaché au domaine, le Gunton Arms, et mit toute sa passion dans la restauration de cette bâtisse historique.

Ne ménageant pas ses effonts, il créèr un hôtel de huit chambres, un tantinet excentrique, situé dans un parc giboyeux de 400 hectares, véritable décor à la Robin des bois. Dans cette villégiature typiquement anglaise, on perçoit le goût de propriétaire qui, au moyen d'œuvres d'art et d'une subtile palette de couleurs, a changé l'esprit des lieux. Là où celui qui deviendrait plus tard le roi Édouard VII organisait jadis des parties de chasse, des Londoniens distingués savourent désormais la paix royale et l'excellente cuisine, qui mise notamment sur le gibier du parc et les célèbres crabes de Cromer. Un vrai délice!

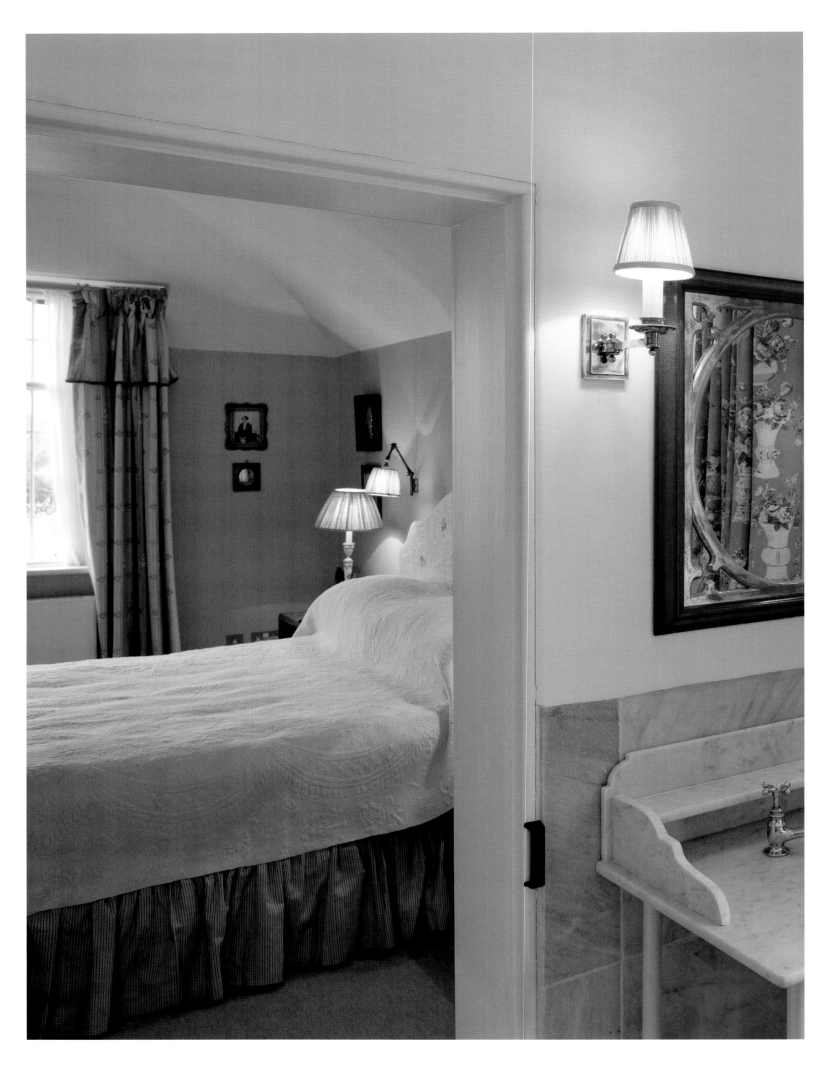

LOCATION
Near the east coast of England, in the county of Norfolk. From Heathrow, it's a 3- to 4-hour drive (head for Norwich/Cromer)

RATES
Double rooms from $145, superior rooms from $250, breakfast included

ROOMS
8 rooms

STYLE
Old inn with superb interiors by design stars Robert Kime and Martin Brudnizki

FOOD
English cuisine at its hearty best—guests can even watch their meat being grilled in the open fireplace

X FACTOR
The sight of the majestic deer outside trumps any painting; in the mornings and evenings, they even come right up to the house

BOOK TO PACK
"The Absolutist" by John Boyne

LAGE
In der Grafschaft Norfolk an Englands Ostküste. Von London-Heathrow sind es 3 bis 4 Stunden Autofahrt in Richtung Norwich/Cromer

PREISE
Doppelzimmer ab 110 €, Superior-Zimmer 190 €, inklusive Frühstück

ZIMMER
8 Zimmer

STIL
Altes Pub, vorbildlich erneuert mithilfe der Interiorstars Robert Kime und Martin Brudnizki

KÜCHE
Englische Küche in ihrer besten, herzhaften Ausprägung; manches Stück Fleisch wird sogar über dem offenen Feuer zubereitet

X-FAKTOR
Besser als jedes Gemälde: das majestätische Wild zu beobachten, das frühmorgens oder abends sogar bis vors Haus kommt

BUCH ZUM ORT
„Das späte Geständnis des Tristan Sadler" von John Boyne

SITUATION
Dans le comté du Norfolk, sur la côte est de l'Angleterre. De Heathrow, à 3 ou 4 heures de voiture en direction de Norwich/Cromer

PRIX
Chambres doubles à partir de 110 €, chambre supérieure 190 €, petit déjeuner compris

CHAMBRES
8 chambres

STYLE
Ancien pub restauré à la perfection avec le concours des stars de la décoration Robert Kime et Martin Brudnizki

RESTAURATION
La cuisine anglaise dans sa plus belle expression rustique, avec des viandes grillées au feu de bois

LE «PETIT PLUS»
Mieux qu'en peinture: le majestueux gibier qui vient jusque sous les fenêtres à l'aube ou au crépuscule

LIVRE À EMPORTER
«Par action et par omission» de P. D. James

THE PIG
UK

Beaulieu Road ~ Brockenhurst ~ Hampshire ~ SO42 7QL ~ United Kingdom
Telephone +44 845 0779 494
info@thepighotel.com
www.thepighotel.com

The English, of course, practically invented country life and, to this day, its traditions are still widely celebrated on weekends. To experience them for yourself, head to this charming Hampshire hotel. As the name suggests, there is a sturdy, rustic feel to The Pig, which, in addition to five well-kept porkers, boasts a first-rate kitchen that sets great store by sustainability and uses produce from its own garden and region wherever possible.

Situated not far from the south coast, it is a place dedicated to simple country pleasures, at which guests can indulge in time-honored aristocratic pursuits, such as fly-fishing, horse riding, and strolling around the grounds in your Wellingtons—but in an atmosphere that is entirely devoid of class snobbishness. Its "witty chic" interiors are always a welcome sight after such outdoor activities, as are the cups of tea that can be enjoyed at the dining room's bare wooden tables.

Die Engländer haben bekanntlich das *country life* erfunden, und bis heute wird es von ihnen an den Wochenenden gediegen zelebriert. Ein besonders schöner Ort dafür ist The Pig. Wie der rustikale Name schon andeutet, geht es hier durchaus ländlich-robust zu: Fünf wohlgehaltene Schweine gehören ebenso zum Hotel wie eine ausgezeichnete nachhaltige Küche, die zu jeder Jahreszeit möglichst viel vom eigenen Garten und Grund verwendet.

Das ganze Haus atmet pure, unverfälschte Lust am Einfachen. So passt der *witty* chic des charmanten Landhauses perfekt, wenn man nach einer Gummistiefel-Wanderung auf blanken Holztischen eine Tasse Tee serviert bekommt. Fliegenfischen, Jagen und ein Ausflug an die nahe Küste sind die Beschäftigungen, mit denen sich die britische Oberschicht seit jeher die Zeit auf dem Land vertrieben hat. Im The Pig wird ihnen ebenfalls gefrönt, und zwar ganz ohne Standesdünkel.

Comme chacun sait, ce sont les Anglais qui ont inventé la *country life*, et ils la célèbrent encore dignement le week-end. Lieu emblématique de cette vie champêtre, The Pig est empreint d'une ambiance résolument campagnarde, comme son nom rustique le suggère : les cinq cochons bien nourris sont ici une institution, au même titre que la délicieuse cuisine «durable» élaborée au fil des saisons avec un maximum de produits du terroir.

Tout l'établissement respire le plaisir pur et authentique des choses simples. Le chic plein d'esprit de ce charmant manoir sonne juste quand, au retour d'une promenade en bottes de caoutchouc, on vous sert une tasse de thé sur de simples tables en bois. Pêche à la mouche, chasse et promenade sur la côte proche, voilà ce à quoi la gentry occupait le plus clair de son temps à la campagne. Et dans cet hôtel, on s'adonne encore à ces occupations, mais sans aucun snobisme.

LOCATION

The hotel is in the New Forest National Park, close to Southampton on the south coast; the journey from London takes less than 2 hours

RATES

Doubles from $200, family rooms from $360

ROOMS

26 rooms: 16 in the main house and 10 in the stable yard, each with forest or garden views

STYLE

House & Garden meets *World of Interiors*

FOOD

The chef is committed to the 25-mile rule—what can't be grown in the kitchen garden is sourced from the surrounding area

X FACTOR

Fly-fishing is a sport long beloved of country gentlemen; the beautiful rivers around The Pig are the perfect place to try it for yourself

BOOK TO PACK

"The Forest" by Edward Rutherfurd

LAGE

Das Hotel befindet sich im New Forest National Park an der englischen Südküste bei Southampton; von London aus in unter 2 Stunden erreichbar

PREISE

Zimmer ab 150 €, Familienzimmer ab 265 €

ZIMMER

26 Zimmer: 16 davon im Haupthaus, 10 im ehemaligen Stall, jeweils mit Wald- oder Gartenblick

STIL

House & Garden trifft *World of Interiors*

KÜCHE

Das Menü folgt der 25-Meilen-Regel: Was nicht im eigenen Küchengarten wächst, wird regional dazugekauft

X-FAKTOR

Seit jeher gehört das Fliegenfischen zu den Gentleman-Sportarten; ihr kann man hier an wunderbaren Gewässern nachgehen

BUCH ZUM ORT

„Der Wald der Könige" von Edward Rutherfurd

SITUATION

Au cœur du New Forest National Park sur la côte méridionale de l'Angleterre, près de Southampton; à moins de 2 heures de Londres en voiture

PRIX

Chambres à partir de 150 €, chambres familiales à partir de 265 €

CHAMBRES

26 chambres, dont 16 dans le bâtiment principal et 10 dans l'ancienne étable, toutes avec vue sur la forêt ou le jardin

STYLE

Mixte de *House & Garden* et de *World of Interiors*

RESTAURATION

En vertu de la règle des 40 km, tout ce qui ne pousse pas sur place est acheté auprès de producteurs locaux

LE «PETIT PLUS»

La région est un paradis pour la pêche à la mouche, sport de gentleman s'il en est

LIVRE À EMPORTER

«La Forêt des rois» d'Edward Rutherfurd

THE WHEATSHEAF INN
UK

West End, Northleach ~ Gloucestershire GL54 3EZ ~ United Kingdom
Telephone +44 1451 860244
reservations@cotswoldswheatsheaf.com
www.cotswoldswheatsheaf.com

The rolling hills of the Gloucestershire Cotswolds are the epitome of picture-book England, a paradise for weekend breaks, in the midst of which lies the Wheatsheaf Inn. Built in traditional Tudor style from the limestone that characterizes the area's architecture, this former village pub was given a new lease on life in 2011. Since then it has pulled off the rare trick of appealing both to locals and to urbanites looking for a relaxing getaway.

With walls featuring Farrow & Ball paints, Lewis & Wood papers, and pictures by contemporary artist Sebastian Krüger, the 14 rooms exude a genuinely romantic air while steering well clear of kitsch. The food is astoundingly good, the garden has its own playground, and there are spare Wellingtons for the kids. In fact, the Wheatsheaf is such a perfectly formed addition to the picturesque Cotswold surroundings, it seems hard to believe it's a relatively new addition to the scene.

Die englischen Cotswolds gelten nicht umsonst als Synonym für ein Landleben wie im Bilderbuch, und mittendrin in diesem Paradies fürs gehobene *weekend* liegt das Wheatsheaf Inn in der Grafschaft Gloucestershire. Das alte Pub wurde im typischen Kalkstein gebaut, und auch die Nachbarschaft ist im schönsten Tudor-Stil erhalten. 2011 wurde die Dorfwirtschaft wiederbelebt und vollbringt mit ihren 14 Zimmern nun einen erstaunlichen Spagat – sie spricht die Einheimischen genauso an wie Städter, die nach einem Plätzchen zum Ausspannen suchen.

Mit Wandfarben von Farrow & Ball, Tapeten von Lewis & Wood und Bildern des zeitgenössischen Künstlers Sebastian Krüger atmen die Zimmer handfeste Romantik, ohne dabei unter Kitschverdacht zu geraten. Die Küche ist bemerkenswert gut, im Garten wartet ein Spielplatz, und für die Kinder stehen Gummistiefel bereit. Würde es das Wheatsheaf Inn nicht wirklich geben, man hätte es in die Bilderbuchwelt der Cotswold hineinzeichnen müssen.

Les Cotswolds sont à juste titre synonyme de vie à la campagne digne d'un livre d'images, et au cœur de ce paradis pour week-ends huppés se trouve le Wheatsheaf Inn, dans le comté du Gloucestershire. Cet ancien pub construit en pierre calcaire locale s'inscrit dans un magnifique ensemble Tudor superbement conservé. Avec ses 14 chambres, cette auberge de village, à laquelle on a insufflé une nouvelle vie en 2011, réussit un étonnant tour de force : elle plaît aussi bien aux personnes du cru qu'aux citadins en quête de détente.

Avec des peintures de Farrow & Ball, des papiers peints signés Lewis & Wood et des tableaux de l'artiste contemporain Sebastian Krüger, les chambres respirent un romantisme pur et dur, sans prêter le flanc aux accusations kitsch. La cuisine est remarquable et dans le jardin, des équipements de jeu et des bottes en caoutchouc attendent les enfants. Si le Wheatsheaf n'existait pas, il aurait fallu le dessiner dans paysage grandiose des Cotswolds.

LOCATION
In the heart of Northleach village, between Gloucester and Oxford; about a 2-hour drive from the center of London in normal traffic

RATES
Rooms between $225 and $370, continental breakfast included

ROOMS
14 rooms, all with power showers or freestanding baths

STYLE
Handsome village pub, furnished with smart, contemporary touches

FOOD
Unpretentious cooking with a commitment to using local, organic (and therefore seasonal) ingredients

X FACTOR
As befits a village pub, the bar focuses heavily on beers, with a whole range of excellent and exotic examples on offer

BOOK TO PACK
"The Cotswolds' Finest Gardens" by Tony Russell

LAGE
Im Herzen des Dorfes Northleach zwischen Gloucester und Oxford. Vom Zentrum Londons aus fährt man bei Normalverkehr ca. 2 Stunden

PREISE
Zimmer zwischen 165 € und 280 €, inklusive kontinentales Frühstück

ZIMMER
14 Zimmer mit Power-Duschen oder freistehenden Badewannen

STIL
Stilvolle Dorfwirtschaft, eingerichtet mit pfiffigen zeitgenössischen Details

KÜCHE
Unprätentiöse Kochkunst, bei der ausschließlich biologische und regionale Zutaten verwendet werden, die saisonal wechseln

X-FAKTOR
Auch das noch: Die Barmannschaft hat Bier zu ihrem Liebling erkoren und bietet deshalb eine ganze Palette ausgezeichneter, rarer Sorten an

BUCH ZUM ORT
„The Cotswolds' Finest Gardens" von Tony Russell

SITUATION
Au cœur du village de Northleach, entre Gloucester et Oxford; par trafic routier normal, à environ 2 heures du centre du Londres

PRIX
Chambres entre 165 € et 280 €, petit déjeuner continental compris

CHAMBRES
14 chambres dotées de douches à jet puissant ou de baignoires sur pieds

STYLE
Élégante auberge de village aménagée avec des détails contemporains futés

RESTAURATION
Art culinaire sans chichi qui fait appel à des produits bio et régionaux, toujours de saison

LE «PETIT PLUS»
La cerise sur le gâteau: grande amatrice de bière, l'équipe du bar propose une palette de raretés excellentes

LIVRE À EMPORTER
«Propos sur le jardin» de Gertrude Jekyll

CASA ZINC
URUGUAY

La Barra ~ Punta del Este ~ Uruguay
Telephone +598 996 20066, ~ +598 427 73003
posada@casazinc.com
www.casazinc.com

He'd originally intended just to open a new showroom for his favorite vacation-home pieces, but somehow antiques dealer Aaron Hojman ended up with an entire hotel. It's perhaps unsurprising then that his *posada* is decorated throughout with hand-picked vintage pieces, and that each of its six rooms is a one-off.

The atmosphere is extremely friendly and relaxed, with everyone dining around a single table and breakfast served until late in the afternoon (guests can even commandeer the kitchen and rustle up dinner themselves). This endearing mixture of the exclusive and the informal has made Casa Zinc one of the hippest spots in all Uruguay. It lies just a few minutes from the busy beach of Punta del Este—and yet seems a million miles away.

Eigentlich wollte der Antiquitätenhändler Aaron Hojman nur einen neuen Showroom für seine schönsten Ferienhaus-Stücke aufmachen. Dieses Vorhaben geriet ihm letztlich zur Eröffnung einen überaus liebenswerten Vintage-Hotels. Folglich ist das *posada* nun von der Türschwelle bis zum Nachtkästchen mit handverlesenen Stücken dekoriert; sechs Zimmer gibt es, und jedes ist eine eigene Welt.

Der Hotelbetrieb wird hier betont familiär und lässig abgewickelt: Man sitzt an einem gemeinsamen Esstisch, und Frühstück gibt es bis spät in den Nachmittag hinein. Wer will, kann sich dann auch gleich selbst in die Küche stellen und sein Abendessen zubereiten. Die sympathische Mischung aus exklusiv und ungezwungen hat das Hotel zu einem der hippsten Plätze Uruguays gemacht, nur wenige Minuten vom quirligen Strand von Punta del Este entfernt – und doch irgendwie ganz woanders.

À l'origine, l'antiquaire Aaron Hojman voulait simplement ouvrir un nouveau show-room pour y présenter ses plus beaux objets de décoration pour maisons de campagne. Mais de fil en aiguille, il en est venu à ouvrir un hôtel vintage absolument charmant. Ainsi, du seuil de la porte à la table de chevet, cette posada est décorée de pièces uniques, chacune des six chambres constituant un univers en soi.

Convivialité et décontraction sont la philosophie clairement affichée par les hôteliers : on prend ses repas à une table commune, et le petit déjeuner est servi jusqu'en milieu d'après-midi. Les hôtes qui le souhaitent peuvent aussi tout simplement s'installer dans la cuisine pour préparer leur dîner. Mariant haut de gamme et simplicité, la posada est devenue un des endroits les plus branchés d'Uruguay, à deux pas de la plage trépidante de Punta del Este. Mais l'on s'y sent tout de même à des années-lumière.

LOCATION
In the former fishing village of La Barra, 25 minutes from Punta del Este airport

RATES
Rooms from $160, "studios" from $360, breakfast included

ROOMS
6 unique rooms—the 1940s-style Estudio Arquitecto is particularly atmospheric

STYLE
Charming mix of the DIY, vintage, and rare

FOOD
The hotel's lavish breakfast is available right through to 4 p.m.

X FACTOR
Frankly, pretty much everything at this charmingly offbeat hotel is special. A particular highlight can be found out on the idyllic patio, though: a magnificent four-ton olive tree that was brought here from an old estancia

BOOK TO PACK
"Blood Pact: And Other Stories" by Mario Benedetti

LAGE
Im ehemaligen Fischerdorf La Barra, 25 Minuten vom Flughafen Punta del Este entfernt

PREISE
Zimmer ab 120 €, Estudios ab 275 €, jeweils inklusive Frühstück

ZIMMER
6 individuell gestaltete Zimmer – zum Beispiel das Estudio Arquitecto im Stil der 1940er

STIL
Best of DIY, Vintage und kuriose Raritäten

KÜCHE
Das Hotel-Frühstück ist opulent und wird bis 16 Uhr serviert

X-FAKTOR
Eigentlich ist alles hier besonders und von schrulliger Liebenswürdigkeit. Der idyllische Patio bietet aber eine besondere Sehenswürdigkeit: einen 4 Tonnen schweren Olivenbaum, welcher von einer alten Estanzia stammt

BUCH ZUM ORT
„Die Gnadenfrist" von Mario Benedetti

SITUATION
Dans l'ancien village de pêcheurs La Barra, à 25 km de l'aéroport de Punta del Este

PRIX
Chambres à partir de 125 €, studios à partir de 275 €, petit déjeuner compris

CHAMBRES
6 chambres personnalisées, dont l'Estudio Arquitecto, dans le style années 1940

STYLE
Excellent travail de bricoleur, vintage et curiosités

RESTAURATION
L'hôtel propose un petit déjeuner royal servi jusqu'à 16 heures!

LE «PETIT PLUS»
Ici, tout est unique et possède un charme excentrique, mais le patio idyllique recèle un vrai monument: un olivier de 4 tonnes provenant d'une ancienne *estancia*

LIVRE À EMPORTER
«La Trêve» de Mario Benedetti

ACE HOTEL
USA

701 East Palm Canyon Drive ~ Palm Springs, CA 92264 ~ USA
Telephone +1 760 325 9900 ~ Fax +1 760 325 7878
enquire.ps@acehotel.com
www.acehotel.com

Portland, Seattle, Midtown New York, London, L.A., Panama, Palm Springs: Going by the locations—and the fans—of the small Ace Hotel chain, you could be forgiven for thinking it was actually a fashionable record label. Situated in the trendiest parts of their respective cities, the hotels are popular with media types, designers, and other cool urbanites who appreciate not only the location but also the effortless way the lobbies become local nightlife hot spots—and the quirky individuality of their interiors.

The Ace Palm Springs, for instance, is a Howard Johnson Motel from 1965 that has been turned into a boutique hotel with an eccentric camping vibe. The rooms are furnished with vintage pieces and industrial accessories, while, outside, there are tarpaulin-shaded patios with fireplaces and hammocks.

Portland, Seattle, Midtown NYC, London, L.A., Panama oder eben Palm Springs: Sieht man sich die Locations und die Anhängerschaft der kleinen Hotelkette Ace genauer an, könnte sie eigentlich auch ein angesagtes Plattenlabel sein. Medienleute, Designer und andere coole Urbanisten steigen bevorzugt hier ab, weil die Hotels stets in den In-Vierteln liegen und sich abends Hotelgäste und lokale Szene wie von selbst in der Lobby vermischen.

Außerdem ist jedes Haus individuell durchgeknallt. Im Falle des Ace Palm Springs wurde zum Beispiel ein Howard-Johnson-Motel aus dem Jahr 1965 in ein Boutique-Hotel verwandelt, das mit schrägem Camping-Ambiente auftrumpft. In den Zimmern findet man Vintage-Mobiliar und Industrie-Accessoires, draußen warten von Zeltplanen überspannte Patios mit Lagerfeuern und Hängematten.

Portland, Seattle, New York, Londres, Los Angeles, Panama ou… Palm Springs : quand on considère cette liste et les adeptes de la petite chaîne d'hôtels Ace, on pourrait croire qu'il s'agit d'un label de musique en *hipster*. Professionnels des médias, designers et autres créatifs apprécient ces hôtels situés dans des quartiers en vogue où, le soir venu, ils se mêlent spontanément aux branchés du coin dans le hall de l'hôtel.

Les hôtels Ace sont décalés, chacun à sa façon. Celui de Palm Springs est un motel Howard Johnson de 1965 converti en hôtel de charme jouant la carte de l'ambiance camping folklo. Dans les chambres, on trouve des meubles vintage et des objets industriels en guise d'accessoires, tandis que dans les patios couverts de toile de tente, feux de camp et hamacs attendent les hôtes.

LOCATION
Located south of downtown Palm Springs,
175 km/109 miles from Los Angeles

RATES
Rooms from $100, breakfast not included

ROOMS
165 rooms and 11 suites arranged around the
pool area. The best have their own private
patios with fireplaces

STYLE
Surfer style with classy retro design

FOOD
The King's Highway is an homage to classic
American roadside diners; the Amigo Room
bar serves beer and cocktails

X FACTOR
The record players with LPs in some of the
rooms. And the Ace fashion line, which is also
available via an online shop—the coyote-print
baby's bodysuit is particularly cool

BOOK TO PACK
"Frank: The Voice" by James Kaplan

LAGE
Südlich von Downtown Palm Springs gelegen,
175 km östlich von Los Angeles

PREISE
Zimmer ab 75 €, ohne Frühstück

ZIMMER
165 Zimmer und 11 Suiten rings um den Poolbereich; die besten haben ihre eigenen Patios
mit Außenkamin

STIL
Surfer-Style mit ambitioniertem Retro-Design

KÜCHE
Das King's Highway ist eine Hommage ans klas-
sische amerikanische Roadside Diner, die
Amigo-Room-Bar serviert Bier und Cocktails

X-FAKTOR
Der Plattenspieler mit Vinyl-LPs in manchen
Zimmern. Und die Ace-eigene Modelinie, die
man auch online bestellen kann. Besonders
cool: Baby-Strampler mit Kojoten-Silhouette!

BUCH ZUM ORT
„Sinatra. Sein Leben, seine Musik, seine Filme"
von Richard Havers

SITUATION
Au sud du centre-ville de Palm Springs,
à 175 km à l'est de Los Angeles

PRIX
Chambres à partir de 75 €, petit déjeuner
non compris

CHAMBRES
165 chambres et 11 suites disposées autour
de la piscine ; les meilleurs hébergements
ont un patio privé avec cheminée

STYLE
Style surfer avec un ambitieux design rétro

RESTAURATION
Le King's Highway rend hommage à la cuisine
de routiers américaine classique, et le bar
Amigo Room sert de la bière et des cocktails

LE «PETIT PLUS»
Le tourne-disque et les vinyles dans certaines
chambres, ainsi que la ligne de prêt-à-porter
Ace, également en vente sur Internet. La gre-
nouillère à motif coyote est craquante !

LIVRE À EMPORTER
«Sinatra» de Richard Havers

AMANGIRI
USA

1 Kayenta Road ~ Canyon Point, UT 84741-285 ~ USA
Telephone +1 435 675 3999 ~ Fax +1 435 675 8999
amangiri@amanresorts.com
www.amanresorts.com/amangiri/home.aspx

Aman Resorts has a reputation for establishing hotels in the world's most beautiful places—and for getting there before anyone else. The Amangiri ("peaceful mountain"), which stands alone in a southern Utah canyon, offers spectacular confirmation, the full-height windows affording stunning views of the desert valley and surrounding rocky plateaus.

Its concrete, stone, and steel structures—by architects Marwan Al-Sayed, Wendell Burnette, and Rick Joy—are carefully integrated into this dramatic environment, while the 34 suites, each boasting a different ambience, with some also having their own pool, feature pale wood and cream-colored soft furnishings. A place of stark contrasts, the Amangiri is both inspiring and wonderfully cosseting at the same time.

Den Edelhotels von Aman eilt der Ruf voraus, auf der ganzen Welt an den schönsten Plätzen zu liegen – und zwar lange, bevor andere sie entdecken. Das Amangiri („friedlicher Berg") in der dramatischen Landschaft Süd-Utahs bestätigt das auf spektakuläre Weise: Die Wüstenlandschaft und die umliegenden Felsenplateaus werden durch die raumhohen Fenster auf eindrückliche Weise in Szene gesetzt. Jede der 34 Suiten fängt andere Stimmungen ein, einige haben auch einen eigenen Pool.

Äußerlich setzten die Architekten Marwan Al-Sayed, Wendell Burnette und Rick Joy die Bauten aus Beton, Stein und Stahl mit idealer Präzision in die Natur; innen bilden helles Holz und cremefarbene Stoffe den weichen Kontrapunkt zu ihrem Felsenstil. Aus diesem Gegensatz entsteht ein Kraftfeld, in dem man sich als Gast ziemlich einzigartig aufgehoben fühlt.

Les hôtels de luxe de la chaîne Aman Resorts ont la réputation de s'implanter dans les plus beaux endroits au monde avant les autres. L'Amangiri («montagne paisible»), dans l'impressionnant Utah méridional, en apporte la preuve spectaculaire: les baies vitrées courant du sol au plafond mettent en scène de manière saisissante le désert et les plateaux rocheux alentour. Chacune des 34 suites – certaines avec piscine privée – est empreinte d'une ambiance différente.

Les architectes Marwan Al-Sayed, Wendell Burnette et Rick Joy ont intégré à la nature les bâtiments en béton, en pierre et en acier avec une précision d'orfèvre. En contrepoint à ce style minéral, ils ont choisi du bois clair et des étoffes crème pour les intérieurs. Dans le champ de forces qui en résulte, les hôtes se sentent enveloppés dans un cocon douillet.

LOCATION
Situated in the Four Corners region, where the states of Utah, Colorado, New Mexico, and Arizona meet. The nearest airport is in Page, a 25-minute drive south of the hotel

RATES
Suites from $1,100, pool suites from $1,650, breakfast not included

ROOMS
34 suites with underfloor heating

STYLE
International Style 2.0: effortlessly sensuous architecture in dramatic surroundings

FOOD
Rustic, seasonal dishes are served in the Dining Room, the centerpiece of which is an open kitchen with a wood-fired oven

X FACTOR
The Amangiri spa, painstakingly carved out of the rock, is both impressive and visually calming

BOOK TO PACK
"Between a Rock and a Hard Place" by Aron Ralston

LAGE
Im Gebiet der Four Corners gelegen, wo Utah, Colorado, New Mexico und Arizona zusammentreffen. Der nächste Flughafen ist Page Airport, 25 Minuten südlich des Hotels

PREISE
Suiten ab 800 €, Pool-Suiten ab 1200 €, ohne Frühstück

ZIMMER
34 Suiten mit Fußbodenheizung

STIL
International Style 2.0: souveräne Sinnlichkeit, eingebettet in eine dramatische Szenerie

KÜCHE
Herzstück des Dining Room ist die offene Küche mit Holzofen – hier werden saisonale, rustikale Spezialitäten zubereitet

X-FAKTOR
Eindrucksvoll und schon allein über das Auge meditativ wirkend: das Spa des Amangiri, mit viel Aufwand direkt aus dem Fels gehauen

BUCH ZUM ORT
„127 Hours im Canyon" von Aron Ralston

SITUATION
Dans la région des Four Corners, où convergent Utah, Colorado, Nouveau-Mexique et Arizona. L'aéroport le plus proche, Page Airport, est à 25 minutes en direction du sud

PRIX
Suites à partir de 800 €, suites avec piscine à partir de 1 200 €, petit déjeuner non compris

CHAMBRES
34 suites avec chauffage par le sol

STYLE
Style international version 2.0 : sensualité royale, dans un cadre spectaculaire

RESTAURATION
Pièce maîtresse du Dining Room, la cuisine américaine équipée d'un fourneau à bois. On y prépare des plats rustiques de saison

LE «PETIT PLUS»
Le spa creusé dans le roc au prix d'un travail titanesque est impressionnant, et sa simple vue invite à la méditation

LIVRE À EMPORTER
«127 heures» d'Aron Ralston

"It's an extraordinary otherworld—a fluid,
sculpted triumph that channels nature
at her loudest and proudest."

TATLER TRAVEL GUIDE, UK

„Dieses Hotel ist eine außerordentliche Gegenwelt – ein fließend skulpturaler Triumph,
inspiriert von der Natur in ihrer stolzesten Ausprägung."

« Cet hôtel constitue un antimonde d'exception : une prouesse sculpturale fluide,
inspirée de la nature dans toute sa majesté. »

BEDFORD POST
USA

954 Old Post Road ~ Bedford, NY 10506 ~ USA
Telephone +1 914 234 7800
inn@bedfordpostinn.com
www.bedfordpostinn.com

As if the historic ambience weren't reason enough to visit the Bedford Post, there's the added bonus of staying in a place co-owned by gracefully graying heartthrob Richard Gere. Together with Tiffany Vassilakis, Gere's ex-wife, Carey Lowell has transformed a picturesque group of farm buildings from 1762 into a country hotel at which first-class cuisine and eco-friendly interior design take the leading roles.

With a location just an hour from Manhattan, in-house yoga classes, and luxurious, romantic rooms, some of which have fireplaces and verandas, the inn attracts upscale bohemian New Yorkers and is packed all year round. Probably, though, that has less to do with a certain Hollywood actor and more with stressed city-dwellers' need for regular escapes with their partner or best friend.

Wenn das kein sexy graumeliertes Argument für einen Besuch im Bedford Post ist: Zu den Besitzern dieses *luxury inn* gehört Richard Gere. Gemeinsam mit Tiffany Vassilakis hat seine Ex-Frau Carey Lowell den malerischen Hof aus dem Jahr 1762 in ein wahrlich filmreifes Land-hotel mit erstklassiger Küche verwandelt.

Oberste Prämisse war dabei umweltfreundli-ches und nachhaltiges Design, schließlich hat man hier die Edelboheme von New York zu Gast. Diese logiert in luxuriös-romantischen Zimmern, einige mit Kamin und Veranda, und nimmt an den angebotenen Yoga-Kursen teil. Nur 60 Minuten von Manhattan entfernt, ist das Bedford Post zu jeder Jahreszeit bestens gebucht. Was nun kaum etwas mit Richard Gere zu tun hat – eher mit der ewigen Lust geplagter Städter auf ein wenig *country life* mit dem Partner oder der besten Freundin.

Sexy, la soixantaine grisonnante... N'est-ce pas un argument en faveur du Bedford Post? En effet, un de ses propriétaires n'est autre que Richard Gere. Avec Tiffany Vassilakis, son ex-épouse Carey Lowell a fait de cette ancienne charmante ferme de 1762 un relais de campagne digne d'un décor de cinéma et dotée d'une table excellente.

Ce faisant, la priorité a été donnée au design écologique et durable, car on reçoit ici la crème des bobos new-yorkais. Ceux-ci logent dans des chambres alliant romantisme et luxe, dont certaines avec cheminée et véranda, et suivent les cours de yoga proposés. À seule-ment 1 heure de Manhattan, le Bedford Post affiche complet en toute saison. Cela tient moins à Richard Gere qu'au fait que les citadins stressés ont des envies de séjour à la cam-pagne en couple ou entre amis.

LOCATION
In the heart of posh Westchester village, 70 km/43 miles northeast of Manhattan

RATES
Rooms from $395, breakfast included

ROOMS
8 rooms, each with its own marble bathroom

STYLE
Dream retreat in Dutch colonial farm ensemble converted with impeccable taste

FOOD
Be it at the casual barn or the more formal The Farmhouse, guests at the Bedford Inn enjoy contemporary U.S. cuisine prepared with environmentally sound ingredients

X FACTOR
In addition to the celebrity factor, there's a large yoga loft with exposed roof timbers in which Vinyasa, Iyengar, or Kundalini classes are held every morning (and sometimes in the afternoons and evenings, too)

BOOK TO PACK
"Infinite Life" by Robert Thurman

LAGE
Im Herzen des reichen Westchester, 70 km nordöstlich von Manhattan

PREISE
Zimmer ab 290 €, inklusive Frühstück

ZIMMER
8 Zimmer, alle mit eigenem Marmorbad

STIL
Traum-Landhaus im Dutch-Colonial-Stil, mit viel Geschmack umgebaut und geführt

KÜCHE
The Barn mit entspannter Atmosphäre und das formellere The Farmhouse servieren moderne US-Küche, natürlich zubereitet aus ökologisch einwandfreien Zutaten

X-FAKTOR
Außer dem Promi-Faktor? Zum Beispiel das großzügige Yoga Loft mit offenem Dachstuhl, wo jeden Morgen (mitunter auch nachmittags und abends) Klassen in Vinyasa, Iyengar oder Kundalini stattfinden

BUCH ZUM ORT
„Grenzenlos leben" von Robert Thurman

SITUATION
Au cœur du sélect comté de Westchester, à 70 km au nord-est de Manhattan

PRIX
Chambres à partir de 290 €, petit déjeuner compris

CHAMBRES
8 chambres, toutes avec salle de bains en marbre

STYLE
Maison de campagne de style colonial hollandais, restaurée et tenue avec goût

RESTAURATION
The Barn, à l'ambiance décontractée, et le très chic The Farmhouse servent de la cuisine américaine moderne à base de produits 100 % bio produits écolabellisables

LE «PETIT PLUS»
Hormis le facteur célébrité, le grand Yoga Loft avec poutres apparentes, où chaque jour sont enseignés le vinyasa, le Iyengar ou le kundalini

LIVRE À EMPORTER
«La Révolution intérieure» de Robert Thurman

EL COSMICO
USA

802 South Highland Avenue ~ Marfa, TX 79843 ~ USA
Telephone +1 877 822 1950
info@elcosmico.com
www.elcosmico.com

When a hotel lists its events under the heading "happenings," you can probably guess what kind of place it will be. El Cosmico certainly lives up to expectations, resembling a hippie outpost in the Texan desert.

Guests stay in spacious trailers or yurts scattered across a 17-acre site, prepare their meals in a communal kitchen, and discover the universally relaxing appeal of the hammock. Accommodation is not exactly luxurious nor is it rudimentary. Anything but: Working with architects Lake/Flato, owner Liz Lambert has created wonderful interiors that re-create in painstaking detail the look of 1950s America. The camp's two tepees, meanwhile, take guests even further back into the country's past.

Wenn ein Hotel in seinem Programm ernsthaft das Kapitel „Happenings" aufführt, dann ahnt man schon ungefähr, was los ist. Und richtig: Auf einem sieben Hektar großen Grundstück in der texanischen Wüste steht mit dem EL Cosmico eine Außenstelle der Hippie-Kultur.

Man wohnt hier in geräumigen Trailern oder Jurten, teilt sich mit den anderen eine Gemeinschaftsküche und erhebt tagsüber die Hängematte zum universalen Aufenthaltsort. Dabei ist der Luxus zwar überschaubar, keinesfalls aber sind die Wohnwagen nur Behelfsunterkunft. Vielmehr hat Betreiberin Liz Lambert mithilfe der Architekten von Lake/Flato ganz wunderbare Interiors geschaffen, die detailgetreu eine Zeitreise ins Amerika der 1950er ermöglichen. Residiert man in einem der beiden Tipis der Anlage, geht die amerikanische Zeitreise sogar noch etwas weiter zurück.

Quand le programme d'un hôtel comporte une rubrique « Happenings » en bonne et due forme, on imagine vaguement ce qu'il en est. Et cela se confirme dans les faits : implanté sur sept hectares dans le désert du Texas, El Cosmico est un poste avancé de la culture hippie.

On dort ici dans de spacieuses caravanes ou sous des tipis, on partage une cuisine avec les autres hôtes et, pendant la journée, on élève le hamac au rang de lieu de vie universel. Sans être luxueuses, les caravanes ne sont pas pour autant des abris de fortune. Au contraire : avec les architectes de Lake/Flato, la gérante Liz Lambert a créé des intérieurs fabuleux qui, avec une grande fidélité dans les détails, vous transportent dans l'Amérique des années 1950. Et dans les tipis, le voyage dans le temps remonte encore plus loin dans l'histoire américaine.

LOCATION
Marfa is located in western Texas, 760 km/ 472 miles from Austin. El Cosmico is on Highway 67, south of the town center

RATES
Trailers from $110 per night per unit, safari tents from $65, and tepees from $80 (all self-catering)

ROOMS
7 trailers, 8 safari tents, and 3 tepees—more trailers are currently being renovated

STYLE
Intriguing contemporary caravanserai filled with Americana accessories

FOOD
Guests share a communal kitchen

X FACTOR
The sense of community that is part of the El Cosmico philosophy. And, of course, the art sites in Marfa that attract Donald Judd disciples from around the world

BOOK TO PACK
"On the Road" by Jack Kerouac

LAGE
Marfa liegt im Westen von Texas, 760 km von Austin entfernt. El Cosmico ist am Highway 67 zu finden, südlich des Ortszentrums

PREISE
Übernachtung im Wohnwagen ab 85 €, im Safari-Zelt 50 €, im Tipi 60 €, jeweils mit Selbstverpflegung

ZIMMER
7 Wohnwagen, 8 Safari-Zelte und 3 Tipis; weitere Wohnwagen werden restauriert

STIL
Absolut sehenswerte, moderne Karawanserei mit vielen Americana-Accessoires

KÜCHE
Die Gäste teilen sich eine Gemeinschaftsküche

X-FAKTOR
Das pfadfinderhafte Gemeinschaftsgefühl, das zur Philosophie des Camps gehört. Und natürlich Marfas Kunst-Pilgerstätten, für die Donald-Judd-Jünger aus aller Welt hierherkommen

BUCH ZUM ORT
„Unterwegs" von Jack Kerouac

SITUATION
Au sud du centre-ville de Marfa, dans l'ouest du Texas, en bordure de la Highway 67 et à 760 km d'Austin

PRIX
Nuitée dans une caravane à partir de 85 €, sous une tente de safari 50 €, dans un tipi 60 € ; aucun repas n'est servi

CHAMBRES
7 caravanes, 8 tentes de safari et 3 tipis ; d'autres caravanes sont en cours de restauration

STYLE
Caravansérail moderne regorgeant d'accessoires Americana. À voir absolument !

RESTAURATION
Cuisine commune à la disposition des hôtes

LE «PETIT PLUS»
L'esprit communautaire, inscrit dans la philosophie de l'hôtel. Sans oublier les lieux de pèlerinage artistique à Marfa, qui attirent des fans de Donald Judd du monde entier

LIVRE À EMPORTER
«Sur la route» de Jack Kerouac

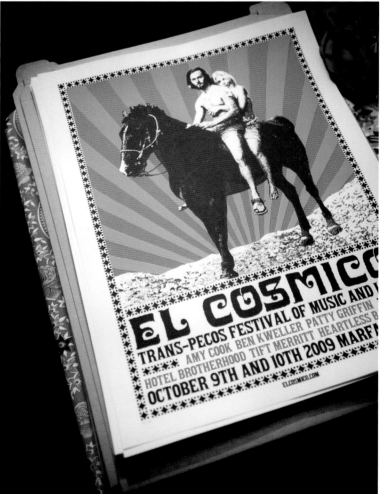

"El Cosmico is part vintage trailer and tepee hotel,
part creative lab and amphitheater—a community space
that fosters artistic and intellectual exchange."

LIZ LAMBERT, FOUNDER

„El Cosmico ist teils Wohnwagen- und Tipi-Hotel,
teils Kreativlabor und Amphitheater – ein Ort der Gemeinschaft,
der künstlerischen und intellektuellen Austausch befördert."

« El Cosmico est à la fois un hôtel de caravanes et de tipis,
un laboratoire de création et un amphithéâtre – un lieu communautaire
qui favorise les échanges artistiques et intellectuels. »

FREEHAND MIAMI
USA

2727 Indian Creek Drive ~ Miami Beach ~ Florida 33140 ~ USA
Telephone +1 305 531 2727 ~ Fax +1 305 531 5651
info.miami@thefreehand.com
thefreehand.com

From the outside, it could be an old-fashioned beach hotel, but, inside, the Freehand Miami is more summery hall of residence for adults, as perhaps imagined by indie director Wes Anderson. This former 1930s Art Deco hotel, just a short walk from Ocean Drive, has been transformed by New York kings of cool Roman & Williams, who also devised the interiors for some of Ace Hotel's creative urban hideouts.

The rooms and lounges offer stylish echoes of a past era, with midcentury furniture and bold retro colors that harmonize beautifully with the Florida sun. There are also functional bunk bed dormitories whose charmingly patinated changing room aesthetic is sure to please Hipstamatic photographers and Mac-toting graphic designers—providing they can get into the spirit of sharing. If so, they'll also benefit from particularly friendly rates.

Nur einen kurzen Spaziergang vom Ocean Drive entfernt liegt ein Hostel, das an Filmsets von Wes Anderson erinnert. Halb *Old-school*-Strandhaus, halb perfektes Schullandheim für Erwachsene: Das ist das Freehand Miami.

Umgebaut wurde das ehemalige Art-déco-Hotel aus den 1930ern von den New Yorker Coolisten Roman & Williams, die schon die Ace-Hotels zu urbanen Herbergen für Kreative machten. Die Zimmer und Lounges sind bildschöne Botschafter einer vergangenen Epoche: Mid-Century-Mobiliar und kräftige Retro-Farben harmonieren bestens mit der Sonne Floridas. Schön funktionale Schlafsäle, teils mit Hochbetten und kunstvoll patinierter Umkleideraum-Optik, vollenden den Charme dieser Unterkunft. Genau das Ambiente, in dem sich Hipstamatic-Fotografen und Grafiker mit Apple-Gerätepark wohlfühlen. Vorausgesetzt natürlich, sie teilen die Begeisterung für Gemeinschaftsatmosphäre – die aber auch für eine sehr friedliche Preisgestaltung sorgt.

À deux pas d'Ocean Drive se dresse une auberge de jeunesse digne d'un film de Wes Anderson qui tient à la fois de la maison de bord de mer un brin désuète et de la parfaite colonie de vacances pour adultes : le Freehand Miami.

Cet ancien hôtel Arts déco des années 1930 a été transformé par les architectes new-yorkais Roman & Williams, qui avaient déjà transformé les hôtels Ace en retraites citadines pour créatifs. Les chambres et les foyers sont les magnifiques ambassadeurs d'une époque révolue, avec du mobilier années 1950 et des tons rétro saturés en parfait accord avec le soleil de Floride. Des dortoirs épurés et fonctionnels, dont certains avec des lits superposés et un look vestiaire patiné avec art, apportent la touche finale. De quoi plaire aux photographes de la génération Hipstamatic et aux graphistes bardés de matériel Apple, à condition, bien sûr, d'aimer la vie en communauté – le gage de prix très raisonnables.

LOCATION
On the corner of 28th Street and Indian Creek Drive, just minutes from the Miami Beach Convention Center and the seafront

RATES
Beds from $35, private rooms from $150

ROOMS
As befits a hostel, the Freehand offers not only private rooms but also beds in shared rooms. There's also a bungalow that sleeps 8

STYLE
Thrown-together aesthetic in which every rug and hook looks just right

FOOD
As we went to press, the restaurant (good food in good company) was still being readied; the Broken Shaker bar was already serving handcrafted cocktails until 2 a.m.

X FACTOR
On weekends, there's barbecued corn on the cob outside—plus a table tennis tournament

BOOK TO PACK
"The South Beach Diet" by Dr. Arthur Agatston

LAGE
An der Ecke 28th Street und Indian Creek Drive, nur wenige Blocks vom Miami Beach Convention Center und 100 m vom Strand entfernt

PREISE
Betten ab 25 €, Privatzimmer ab 115 €

ZIMMER
Als Hostel bietet das Freehand neben einzeln buchbaren Zimmern auch Schlafsäle und einen Bungalow für 8 Personen

STIL
Wild zusammengewürfelt, und doch: Jeder Häkelteppich, jeder Haken stimmt

KÜCHE
Am Restaurant (good food and in good company) wurde bei Drucklegung noch gearbeitet; die Bar Broken Shaker mit *handcrafted* Cocktails bis 2 Uhr früh war bereits in Betrieb

X-FAKTOR
Am Wochenende gibt es im Innenhof Mais vom Grill ... und natürlich ein Pingpong-Turnier

BUCH ZUM ORT
„Die South-Beach-Diät" von Dr. Arthur Agatston

SITUATION
À l'angle de la 28e Rue et d'Indian Creek Drive, à quelques rues du Miami Beach Convention Center et à 100 mètres de la plage

PRIX
Lits à partir de 25 €, chambre individuelle à partir de 115 €

CHAMBRES
Outre les dortoirs, chambres individuelles et 1 bungalow pour 8 personnes

STYLE
Hétéroclite, mais chaque tapis au crochet et chaque patère est ici à sa place

RESTAURATION
Le restaurant (bonne cuisine et convivialité) était encore en travaux lors de la mise sous presse ; le bar Broken Shaker propose ses cocktails maison jusqu'à 2 heures du matin

LE «PETIT PLUS»
Le week-end, maïs grillé... et bien sûr tournoi de ping-pong dans la cour intérieure

LIVRE À EMPORTER
«Régime Miami» d'Arthur Agatston

GREENWICH HOTEL
USA

377 Greenwich Street ~ New York, NY 10013 ~ USA
Telephone +1 212 941 8900 ~ Fax +1 212 941 8600
info@thegreenwichhotel.com
www.thegreenwichhotel.com

Robert de Niro has done much to establish Tribeca's reputation as one of the hottest neighborhoods in New York; not least with his Greenwich Hotel, in which none of the 88 rooms are alike. While the building's brick facade still echoes the area's industrial past, the inside is a rather more sophisticated melting pot of styles. The lobbies and bathrooms lean toward Mediterranean chic, but these are contrasted by interior designer Samantha Crasco's guest rooms, which feature comfortable DUX beds from Sweden and silk rugs from Tibet.

In the evenings, the courtyard is as vibrant as the alleyways of Naples. The spa, on the other hand, offers Oriental calm—de Niro had an old wood-and-bamboo Japanese farmhouse transported to the U.S. and then installed in his hotel. As you calmly swim your lengths beneath its timbered roof, the wailing sirens on the nearby streets will seem far, far away.

Robert De Niro hat einiges dafür getan, dass Tribeca heute zu den begehrtesten Vierteln New Yorks gehört; unter anderem mit seinem Greenwich Hotel, das 88 Zimmer umfasst, von denen jedes ein Unikat ist. Während die Backsteinfassade des Hauses noch mit dem früheren Industriecharakter der Gegend flirtet, geht es drinnen mondän zu. In den Empfangsräumen und Bädern dominiert noch mediterraner Chic. In den Zimmern steuerte die Designerin Samantha Crasco mit gemütlichen DUX-Betten aus Schweden und Seidenteppichen aus Tibet erfolgreich dagegen, sodass Gäste nun in einem *melting pot* residieren.

Im Innenhof herrscht abends ein buntes Treiben wie in den Gassen von Neapel, im Spa dagegen fernöstliche Ruhe – De Niro ließ ein altes japanisches Bauernhaus aus Holz und Bambus importieren, erst in die USA und dann in sein Hotel. Unter dessen Balken zieht man nun morgens seine Kraulbahnen, so weit und doch so nah vom Heulen der Polizeisirenen draußen vor der Tür.

Robert De Niro n'est pas étranger au fait que Tribeca compte parmi les quartiers les plus sélects de New York, notamment avec son Greenwich Hotel, dont chacune des 88 chambres est une perle rare. Si la façade en briques reflète le passé industriel du quartier, l'intérieur est raffiné, avec des salons et des salles de bains sacrifiant au chic méditerranéen. Une règle dont la décoratrice Samantha Crasco s'est brillamment affranchie dans les chambres en les équipant de confortables lits suédois DUX et de tapis de soie tibétains, si bien que les hôtes baignent dans une authentique ambiance «melting-pot».

Le soir, la cour intérieure s'anime comme les ruelles de Naples, tandis qu'il règne dans le spa un calme asiatique. De Niro a fait venir du Japon et intégrer à son hôtel une vieille ferme en bois et bambou, sous la charpente de laquelle il a aménagé une piscine: on y fait ses longueurs si loin de tout et pourtant à quelques pas seulement du hurlement des sirènes de police dans la rue.

LOCATION
In downtown Manhattan's "TRIangle BElow CAnal Street"; some rooms have river views

RATES
Rooms from $550, suites from $1,350

ROOMS
75 rooms, 10 suites, 3 penthouse

STYLE
Eclectic neo-authentic look composed by Grayling Design and Samantha Crasco

FOOD
The Locanda Verde does justice to the de Niro name, with first-class Italian specialties and excellent wines

X FACTOR
The feeling of living like a famous New York artist or new-media mogul: The suites (and their bathrooms) are so fabulous you'll wish you could move in. Just don't wheel out the old "You talkin' to me?" line should you bump into the owner in the foyer

BOOK TO PACK
"Cosmopolis" by Don DeLillo

LAGE
Im „TRIangle BElow CAnal Street" in Downtown Manhattan; einige Zimmer haben Hudson-Blick

PREIS
Zimmer ab 405 €, Suiten ab 1000 €

ZIMMER
75 Zimmer, 10 Suiten und 3 Penthouse

STIL
Eklektische Neo-Authentizität, komponiert von Grayling Design und Samantha Crasco

KÜCHE
Der Name De Niro verpflichtet: In der Locanda Verde werden beste italienische Spezialitäten und exzellenter Wein serviert

X-FAKTOR
Das Gefühl, tatsächlich wie ein New Yorker Starkünstler oder *new media*-Mogul zu residieren. In die Suiten (und deren Bäder) würde man gern auf Dauer einziehen. Ein Tipp, falls man dem Besitzer mal im Foyer begegnet: Bloß nicht mit „You talkin' to me?" ansprechen!

BUCH ZUM ORT
„Cosmopolis" von Don DeLillo

SITUATION
Dans le «TRIangle BElow CAnal Street», dans le centre de Manhattan; certaines chambres ont vue sur l'Hudson

PRIX
Chambres à partir de 405 €, suites à partir de 1 000 €

CHAMBRES
75 chambres, 10 suites et 3 penthouse

STYLE
Néo-authenticité éclectique composée par Grayling Design et Samantha Crasco

RESTAURATION
De Niro oblige, la Locanda Verde sert des spécialités et des vins italiens exquis

LE «PETIT PLUS»
L'impression d'être logé comme un grand artiste new-yorkais ou un magnat des nouveaux médias. On vivrait bien à demeure dans les suites. Un conseil: si vous croisez De Niro, abstenez-vous de lui sortir: «You talkin' to me?»

LIVRE À EMPORTER
«Cosmopolis» de Don DeLillo

"The Greenwich has the atmosphere
of a discreet members' club
and a delicious feeling of space and serenity."

CONDÉ NAST TRAVELLER

„Das Greenwich hat die Atmosphäre eines diskreten Clubs
und vermittelt ein köstliches Gefühl von Raum und Ruhe."

«Le Greenwich a l'atmosphère d'un club feutré
et donne une impression agréable d'espace et de sérénité.»

HOTEL BEL-AIR
USA

701 Stone Canyon Road ~ Los Angeles ~ California 90077 ~ USA
Telephone +1 310 472 1211 ~ Fax +1 310 909 1601
reservations.hba@dorchestercollection.com
www.hotelbelair.com

Given all the movies the Bel-Air has played some part in, it's a wonder this L.A. institution hasn't already made it onto the "Walk of Fame." Today, it remains a popular hangout for Hollywood players, not to mention something of a catwalk and casting hot spot; despite that, it has managed to remain a largely paparazzi-free zone.

Situated just over half a mile from Sunset Boulevard and surrounded by verdant gardens, the hotel recently underwent a major face-lift, though the surgery doesn't show. In fact, the two teams responsible for the redesign carefully complemented the '30s, '40s, and '50s glamour with perfectly chosen furniture and colors, and with a restoration that blends the indoor and outdoor experiences. Here, guests can relive the glory of Tinseltown's golden age—and perhaps bump into some of its famous figures from the present day.

Wäre das Bel-Air in den Abspännen aller Filme genannt worden, zu denen es irgendwie beigetragen hat – es hätte längst seinen eigenen Stern auf dem „Walk of Fame". Bis heute ist das Hotel eine Oase des Hollywoodpersonals, dazu Laufsteg und Castingbörse. Dennoch ist es weitgehend paparazzifreie Zone geblieben.

Nur einen knappen Kilometer vom Sunset Boulevard entfernt und umgeben von üppigen Gärten, schlägt nach umfassender Renovierung heute schon das zweite Herz in dieser runderneuerten Diva – was man ihr allerdings nicht ansieht. Die beiden Designteams ihres Liftings haben Innen und Außen zusammengezogen, der Glamour der 1930er- bis 1950er-Jahre wird durch perfekt ausgewählte Möbelstücke und Farben pointiert aufgenommen. Wer hier eincheckt, begegnet noch vielem, was einst den Glamour der goldenen Ära Hollywoods ausgemacht hat – und mit ein wenig Glück auch dessen heutigen Promi-Vertretern.

Si le Bel-Air avait été cité dans les génériques de tous les films auxquels il a un tant soit peu contribué, il aurait déjà son étoile sur le « Walk of Fame ». Éternel refuge pour le gratin d'Hollywood, cet hôtel assume aussi son rôle de podium de défilé de mode et studio de casting, et ce à l'abri des paparazzi.

À un petit kilomètre de Sunset Boulevard, parmi des jardins luxuriants, c'est un cœur neuf qui, mine de rien, bat dans cette diva retapée des pieds à la tête. Les deux équipes chargées de son lifting ont accordé intérieur et extérieur, faisant ressortir de manière pertinente le glamour des années 1930 à 1950 au moyen de meubles et de coloris choisis à la perfection. Le voyageur qui pose ses valises dans ces lieux retrouve de nombreuses réminiscences du glamour de l'âge d'or d'Hollywood, et avec un peu de chance, croise le chemin de ses représentants célèbres d'aujourd'hui.

LOCATION

In the Bel-Air hills above Los Angeles, about 35 minutes from LAX

RATES

Rooms from $515

ROOMS

58 rooms and 45 suites, including 7 "specialty suites"

STYLE

Ultra-glam residence with Hispanic colonial architecture

FOOD

The kitchen of renowned Academy Awards chef Wolfgang Puck blends Californian cuisine with European/Mediterranean influences

X FACTOR

The alcoves with views of the lake are a particularly fine place to dine (try the famous tortilla soup). For the perfect souvenir, pick up some striped pajamas with Bel-Air monograms

BOOK TO PACK

"Who the Devil Made It" by Peter Bogdanovich

LAGE

In den namensgebenden Hügeln von Bel-Air über Los Angeles, rund 35 Minuten von LAX

PREISE

Zimmer ab 395 €

ZIMMER

58 Zimmer und 45 Suiten, darunter 7 Specialty Suites

STIL

Ausgesprochene Glam-Residenz in hispanischer Kolonialarchitektur

KÜCHE

Kalifornische Küche mit europäisch-mediterranen Einflüssen unter der Leitung des berühmten Academy-Awards-Kochs Wolfgang Puck

X-FAKTOR

In Alkoven mit Blick auf den Schwanenteich lässt sich besonders schön dinieren, etwa die berühmte Tortilla-Suppe. Als Souvenir kauft man den Streifenpyjama mit Bel-Air-Schriftzug

BUCH ZUM ORT

„Wer hat denn den gedreht?" von Peter Bogdanovich

SITUATION

Dans les collines du même nom sur les hauteurs de Los Angeles, à environ 35 minutes de l'aéroport international de Los Angeles

PRIX

Chambres à partir de 395 €

CHAMBRES

58 chambres et 45 suites, dont 7 suites spéciales

STYLE

Résidence résolument glamour dans le style colonial espagnol

RESTAURATION

Cuisine californienne avec des influences méditerranéennes sous la conduite de Wolfgang Puck, le célèbre chef des Academy Awards

LE « PETIT PLUS »

Le dîner servi dans les alcôves avec vue sur l'étang (célèbre soupe aux tortillas). Le pyjama siglé Bel-Air, en vente à l'hôtel comme souvenir.

LIVRE À EMPORTER

« Le Roman de Hollywood » de Jacqueline Monsigny et Edward Meeks

"If I could, I would marry the Bel-Air tomorrow. She makes my bed every day, feeds me … and puts my laundry in the little boxes tied up with ribbon."

TONY CURTIS

„Wenn ich könnte, würde ich das Bel-Air heiraten. Es macht täglich mein Bett, gibt mir zu essen … und liefert meine frisch gewaschene Wäsche in Kartons mit Bändchen."

« Si c'était possible, j'épouserais le Bel-Air. Il fait mon lit tous les jours, cuisine pour moi… et me rend mon linge lavé et repassé, présenté dans des boîtes avec ruban. »

SUNSET BEACH
USA

35 Shore Road ~ Shelter Island ~ Long Island, NY 11965 ~ USA
Telephone +1 631 749 2001 ~ Fax +1 631 749 1843
reservations@sunsetbeachli.com
www.sunsetbeachli.com

If there's one place in the northern hemisphere where it's OK for guests to go barefoot to dinner, then this picture-book Hamptons beach hotel, at which American preppy style meets the nonchalant air of old French movies, is surely it. Apart from shoeless diners, summer at the Sunset Beach on Long Island means pastels galore, beach dresses, rolled-up linen pants. And his-and-hers Ray-Bans reflecting the sunset.

The latter, as the hotel's name suggests, is famed throughout New York. Other attractions include rooms that are a perfect match for the romantic Technicolor skies, with retro decor and Hamptons classics, such as the Hardoy Butterfly Chair and a restaurant offering (what else?) French specialties such as moules-frites and salade niçoise. The only thing missing is Alain Delon with Jackie Kennedy on the sundeck.

Wenn man je irgendwo auf der Nordhalbkugel barfuß zum Dinner gehen kann, dann in diesem Bilderbuch-Strandhotel in den Hamptons. Im Sunset Beach auf Long Island wird bis aufs kleinste Detail dem Preppy-Stil gehuldigt. Für den Gast bedeutet das im Sommer ein Lebensgefühl, wie man es sonst nur aus alten französischen Filmen kennt: viele Pastellfarben, Strandkleidchen, aufgekrempelte Leinenhosen. Und in den Ray-Ban-Brillen von ihr und ihm spiegelt sich der Sonnenuntergang.

Letzterer gilt, der Hotelname verrät es, in ganz New York als eine der größten Annehmlichkeiten des Ortes. Passend zur Technicolor-Romantik sind die Zimmer im Retro-Look und mit Hamptons-Klassikern wie dem Hardoy Butterfly Chair eingerichtet. Das Restaurant kocht – natürlich – französische Gerichte wie Moules-frites und Salade Niçoise. Fehlen eigentlich nur noch Alain Delon und Jackie Kennedy auf dem Sonnendeck.

S'il est un lieu dans l'hémisphère Nord où l'on peut se rendre à table pieds nus, c'est bien dans ce charmant hôtel balnéaire des Hamptons. Le Sunset Beach, à Long Island, est un hymne au style «preppy». En été, couleurs pastel, robes légères et pantalons de lin retroussés fleurent bon le vieux film français. Et dans les Ray-Ban de Madame et de Monsieur se reflète le coucher de soleil.

Ici, comme le suggère le nom de l'établissement, le coucher de soleil est une attraction connue du Tout-New York. En accord avec ce romantisme en Technicolor, les chambres rétro sont meublées de classiques des Hamptons, comme le siège Butterfly signé Hardoy. Le restaurant propose bien sûr des plats typiquement français comme les moules-frites et la salade niçoise. Il ne manque plus qu'Alain Delon et Jackie Kennedy sur le solarium.

LOCATION
In a delightful Shelter Island bay, 170km/
106 miles east of New York City. The island can
be reached by ferry from Greenport in just
7 minutes

RATES
Rooms from $345, breakfast not included,
minimum stay of two nights on weekends

ROOMS
20 rooms, all with private sundecks and
sea views

STYLE
Simple but sophisticated retro idyll

FOOD
Guests can enjoy Côte d'Azur classics, such
as bouillabaisse and salade niçoise—served
with rosé from hotel founder André Balazs's
own range

X FACTOR
The bar at which guests can enjoy evening
cocktails while watching day turn to night

BOOK TO PACK
"Montauk" by Max Frisch

LAGE
An einer herrlichen Bucht auf Shelter Island
gelegen, 170 km östlich von New York City.
Ab Greenport ist die Insel per Fähre erreichbar,
die Überfahrt dauert ganze 7 Minuten

PREISE
Zimmer ab 255 €, ohne Frühstück, an den
Wochenenden 2 Nächte Mindestaufenthalt

ZIMMER
20 Zimmer, alle mit privatem Sonnendeck
und Meerblick

STIL
Schlichtes, aber *sophisticated* Retro-Idyll

KÜCHE
Zu Klassikern von der Côte d'Azur wie Bouillabaisse und Salade Niçoise lässt Hotelerfinder
André Balazs Rosé-Wein aus eigener Herstel-
lung ausschenken

X-FAKTOR
Die Bar mit Blick auf die untergehende Sonne.
Sundowner trinken, wo sie erfunden wurden!

BUCH ZUM ORT
„Montauk" von Max Frisch

SITUATION
Dans une superbe baie sur Shelter Island,
à 170 km à l'est de New York. La traversée
en bac au départ de Greenport dure 7 minutes

PRIX
Chambres à partir de 255 €, petit déjeuner
non compris. Le week-end, séjour de deux
nuits minimum

CHAMBRES
20 chambres, toutes avec terrasse-solarium
et vue sur mer

STYLE
Sobre avec une touche rétro raffinée et idyllique

RESTAURATION
Le créateur de l'hôtel, André Balazs, fait servir le
rosé de sa propre production en accompagne-
ment de la bouillabaisse et de la salade niçoise

LE « PETIT PLUS »
Le bar faisant face au soleil couchant. Siroter
le Sundowner là où il a été inventé !

LIVRE À EMPORTER
« Montauk » de Max Frisch

WASHINGTON SCHOOL HOUSE
USA

543 Park Avenue ~ Park City, UT 84060 ~ USA
Telephone +1 435 649 3800 ~ Fax +1 435 649 3802
reservations@washingtonschoolhouse.com
www.washingtonschoolhouse.com

Were prizes awarded for the nicest descriptions on a hotel home page, the Washington School House would definitely be among the winners. What's more, this school-turned-hotel and its owners are equally charming in real life. The interiors alone—fresh yet vintage look, lots of white, choicest antique furniture—deserve an A+. The quarried limestone facade, meanwhile, is an attraction in itself, not least because it's one of the few structures that survived Park City's Great Fire of 1898.

In contrast to the rugged exterior, the inside of this peaceful hotel is designed for relaxation and stress-free socializing. And don't worry: The owners' threat to prize you out of your room lest you miss out on the fantastic mountains and pistes is, of course, just a schoolmasterly joke.

Wenn es einen Preis für die netteste Begrüßung auf der Homepage gäbe, dann hätte ihn das Washington School House schon gewonnen. Genauso charmant sind das zum Hotel umgewandelte Schulgebäude und seine Betreiber in echt. Allein die Einrichtung – frischer Vintage-Style, viel Weiß und dazu ausgesucht schöne, authentische Möbel – verdient die Note 1+. Die gehämmerte Kalksteinfassade des Hauses ist fast eine Sehenswürdigkeit für sich und eine der wenigen Mauern, die dem großen Stadtbrand von Park City im Jahr 1898 trotzten.

Hinter diesen hart geprüften Steinen lässt sich ausgezeichnet der Tag verdösen, alles in dem friedlichen Boutique-Hotel ist auf Erholung und stressfreies Miteinander ausgelegt. Und dass die Betreiber ankündigen, sie würden ihre Gäste eigenhändig aus dem Bett zerren, wenn die nicht in die Gänge kommen, um die herrlichen Berge und Skigebiete in der Umgebung zu besuchen, ist natürlich nur ein schulmeisterlicher Scherz.

S'il y avait un prix pour la page d'accueil la plus sympathique, le Washington School House l'aurait déjà remporté. Cet hôtel créé dans une ancienne école et ses gérants sont tout aussi charmants dans la vie réelle. La décoration, dans un style vintage rafraîchissant avec beaucoup de blanc et de beaux meubles d'époque triés sur le volet, mérite à elle seule un 20/20. Presque une curiosité en soi, la façade en moellons de calcaire compte parmi les rares murs ayant défié le grand incendie qui a ravagé Park City en 1898.

À l'abri de ces pierres mises à rude épreuve, les hôtes coulent des jours tranquilles, tout dans ce paisible hôtel de charme étant conçu pour la détente et une cohabitation harmonieuse. Et quand les gérants menacent de tirer du lit *manu militari* les hôtes qui ont du mal à s'activer pour partir à la découverte des superbes montagnes et domaines skiables de la région, il ne s'agit là, bien sûr, que d'une plaisanterie bienveillante.

LOCATION
Just a short walk from the town center, 45 minutes from Salt Lake City airport

RATES
Rooms from $295, suites from $475

ROOMS
12 rooms and suites

STYLE
Informal mountain retreat with extremely friendly hosts

FOOD
A light and contemporary take on classic American cuisine

X FACTOR
Après-ski drinks enjoyed around the hotel's outdoor fire. The fire pit itself has a rather unusual history—it was one of the steel torches used for the 2002 Winter Olympics in Salt Lake City

BOOK TO PACK
"Utah Curiosities: Quirky Characters, Roadside Oddities & Other Offbeat Stuff"
by Brandon Griggs

LAGE
Wenige Gehminuten vom Stadtkern entfernt, 45 Minuten von Salt Lake City Airport

PREISE
Zimmer ab 215 €, Suiten ab 350 €

ZIMMER
12 Zimmer und Suiten

STIL
Lässiges Mountain-Retreat mit äußerst sympathischen Gastgebern

KÜCHE
Klassisch-amerikanische Küche, leicht und modern interpretiert

X-FAKTOR
Die Outdoor-Feuerstelle, an der man hervorragend Après-Ski machen kann und die eine eigene Geschichte erzählt: Sie war eine der Stahlfackeln bei den Olympischen Winterspielen 2002 in Salt Lake City

BUCH ZUM ORT
„Utah Curiosities: Quirky Characters, Roadside Oddities & Other Offbeat Stuff" von Brandon Griggs

SITUATION
À quelques minutes à pied du centre-ville, et à 45 minutes de l'aéroport de Salt Lake City

PRIX
Chambres à partir de 215 €, suites à partir de 350 €

CHAMBRES
12 chambres et suites

STYLE
Refuge de montagne décontracté tenu par des hôtes très sympathiques

RESTAURATION
Interprétation moderne et allégée de la cuisine américaine classique

LE « PETIT PLUS »
Le brasero à l'extérieur, autour duquel on se réchauffe après le ski et qui a une histoire : Il s'agit d'une des torches olympiques en acier des Jeux d'hiver de Salt Lake City en 2002

LIVRE À EMPORTER
« L'Œil de l'Utah » de Georges Simenon

THE NAM HAI
VIETNAM

Hoi An ~ Hamlet 1, Dien Duong Village ~ Dien Ban District, Quang Nam Province ~ Vietnam
Telephone +84 510 394 0000 ~ Fax +84 510 394 0999
reservations@thenamhai.com
www.thenamhai.com

With the ancient settlements of Hoi An and My Son close by, both UNESCO world heritage sites, and the delights of modern-day Vietnam, too—such as Hoi An's express tailors, who will run up a made-to-measure suit in just two days—the area around the Nam Hai is well worth exploring.

It can, though, be hard to tear yourself away from the hotel's own grounds. The spacious guest villas, some of which have fabulous private pools, are set in a beautifully laid out palm tree garden, while the beachfront fish restaurant and first-class spa offer two more good reasons to never leave this dream resort, which was created by architect Reda Amalou and designer Jaya Ibrahim. Still, every good visitor should get to know their host country at least a little, and the tours offering insights into the daily life of local residents are the ideal opportunity.

Rund um dieses Resort gibt es allerlei zu erleben. Einmal die UNESCO-Welterbe-Stätten Hoi An und My Son – spektakuläre Zeugnisse vergangener Hochkulturen. Daneben modernes Vietnam in Form der *high-speed*-Schneider der Küstenstadt Hoi An, die in zwei Tagen einen maßgefertigten Anzug hinkriegen.

Man sollte also auf jeden Fall das Hotelgelände verlassen, auch wenn es schwerfällt – schließlich handelt es sich um einen wunderbar angelegten Palmengarten, in dem großzügige Privatvillen liegen, teilweise mit herrlichen eigenen Pools. Das Fischrestaurant am Strand und das exzellente Spa komplettieren die Annehmlichkeiten des Resorts, das der Architekt Reda Amalou und der Designer Jaya Ibrahim an diesem Traumplatz geschaffen haben. Zu richtigen Ferien gehört eine Portion Landeskunde, weshalb Gäste hier auch Touren buchen können, bei denen sie am Alltag der Einheimischen teilnehmen.

Les environs de ce complexe recèlent bien des curiosités : les sites de Hoi An et de Mi Son, classés au patrimoine mondial de l'UNESCO et témoins grandioses de civilisations anciennes, mais aussi le Vietnam moderne, incarné par les tailleurs express de la ville côtière de Hoi An, qui confectionnent un costume sur mesure en deux jours.

Aussi faut-il absolument sortir de l'hôtel, aussi difficile soit-il de s'arracher à cette palmeraie divine abritant de spacieux bungalows, dont certains disposent d'une superbe piscine privée. Le restaurant de poisson sur la plage et l'excellent spa complètent les agréments de ce complexe créé dans cet endroit de rêve par le fondateur Adrian Zecha, l'architecte Reda Amalou et le décorateur Jaya Ibrahim. De vraies vacances ne s'entendant pas sans une dose de civilisation, les hôtes peuvent aussi participer à des excursions au cours desquelles ils sont peuvent partager le quotidien des habitants.

LOCATION
Situated on Ha My Beach near Hoi An, 30 minutes south of Da Nang airport

RATES
Villas from $800, breakfast and minibar included

ROOMS
60 one-bedroom villas and 40 pool villas with between 1 and 5 bedrooms

STYLE
Sleek, sensuous interiors in white and brown

FOOD
The main restaurant offers fine Vietnamese cuisine and a sundeck with panoramic views; the beach restaurant serves fish and seafood

X FACTOR
The truly unusual range of tours and activities organized by the hotel: Guests can take to the water with a Vietnamese fisherman, for instance, or visit and work with a local farmer for a day

BOOK TO PACK
"The Quiet American" by Graham Greene

LAGE
Am Ha My Beach nahe von Hoi An, 30 Minuten südlich des Flughafens Da Nang

PREISE
Villen ab 600 €, inklusive Frühstück und Minibar

ZIMMER
60 Villen mit jeweils 1 Schlafzimmer sowie 40 Pool-Villen mit 1 bis 5 Schlafzimmern

STIL
Klare Sinnlichkeit in Weiß- und Brauntönen

KÜCHE
Das Hauptrestaurant mit Panoramaterrasse serviert feine vietnamesische Menüs, das Strandrestaurant Fisch und Meeresfrüchte

X-FAKTOR
Die Aktivitäten, die das Hotel anbietet, sind wirklich außergewöhnlich: Unter anderem kann man mit einem Fischer rausfahren oder einen vietnamesischen Bauern besuchen und für einen Tag mitarbeiten

BUCH ZUM ORT
„Der stille Amerikaner" von Graham Greene

SITUATION
Sur la plage de Ha My, près de Hoi An, à 30 minutes au sud de l'aéroport de Da Nang

PRIX
Bungalows à partir de 600 €, petit déjeuner et minibar compris

CHAMBRES
60 bungalows d'une chambre et 40 bungalows avec 1 à 5 chambres et piscine privée

STYLE
Sensualité épurée dans des tons de blanc et de brun

RESTAURATION
Le restaurant principal avec terrasse panoramique sert des menus vietnamiens raffinés, le restaurant de la plage des produits de la mer

LE « PETIT PLUS »
Les activités atypiques proposées par l'hôtel, comme les sorties en mer avec un pêcheur ou la journée de travaux chez un fermier local

LIVRE À EMPORTER
« Un Américain bien tranquille » de Graham Greene

"Request one of the 16 freestanding bungalows along Hoi An's famed powdery-white shore for the best beach access."

TRAVEL + LEISURE

„Sie wünschen sich direkten Zugang zum Strand? Fragen Sie nach einem der 16 Bungalows, die Hoi Ans berühmte pudrig-weiße Küste säumen."

«Vous souhaitez avoir les pieds dans l'eau? Demandez un de nos 16 bungalows qui jalonnent la célèbre côte blanc poudré de Hoi An.»

CREDITS / IMPRINT

366–373 all photos supplied by the hotel 374–381 Mirjam Bleeker, www.mirjambleeker.nl 382–391 all photos supplied by the hotel 392–401 Stefano Scata' and Adriano Bacchella/all photos supplied by the hotel 403 Photo supplied by the hotel 404–407 Gianni Basso/TASCHEN GmbH, www.vegamg.it 408–413 all photos supplied by the hotel 414–419 Patrizia Mussa/TASCHEN GmbH, www.livio.it 420–427 Jimmy Cohrssen 428–433 all photos supplied by the hotel 434–439 all photos supplied by the hotel 440–447 Eddy van Gestel/all photos supplied by the hotel 448–453 Undine Pröhl/all photos supplied by the hotel 454–459 all photos supplied by the hotel 460–467 Jae Feinberg, all photos supplied by the hotel 468–477 all photos supplied by the hotel 478–485 COTE SUD, Bernard Touillon, Cécile Vaiarelli 486–491 all photos supplied by the hotel 492–499 Knut Slinning and Olav Jensen/all photos supplied by the hotel 500–505 Tuca Reinés/TASCHEN GmbH, www.tucareines.com.br 506–515 Paul Barbera/all photos supplied by the hotel 516–521 Ricardo Labougle/TASCHEN GmbH, www.ricardolabougle.com 522–527 all photos supplied by the hotel 528–533 all photos supplied by the hotel 534–539 Ricardo Labougle/TASCHEN GmbH, www.ricardolabougle.com 540–547 Johan Hellström/all photos supplied by the hotel 549, 556–557 Inredningsgruppen ©Treehotel 550–551 Sandell Sandberg ©Treehotel 552–553 Mårten and Gustav Cyrén ©Treehotel 552, 554 Åke E:son Lindman ©Treehotel 555 Tham & Videgård Arkitekter ©Treehotel 558–563 all photos are supplied by the hotel 564–569 all photos supplied by the hotel 570–575 all photos supplied by the hotel 576–581 Mirjam Bleeker, www.mirjambleeker.nl 582–591 all photos supplied by the hotel 592–597 Ali Bekman/all photos supplied by the hotel 598–603 all photos supplied by the hotel 604–609 all photos supplied by the hotel 610–615 Alex Beer/all photos supplied by the hotel 616–621 all photos supplied by the hotel 622–627 David Griffin/all photos supplied by the hotel

628–633 all photos supplied by the hotel 634–639 Jake Eastham/all photos supplied by the hotel 640–645 Ricardo Labougle, www.ricardolabougle.com 646–651 Douglas Lyle Thompson and Jon Johnson/all photos supplied by the hotel 652–661 Ken Hayden and Richard Se/all photos supplied by Amanresorts 662–667 Michael Weschler/all photos supplied by the hotel 669, 672 (above left, below right), 673, 675 Nick Simonite/all photos supplied by the hotel; 670, 672 (above right) Eric Ryan Anderson/all photos supplied by the hotel 671, 672 (below left), 674 Allison von Smith/all photos supplied by the hotel 676–681 Adrian Gaut/all photos supplied by the hotel 682–689 Poul Ober/TASCHEN GmbH, www.poulober.com, 685 (left), 686 (above) Herbert YPMA/all photos supplied by the hotel 690–695 all photos supplied by the hotel 696–701 all photos supplied by the hotel 702–709 Michael Spengler/all photos are supplied by the hotel 711, 714, 715 (above) Mirjam Bleeker www.mirjambleeker.nl 712–713, 715 (below), 716–717 all photos supplied by the hotel

To stay informed about TASCHEN and our upcoming titles, please subscribe to our free magazine at www.taschen.com/magazine, download our magazine app for iPad, follow us on Twitter and Facebook, or e-mail your questions to contact@taschen.com.

© 2014 TASCHEN GmbH
Hohenzollernring 53
50672 Köln
www.taschen.com

EDITOR
Margit J. Mayer

ART DIRECTION & DESIGN
Diane Bergmann, Berlin

TEXT
Max Scharnigg, Munich; with contributions by Eliza Apperly; Christiane Reiter, Paris; Kristin Rübesamen, Berlin; Julia Strauß, Munich

BARCODE ILLUSTRATION
Robert Nippoldt

PROJECT MANAGEMENT
Stephanie Paas

EDITORIAL ASSISTANT
Falkmar K. Finke

ENGLISH TRANSLATION
Iain Reynolds, Berlin

FRENCH TRANSLATION
Sabine Boccador, Saint-Maur-des-Fossés
Christèle Jany, Cologne

PRODUCTION
Frauke Kaiser

PRINTED IN CHINA
ISBN 978-3-8365-4397-2